SEATHWAITE WAD

and The Mines of the Borrowdale Valley

"First sight of the wad" J Tyler
Executed in raw graphite from Seathwaite mine.

SEATHWAITE WAD

and The Mines of the Borrowdale Valley

by Ian Tyler

BLUE ROCK PUBLICATIONS

1995

ISBN 0 9523028 1 0

Published by **BLUE ROCK PUBLICATIONS**

33 Townhead Road
Cotehill
Carlisle
CA4 0DF

Printed in Great Britain by

THE AMADEUS PRESS LTD

517 Leeds Road, Huddersfield, West Yorkshire HD2 1YJ

Contents

Stylised map of Cumberland circa 1790. Caldbeck Mining Museum Collection

Acknowledgements

This, my fourth book in the Lake District Mining series has been, without doubt, the most difficult to produce. The complexity of the physical workings of the graphite mine was challenging enough, but the breakdown of the dozens of sub-lettings over the period was a minefield in itself. The names of Brandlehow, Brandley and Old Brandley have been misused to great effect in documentation to confuse the historian.

We have tried to unravel the web of intricacies and hopefully delivered to our readers a chronological account of the mines investigated. This has not been done without help from various sources and therefore I have pleasure in acknowledging the following people and organisations without whose co-operation the book could not have been written.

A special mention must be made of a very dear friend David Blundell who sadly passed away during 1994. Dave was instrumental in my undertaking of the surveying of nearly all the mines in the Lake District. The survey of the wad mine, made some years ago, was a long and arduous task which entailed us becoming soaked week after week. The information was gained before SRT was fashionable and the pitches were all done with electron ladders and safety line. The information from these early surveys has been invaluable to the understanding of the wad mine and could never have been achieved without Dave's participation and companionship.

Thanks go to Mike Davies-Shiel who was most kind in giving me detailed information of the watermills of the river Greta, in particular the Greta Bridge Mill, Greta Hamlet Mill, Greta Mill, Forge Mill and Wren's Mill.

To Mines of Lakeland Exploration Society, in particular Ian Hebson and Peter Blezard, who trailed the Borrowdale valley in what can only be described as truly appalling weather week after week, and others who assisted over the many weeks: Peter Sedgewick, Kirsten Crowther, Jean Tyler. To Roy Fellows and Ian Hebson for their photographic expertise. To my good friend Norman Thompson for helping with the geological notes. To Graham Hodgson, Dave Ramshaw and John Adams for exploration. To Carlisle PRO, in particular Barbara Clark, Susan Dench and David Bowcock. To Dorset PRO and County Archivist David C Reeve. To Carlisle Library and in particular Stephen White for his help and interest in the project. To Colin Richardson of Tullie House Museum for permission to photograph the coin moulds. To the 'K' Farers Rambling Club for use of their photograph. To Bill Creighton of Cockermouth for local information. To Lord Egremont for permission to use his archive. To George Bott of Keswick for his local information and knowledge freely given. To Reverend Johns and Reverend Rook of Borrowdale Church for permission to use an article from the Parish Magazine. To David Felton of Chapel House, Borrowdale for allowing me to photograph his house. To double glazing firm Lakeland Superglaze in Keswick for allowing me to take photographs on their site. To Miss Betty Walker at Ellers, for her interest and for allowing us to walk her land and take photographs. To Mr Alan Leyland at Manesty for allowing us to walk his land and take photographs. To Paul and Jenny Clarke of Brandlehow for showing us around their property and other useful information freely given. To Keswick Museum for information given. To Mr David Sharrock, Managing Director of the Cumberland Pencil Co for his help and permission to use his photographs. To Mrs Barbara Reynolds at Keswick Pencil Museum for her help and assistance. To Mr Stan Edmondson of Seathwaite, for his local knowledge and advice and permission to use his photograph. To Stewart Bland of Thorneythwaite for his information and permission to use his photographs. To Mr Neil Dowie of the Royal Oak Inn, Rosthwaite for his information and permission to use his photograph. To Caldbeck Mining Museum Archive for the use of their plans, documents and photographs.

To John Price for his invaluable expertise in producing the typescript.

Finally thanks go to my wife who has spent hours in front of our somewhat antiquated word processor editing the manuscript, and for her care and attention to the detailed drawings.

WARNING

It is important to understand that this book is a history of the Wad Mine and numerous other mines in the Borrowdale Valley, and is in no way intended as an underground guide.

Derelict mines are in many instances places of extreme danger, and many of the sites described in the following pages are riddled with deep shafts and flooded sumps, and therefore out of bounds to the inquisitive amateur. Some sites are on private property and to visit them, permission must be obtained otherwise this will constitute the law of trespass.

Foreword

AFTER WRITING the previous books in the Lake District series, *Force Crag*, the last working mine in the Lakes, *Greenside*, the largest lead mine in the Lakes and *Honister*, the biggest underground slate mine in the Lakes I found myself with the new challenge of what to research and explore for our next publication. The answer was obvious, it was literally just over the hill from Honister where I and my friends in M.O.L.E.S had spent so many months doing our last research........the Wad Mine.

Little has been written about this incredible place and its attendant industry, and it was unique in that it had the distinction of supplying a substance which, pound for pound, was the most valuable ever taken from Cumbrian soil. Also, it had actually been worked for longer than any other mine in the county. There had to be a story to tell, but initially we had woefully little to go on apart from the Carlisle archive material which I had researched many years ago. My underground exploration had taken me to every accessible part of the mine, and it had all been surveyed. None of this however was enough to make a complete history ....we had to have more facts.

The writing had started by the time *Honister Slate* had hit the shelves, and by August we had a manuscript virtually complete when I was told of an archive in Dorset. It was a bonanza strike! Hundreds of original documents giving intricate details and intimate insights into the Wad Mine and the people who worked it, owned it, ran it and robbed it. With these documents we have been able to weave one of the most fascinating historical accounts of a mine so long since closed, and I trust that you will find that we have done justice to it and to the intriguing characters who were involved all those many years ago "wi' t'wad'oles up on t'moor"

It seemed to make sense also to include those other long since finished mines in Borrowdale, and to tell their story too.

From the earliest copper miners to the adventurers of the last century, from the Seathwaite shepherds to the Keswick pencil manufacturers, they all played a part in the story of Lake District mining and to all of them this book is dedicated.

IAN TYLER March 1995

Geology of Borrowdale

THE GEOLOGY of Borrowdale is a major exercise in itself and to do the subject justice would require a separate book. We therefore offer our readers a brief insight into the basic structure in the text that follows. Should the reader wish to find more detailed information there are numerous written sources to study.

Seathwaite.
At the wad mine, the graphite occurs as irregular nodules varying in diameter from a few millimetres to over 1 metre. The nodules occur in association with a diabase intrusion in the Borrowdale Volcanic Series. Numerous quartz veins traverse the formation but appear to have no direct connection with the graphite. The larger deposits of graphite are found in a series of pipes, some of which extend to a depth of more than 100 metres. This deposit appears to be quite unique and so far, no universally accepted theory of its origin has been produced.

Brandlehow
This mine worked the Brandlehow Lode which trends approximately N/S. The lode occurs as a quartz vein containing galena, cerrusite and some sphalerite and was unusual in carrying at its northern end, a saline spring containing a high concentration of calcium chloride.

Old Brandley
This is about 800 metres north of Brandlehow and worked the same lode. Near Coates' Shaft, the Brandlehow Lode divides into two and changes direction to run N/W across Skelgill Bank. The Old Brandley Mine worked the northern branch. The vein carried galena and in the upper levels abundant fluorite occurs.

Salt Well
This lies about 1,200 metres south of Brandlehow. The vein runs ENE/WSW and contains copper minerals. About midway along the vein it is cut by the lead-bearing Brandlehow Vein.

Copper Plate
This is about 800 metres SW of Salt Well and worked two approximately E/W parallel copper veins containing chalcopyrite and arsenopyrite.

The Remote Trials

IN THE high foothills and mountains at the head of Borrowdale lie hidden some of the most obscure mine sites in the Lake District. They are passed by each year by thousands of fell walkers, totally unaware that hundreds of years ago some poor souls dragged their bodies to these remote areas, to find their fortunes. These were certainly not the adventures of well backed companies, but of groups of individuals who, at various times, tried these elusive veins.

Driedley Gill Trial.

This small trial which extends no more than 30 feet, is to be found at about 2,100 feet south east of Glaramara summit in a small gill off Driedley Gill. The entrance was at one time timbered, but this has now rotted away. There is no real sign of mineralisation, but a few yards to the south in Driedley Gill itself, is a large quartz vein of considerable proportions. Whether or not this was the eventual target of the level we will never know, nor whether for iron or copper or perhaps the elusive wad which made these early adventurers struggle to this lonely spot.

Glaramara Crystal Cave

Just south east of the summit of Glaramara is a sort of small cave, not big enough to enter as it is partially water filled, but the host rocks are covered in quartz crystals.

Ruddy Gill

Directly under the bastion of the north face of Great End lies the head of Grains Gill, known as Ruddy Gill and aptly named, for here the ground runs red in the rainy season staining the boots of walkers with haematite rouge. It is possible that this area was mined directly from the surface in the early days, for the iron ore is very obvious. I have been unable to trace any take notes or leases for extraction, but the ground does appear to have been disturbed and not just by the passage of time. Certainly, just to the south-east, the vein was worked at Ore Gap a mile and a half away.

Grains Gill

Sited just half a mile above Stockley Bridge and on the western bank of Grains Gill, is the evidence of a small trial. The level was initially driven through the glacial moraine, and then almost surely due east to intersect the large quartz vein lying in the bed of the gill. The remains of a small stone hut built by the miners, is now a refuge for the local Herdwicks. It is difficult to assess the distance the level was driven, as much of the dump material has gone into the gill. An educated guess would be some 50 yards, and there is malachite and haematite to be found on the dump. Across the gill at about this point is to be found another level, cut into solid rock and following a small quartz stringer. The level was certainly hand drilled and blasted by gunpowder, and both these workings were opened up prior to 1850.

Langstrath Smelter

At the bifurcation of Langstrath and Greenup Gills is an area called Smithymire Island, and here can be seen the old charcoal mounds used for smelting haematite ore. There is an abundance of slag and clinker, and the site is well overgrown with bracken and trees. Many people are of the opinion that the smelter was much further up the Langstrath valley, but having spent hours at a time exploring the upper reaches, I have been unable to locate anything there.

This site is believed to be where the ore was smelted from the Langdale trials under Loft Crag and the surface trials at Ore Gap and, possibly, the early trials at Red Tarn. All these locations are connected by old pack horse routes which pass right by the smelt site.

Rigg Head Copper Mine

The jaws of Borrowdale hide many interesting nooks and crannies, some of them well known by the Lakeland visitor, but one small and remote copper mine eluded discovery by mine explorers for years. The magnificent ravine of Tongue Gill, which sweeps virtually due east into the river Derwent, is not entirely as nature made it. For at least one hundred and fifty years, it was subjected to the ravages of the quarrymen, becoming known as Rigg Head quarries which worked the Yew Crag and Honister slate veins. The quarries were owned by the Leyland family who for years extracted the slate, and it is an interesting fact that they were direct descendants of the Dixon family who had toiled for two centuries at the wad mine.

Prior to the quarrymen coming to extract the slate and open up the cavernous closeheads that can be seen today, the hard rock miners were here first to despoil this area of natural beauty. It is conceivable that the copper lode was spotted by the early adventurers travelling over into the Newlands valley from Rosthwaite and Stonethwaite. Even in those early days both hamlets were substantial settlements, housing many of the local miners and quarrymen.

Here the old men have hacked and chipped the hard rock to get at the vein. The level is very old, and I would estimate it to have been driven around 1700. The reason for this date is by virtue of the level size being no more than 5 feet 6 inches high and 2 feet wide. It is not a coffin level as there are a few hand drilled holes, although these are so small and infrequent that some parts of the level must have been either chipped out or split using stope and feathers, so saving valuable gunpowder. The existing level is 30 yards long although the original drive was considerably longer, possibly 50 yards or more. Unfortunately, this was totally demolished when, in about 1850, a slate level was driven through it. Consequently, the old tunnel with its original waste heap was totally obliterated and is now covered by tons of debris, thus making the entrance to the adit virtually impossible to locate.

These hardy adventurers did not go away empty handed, for attached to the splintered quartz is rich chalcopyrite.

Castle Crag Lead Level

On the eastern shoulder of Castle Crag lies a small working which is referred to on the OS as a lead level, however this appears to be a quarry working.

The Mines of the Borrowdale Valley

Copperplate Mine at Ellers

OVER THE old bridge from the Borrowdale Keswick road lies the delightful village of Grange, home of quarrymen and miners for hundreds of years and behind it, facing eastwards and filling the sky is to be seen the massive eastern flank of High Spy and Maiden Moor. Here, copper ore has been mined from very early days both by surface workings and by the driving of tunnels and in fact, these are some of the finest examples of coffin levels in Cumbria. They have been driven forward without the aid of gunpowder, hand-chipped inch by inch through hard rock using the most basic tools. The miners came from the area of Augsberg in Germany under the leadership of mining steward and engineer Daniel Hechstetter, who had been instrumental in setting up the Company of Mines Royal. The company had been indentured by Queen Elizabeth I to dig for mineral all over Great Britain.

The veins of the Copperplate mine were discovered in August 1567, and no sooner had the miners cut the sod than objections were winging their way to London from the powerful Earl of Northumberland. He was again suffering a grievance over the rights to mine in the area having previously tried to stop the mining at Goldscope. The land belonged to him and he was to fight for the mining rights against the Crown in a law case which finally went against him in 1568. He did however, revoke the restraint on Ellers and work was permitted to continue. The judgement against him ended tragically leading to rebellion against the Queen, and Thomas Percy, the 7th Earl of Northumberland, finally met his end on the block at York in 1571.

The mine was known by the Germans as Kupferplaten, the Copperplate Mine, partly for the quality of the copper discovered, but also because copper sheeting was now required to partially plate the wooden warships of the day. This would have a streamlining effect below the waterline, enabling the ships to sail more speedily. It was supposed also, that the copper sheeting would help to resist infestation by marine growth and yet another aspect was that it strengthened the hull substantially, serving as an early type of armour plate.

The mine sett worked three and possibly four separate veins, and due to the steep and undulating ground, they would have been easily spotted by the early prospectors. Although the lower tree line at this early date may have hampered things a little, the bold rock outcrops with the tell-tale streaks of quartz running through them would have stood out well as in fact they still do today.

The most northerly of the veins bisects the valley in a north-westerly direction from behind the area known as Ellers. Here, the mineralised vein can be seen and followed up the fell, and at OD 550 feet a small hand-picked level is to be found. This small trial is from the earliest period of mining, certainly of Elizabethan origin and there is also evidence of other small surface workings on the back of the vein.

The southern-most vein lies exposed on Swanesty Bank at OD 450 feet, and here a large hand-chipped open-work was cut by the German miners directly on the exposed vein and an amount of copper taken from it. The working is of considerable size being some 20 yards long, 4 feet wide and approximately 15 feet deep. Directly above this working there appears to be a small reservoir chipped out of the solid rock from which a groove has been cut. Down the face to just above the aforementioned work, is a small pile of ore indicating the site of an early dressing and washing floor. Nearby on the outcrops, other areas have been obviously picked.

A few hundred yards to the north-west and higher up the fell at OD 600 feet the vein again outcrops, and here the ancient miners first worked the open vein. Realising then the importance of their discovery, they pursued the copper by tunnelling a coffin level. This was hand-chipped forward a laborious 28 yards, the height of the level about 8 feet 6 inches and the width no more than 3 feet. It is possible that this is the working known by the German miners as the Hamblin. It was driven by two miners, Schopf and Wurzer, and near the entrance is a small dressing floor and also the remains of a crude hut.

The vein on which the Copperplate Mine proper was worked, lies about 150 yards to the north. The Borrowdale workings had of course been under the stewardship of Daniel Hechstetter since 1564/5, and the importance of the mining sett is reflected in the capital outlay of £749 14s 6½d. This amount was more by far than would be spent on any of the other Mines Royal ventures over the next few years with the exception of Newlands, thus establishing the importance of the sett and the neighbouring workings. The Copperplate Mine consists of numerous trials and adits worked along the length of the vein, and the highest trial cut on this vein is at OD 550 feet. The German miners have opened up the vein on surface, creating an open-cut nearly 4 feet wide, 15 feet high and nearly 20 yards long. The lode was proving very rich as the workings continued, and the Germans decided to drive a horizontal level forward directly into the lode. The level cut varies from 7 to 8 feet in height and is 3 feet wide. Small stemple holes can be seen in the walls indicating the possibility of a return airway for 'fire setting'. This was an early method of breaking ground necessitating the building of a fire at the working face. When the rock was very hot, a mixture of vinegar and water was thrown onto it which split the rock thus allowing the miners to place wedges. The level roof would be partitioned off with boards to make a return airway to remove the smoke and fumes.

The level was driven for a distance of 37 yards, and such was the quality of the copper that in the sole near the entrance, the vein has been pursued by a shaft working to a depth of about 20 feet. This was one of the main early workings, and just beside the level mouth lie the remains of a large bothy which appears to have been a single-storey, three roomed house where the workforce would have lived.

Just below this point, the early miners have excavated a large surface work on the vein, which they have worked down to Ellers Beck. The vein at this point is some 6 feet wide and can be seen clearly in the stream bed. Here, the Germans have driven levels both on the east and west banks of the beck. On the western bank, a coffin level was driven to undercut the open workings and two rises put up, which effectively drained the workings above. The main objective of this 57 yard level was to drain the shaft in the higher working, but this connection with the adit and sump working was never made.

The level on the eastern bank again follows the copper vein, and the copper exposed in the rock above the level has been hand-picked out leaving a groove of some 9 inches. The level continues for a distance of 32 yards (level is collapsed here), and at one point the overhand stoping has been so vigorous that the ground cover has been broken through.

Some 200 yards to the north-east, another small hand-picked open work can be found beside the road.

During this period of working, the Copperplate Mine played a very important part in the history of the Mines Royal in so much that some of the 174 cwt of copper ore dispatched to the smelter at Brigham during October 1567, was the first to be smelted efficiently.

By the end of 1568, the Borrowdale workings including Copperplate Mine had been opened up for about 4 years and had been an important venture costing some £1,492 17s 11½d. The expenditure during this same period was exceeded only by the Newlands valley workings.

During 1569, the smith working at Copperplate was Wolff Hund, and he employed two Englishmen who worked for 5d per shift. General labourers were paid 4d or 5d a day. An interesting point is that during this period the valley was still a wild place and so roads and paths had to be constructed. The road-making near Grange was in fact being carried out by Thomas Fischer, John Langstrath, John Judall (Youdale, an old Borrowdale family) and John Fischer and they were being paid 10/- for the job.

By 1571, the Copperplate workings were under the control of foreman W Hochholzer, under-foreman Franz Dorn, a partnership of Jacob Hofer and Jorg Bachmair, another one of U Schlegel, S Buechberger, J Colmanstetter and H Moser and a third one of W Binder and J Heisel. It appears that, just as in later years, the workforce of the day was divided into teams to work different parts of the mine and its area.

Around 1602, the mines were visited by George Bowes and Francis Needham, who came from Carlisle via Bolton, where they visited the colliery which supplied much of the area with coal, in particular the Keswick smelter at Brigham.

These locations cover the full extent of the period of the Mines Royal operations at the Copperplate workings, however, there may well be other very small trials hidden under the 400 years of scree and ground cover.

During 1819, the lease for the sett was taken over by Mr John Tebay from Whitehaven and this included the Copperplate Mine at Ellers. The royalty dues were now paid to the Earl of Egremont, and the new owners were hoping to enjoy a success similar to that of the previous tenants 250 years before. Unhappily, this adventure was to be brief and fruitless.

Initially, a small pilot trial was driven into a vein some 50 feet above the upper Copperplate working. This time though, the level was not hand-picked but blasted forward by hand-drilling with the aid of gunpowder and was of much larger dimensions being 6 feet high and 4 feet wide. The trial, following a quartz vein proved unsuccessful and was only driven 14 yards taking probably no more than 3 to 4 weeks to complete.

A more serious attempt was directed at the German level on the eastern bank of Ellers Beck. The marvellous hand-chipping of the German miners was however desecrated here, as the miners now blasted the level wider in order to use wheelbarrows. Had it been successful, then it would have been railed out for tubs. Just inside the entrance, the portal of the level was enlarged to form a small chamber measuring approximately 4 feet wide by 8 feet long and cut upwards to at least 6 feet high. On the right hand wall is a small inscription which looks like the letter 'F'. It is doubtful that this dates from the Elizabethan period in view of the later widening. Within the entrance chamber, a shaft has been sunk just in from the portal and is 4 feet by 3 feet and 20 feet deep. This was to explore the vein at depth in much the same way that the Germans had done all those years before. In the higher workings however, they were not as successful, the copper not being in sufficient quantity, and the trials were soon abandoned.

During 1871, when the foundations of the house now known as Ellers were excavated, a collection of artefacts was discovered.

Salt Well and Manesty Mine

HERE A saline spring cuts the vein, and a series of shafts and surface trials were put down to exploit the lead and copper ores. The Manesty/Salt Well vein hades NE/SW and is bisected by the Brandlehow Lode NW/SE; approximately at this point is the Salt Well.

The water of the Salt Well is similar in quality to that of Brandlehow, and in about 1820 the then owner of the land, Sir John Woodford K C B sank the well and built a small house over it. The house was of stone construction and was about 10 feet square, the roof of local slate with sandstone copings. The actual bathing area fills the floor, and for the convenience of the public it was divided into two pools, both about 3 feet deep. The local populace however, were not very impressed with the waters, and in fairness, the site is rather remote being in the middle of a field and well off the beaten track. Those few people who did avail themselves of its therapeutic qualities must have been hardy souls indeed, and as time went by, the building gradually fell into disrepair.

The group of mine workings here is by and large forgotten, as the land is flat and subject to flooding, not ideal conditions for mining. Some of these trials are pre-gunpowder workings by the German miners, and are hand-chipped surface excavations which were without doubt, done well prior to the turn of the 16th Century.

If we trace the proven workings from the edge of Derwentwater at Great Bay, we can see the work of the Elizabethan miner at first hand without risking an underground foray. It is at this promontory on the very shores of the lake that the vein is exposed, and here the early miners have hand-chipped their way directly into the copper lode. A few yards inland is the site of a water-filled shaft which has been put down directly on the vein. The spoil area here is a considerable size, and it appears that a level has been put in lower down to cut the shaft. It has not been possible to ascertain whether this shaft is of Elizabethan origin, or work done at a later period. Also on the vein is another small hand-chipped open-work with a small sump and nearby are some other well-grassed surface trials. Just 60 yards north is another vein running parallel, and at this point the German miners have excavated an open work on the back of the vein.

The vein continues westward, and beyond the area of the Salt Well is the site of another mine, known as Manesty Mine. The name derives from Manesty Band, the rib of rock extending steeply up the eastern shoulder of Maiden Moor, where brown streaks reveal the course of the mineralised vein. It is here, close to the Salt Well and at virtually the lowest point that the German miners have attacked the rock with their primitive tools and driven forward a level. Its success is unrecorded possibly because of its close proximity to Copperplate but successful it must have been, for a large amount of dressed copper ore ready for the Keswick smelter still lies at the entrance.

During the year of 1783, this area of land to the south of Manesty Park was owned by Joseph Banks, and the land just to the west where the Salt Well is was owned by Abraham Banks. It is worthwhile mentioning that the northern copper vein is skirted by the remains of a substantial wall, which leads to the edge of Manesty Park, then known as John Watkins Park. Here are the remains of a small house now in ruins, which may well have been for the miners. The only other indigent workers here at this time would have been foresters and one assumes that their shelter would have been inside the forest itself.

It is interesting to see where the veins on this low area break to the surface, the flashes of white quartz being the give away to the early prospectors. Although this land would have been well covered with woodland, the rock outcrops would have stood proud making their job much easier.

The veins going west towards the Salt Well intersect a north-south lead vein, and here on the surface is a hand-chipped trial on an exposed vein. The early workings attracted the attention of John Tebay, who decided to sink a considerable shaft onto the Brandlehow Vein. No records are available as to the success or otherwise of this venture and it is possible that the Keswick Mining Company continued to work the mine after the termination of Mr Tebay's lease. At least three stone buildings were erected very adjacent to the site but unfortunately, this is now agricultural land and has been reclaimed. When, in the early 1960s, the shaft was filled it took a JCB more than a day to do the job, and the spoil heap, which would have given some indication of the depth of the working, was taken away for infill and road hardcore.

Manesty Park

JUST NORTH of Manesty lie two very small trials, the first spoil heap lying just behind the wall of the caravan park beside the road. Unfortunately, the actual ancient tunnel leading to the open stope and pit working was partially destroyed when the road was put through. By the nature of the working this could be very old. Just along the road and on the old road to Brandlehow mine, is a small shaft sunk directly on the vein but to what depth this has been developed is impossible to tell.

Black Crag Mine & Trials

THE CRAGS on the eastern flank of Catbells are known as Black Crags and here, high above the hanging screes, the Yewthwaite vein bisects the mountain in a NW/SE direction, bringing with it lead, zinc and pyrite. Beside the rock band is a ravine, and here in this remote and virtually inaccessible place the miners practised their skills.

This is the territory of the buzzard, the peregrine and the raven as they soar and dive high above the fell tops, and here the access to the crags is barred except for the 800 feet of unremitting slog through the scree or the ascent from Yewthwaite Mine over the other side of the ridge. Remote though it is, two miners Wyllen Fischer and Matthew Hodg were working the vein of lead in

1569 and to them goes the honour of being the first. But it is to John Tebay's miners in 1820 that the credit for endurance and tenacity must go. Here there are no paths, no easy way, no protection from Borrowdale's inhospitable weather and at 1,200 feet the privations can be well imagined. It is more than likely that the miners lived at the bothy at Yewthwaite Mine and daily trudged up the 500 feet over Hause Gate carrying powder, drill steels, hammers and provisions for the day's work. At Black Crag Mine itself there is no trace of a hut or indeed any sort of shelter. From here the men would have traversed the crag to the vein and continuing the earlier efforts, which would have been no more than a scrape, they have worked down in the vein a depth of 20 feet along a course of 20 yards between 2 and 4 feet in width. This would have taken many weeks of drilling and blasting and one can imagine the stillness of this silent place being disturbed by the violent explosions.

Eventually, the vein was worked to capacity, and so a sump was put down to retrieve the lead and now water was the enemy, cascading down the natural ravine and pouring relentlessly into the new working. Therefore a cross cut was blasted 28 yards through the rock to cut the higher workings. The level was cut to about 4 feet wide and 5 feet 9 inches high and on reaching the vein it was tried north for 6 yards, however this proved barren. The vein was then pursued south and a bunch of ore was found in the sole and taken out. The level was continued and the drive cut a natural watercourse which drained the workings above, making conditions slightly more comfortable for the men. However, the vein soon pinched in and although more work was done in the sole of the level no further success was forthcoming.

This fascinating trial is a credit to the men who worked here although their efforts were overshadowed by Yewthwaite and Goldscope mines which were included into the same sett. On top of that, all the lead produced here was added into the Yewthwaite and Brandlehow production figures.

One mystery remains however, for there seem to be no trods or tracks to indicate where the ore was taken to after being brought to surface. One strong possibility is that it could have been sledded down the scree to the mine road from where it would have been transported onwards.

Two other small trials have been identified in this area, one in the same ravine just 5 yards south of the crosscut entrance. It is possible that this may have been the original starting place for the crosscut, although it was started directly on an E/W vein and this is visible in the face. Just above this trial, which is no more than an indentation in the rock, the area has been excavated to take the water away from the aforementioned crosscut. Here the ground is quite steep and alluvial landslip must have been an ever present danger. The other trial is at the same horizon but is in the crags about 150 yards to the north, and here the miners have driven a level about 5 yards.

Black Crag Mine and surface work

Surveyed and drawn Ian Tyler 1995

Scale: 1/8th inch = 1 yard approx.

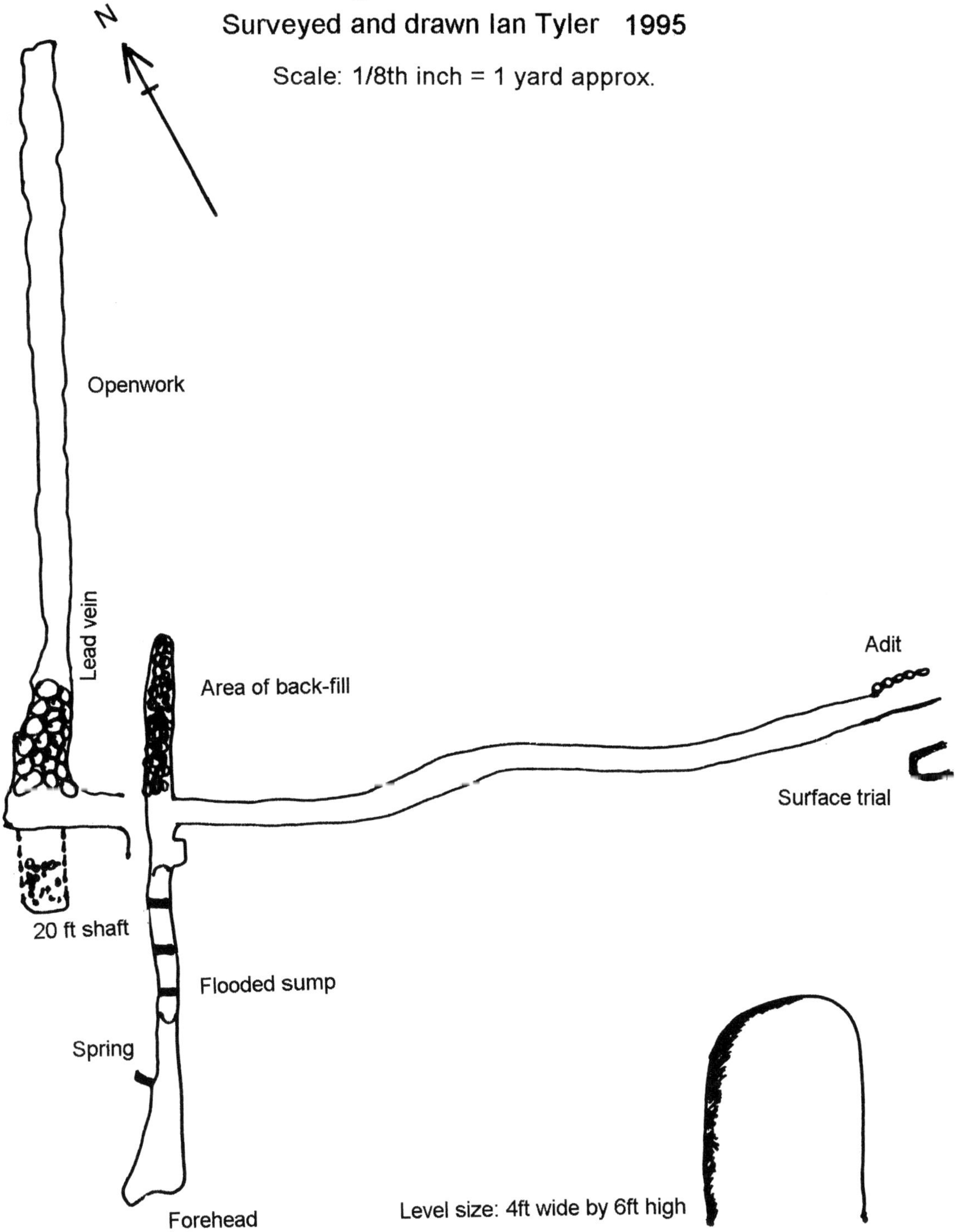

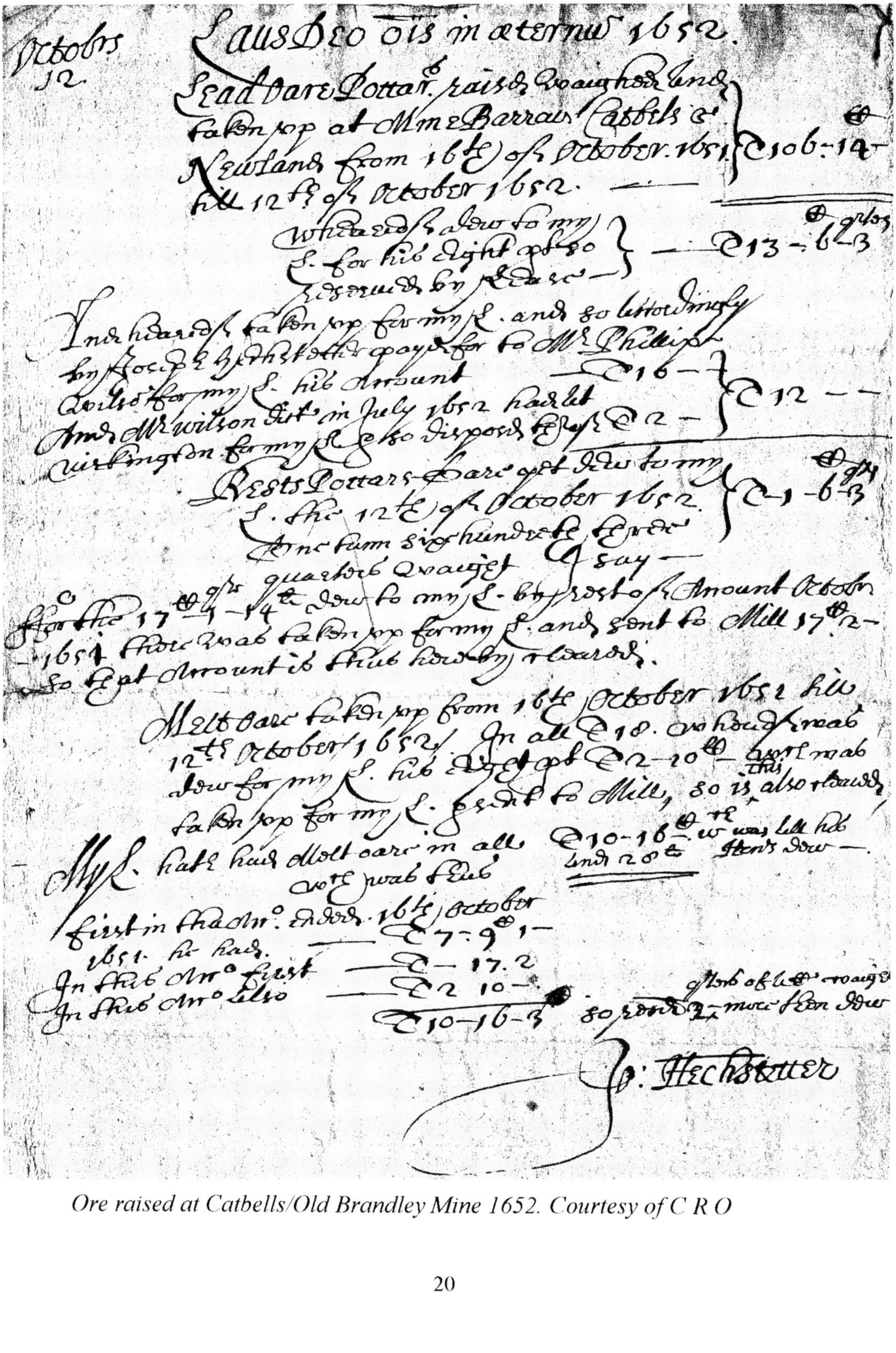

Octobr 12 Laus Deo o[mn]is in aeternu[m] 1652.

Lead Oare Pottar raised weighed and taken up at Mine Barraus Catbels & Newland from 16th of October 1651 till 12th of October 1652. — 106 – 14 –

[illegible]

Rests Pottars Oare [illegible] the 12th of October 1652. — 1 – 6 – 3

[illegible]

Melt Oare taken up from 16th October 1651 till 12th October 1652 [illegible]

My L. hath had Molt oare in all — 10 – 16 – [illegible]

first in the Acc^o. ended 16th October 1651 he had — 7 – 9 – 1 –

In this Acc^o first — – 17 . 2

In this Acc^o also — 2 10 –

— 10 – 16 – 3

[illegible]

Jo: Hechstetter

Ore raised at Catbells/Old Brandley Mine 1652. Courtesy of C R O

Skelgill Bank and Minersputt

THE POPULAR green mountain of Catbells overlooking Derwentwater is a firm favourite with most fell-walking visitors to the Lake District. However, many people are totally unaware of the mineral vein bisecting the northern shoulder of the fell in a NW/SE direction, and of the history attached to it. This started with the Elizabethans who worked the vein on both sides of the mountain.

It is thought that on the NW shoulder of the fell was a working called Minersputt on Skelgill Bank where the mineral extracted was galena. Its first record of working was during 1567 when the sum of £14 0s 0d was spent on opening up the work. The mine consisted of a series of open works directly over where the vein was exposed at surface. None of them penetrated deep into the heart of the mountain, but were literally pickings on the back of the vein.

During October 1651, Joseph Hechstetter leased the mine to Hugh Pottar and Richard Tickell who were to work it with miners William Tickell and John Fisher. From then until the 12th of October 1653 a total of 21 tons 4 cwt 2 qrs of lead ore were taken from the mines of "Barrow and Miners Pitts". By the 13th of October 1654 a further 9 tons 4 cwt had been extracted. These ore receipts were signed by J Hechstetter and the royalty dues paid were one eighth. By 1657 the mine was being worked by Thomas Tickell and a Colonel Beal and during this year 4 tons 7 cwt of lead ore were raised. It may well have been that the workings for the period did in fact actually expose the great lode on the crest of the ridge. Here the orebody was good and the pickings rich for the early adventurers, and it was on the eastern side that the later companies came to develop the vein with more skilled methods of extraction. This eastern side was to become known as Old Brandley.

Old Brandley

LOOKING TOWARDS the eastern flank of Catbells, one cannot fail to see where the mining activity has taken place. The soft rolling lines of the fell have been scarred and pockmarked by hundreds of years of man's relentless search for the mineral wealth lying within the veins. The Elizabethan miners could not have missed the vein streaking diagonally across the fell, and although their initial interest was in copper, there was silver to be had in the lead of Old Brandley. In the Lake District, considerable amounts of lead had been taken already for its silver content, and between 1570 and 1580 around 4,344 oz of silver had been smelted. This continued until the turn of the century but at a decreasing rate, and between 1580 and 1600 it appears that only 820 oz of silver were made.

It is reasonable to assume that the men working Skelgill Bank had taken more than a cursory glance at this side of the mountain and had probably taken lead where it out-cropped on surface. Certainly the open works which are about 15 feet deep at the crest bear signs of hand-picking thus establishing pre-gunpowder working. At this horizon and at a later date the miners have dug what appears to be a water-leat or trough to retain a certain amount of water, possibly for washing the ore and at a later date to act as a water-blast for here, high on the fell, water for washing would be at a premium. The mine worked intermittently from 1701 to 1705 during which time 35 tons 7 cwt of lead were drawn, although it is not possible to ascertain who held a lease to work it at the time. It is likely however, that this was when the small level was initially driven 50 feet down from the ridge to undercut the ancient upper surface workings. The level has been blasted out, using very small drill steels, to 5 feet 9 inches high by 3 feet wide. Around 1810 only 5 tons 12 cwt of lead ore were extracted indicating that little was happening and it is possible that this was when the trial was driven from an ancient open work much lower down the fell at OD 670 feet. This trial was driven directly following the vein, and the level cut to very small dimensions when it was blasted forward all those years ago. It meanders on for a distance of 130 yards and the roof has been stoped out in two places in an attempt to win the lead.

During 1819, the mine lease was taken up by John Tebay of Whitehaven who was an experienced miner, and it was he who decided to drive a main crosscut in an attempt to expose the vein at depth. This was Coates Level, named after the local miner who drove it and it was driven into the flank of Catbells at about OD 880 feet. It did intersect the vein and some lead was extracted but the miners were surprised at the amount of amber fluorspar which was found within the vein. This of course had no commercial value at that time and simply hindered extraction and dressing. There were rewards however and by 1833 there had been a return of 210 tons of lead drawn, at a royalty payment to Lord Egremont of one eighth.

The nearby Stoneycroft smelter was by now closed, and it seems that it was more efficient to transport the lead by sea from the West Coast ports than to transport it overland to Alston as so many of the Cumbrian mines did. At this time the lead was being sold to various companies, among them H Jenkins of Liverpool and Dee Bank and Co of Bagillt. This last was in the heart of the North Wales lead mining field and was already a well established lead smelting area. In fact Messrs Walker Parker of Newcastle were in the process in 1834, of taking over the lease of the Dee Bank smelters from the Halkin adventurers. This site was not massive but it had great potential due to its close proximity to the Welsh mines and the accessibility to the River Dee for shipment.

The mine continued to work and during 1834, lead extracted amounted to 53 tons 17 cwt 2 qtrs. There were probably no more than three or four men working at any one time, and certainly the levels were kept to small dimensions and up to then were never railed out. All the ore was hand-dressed at the level mouth and the rubbish and quartz spoil thrown down the steep fellside. Two further adits were driven by John Tebay, one at OD 740 feet but this was literally no more than a trial. A more serious attempt was made at OD 690 feet and it is from here that 16 tons 15 cwt of ore were drawn in 1836 from the sole of the level. This was the last lead ore to be raised by this adventurer for despite the modicum of success achieved here by John Tebay, his other mining ventures had clawed away at his cash resources, stretching them to the limit. John was unable to continue with the venture and the mine was abandoned.

It appears that the mine remained closed until about 1847, when the Keswick Mining Company was formed, the major shareholders being Samuel Merryweather, a mining engineer of some note and his two partners Messrs Richardson and Langton. Lead was fetching around £12 10s 0d per ton, and the silver content of the Brandley lead, although not great, came in at between 7 and 10 oz per ton. The new company decided to undercut all Tebay's drivings and the old workings above in the hope of finding the rich mother lode. The new level, driven from OD 630 feet, was known as the Low Level and was blasted forward a distance of some 200 yards, however little lead was found despite the efforts made and by 1849 only 3 tons 10 cwt had been raised. It must therefore be assumed that the vein here at depth had pinched out and that it was worthless pursuing the venture further

The price of lead was fluctuating and by 1854 was around £13 10s 0d per ton. From then until 1860, the Keswick Mining Company was selling lead ore to Locke Blackett & Co, Shield Turnbull and Co, the Washington Chemical Co and W J Cookson and Co among others. Carriage was 6/- per ton, storage at Cockermouth 1/- per ton and the ore was dispatched in wooden casks.

In July 1869, a take note was agreed at a royalty of one tenth and a rent of £50 0s 0d. Two men were to be employed throughout the term of one year, however the adventure seems to have fizzled out without much work being done.

A more serious enquiry was made in 1873 by Messrs H K Spark and Benjamin Plummer of Braithwaite, both well known men on the Cumbrian mining scene. Initially the work went well and both the Low Level and Coates Level appear to have been cleaned out and got ready for further work. Unfortunately then it seems that finances ran short leaving them no alternative but to pack up. During this tenure only a small amount of ore appears to have been raised and that apparently was the last time that Brandley Mine was worked.

Below the Low Level are two further trial levels, the first about 60 feet below with the ruins of a small house beside it, but the tip is well grassed over and there is no sign of ore on the dump. Below this level is another trial which is to be found behind the wall on the far side of the lake road. Both have been driven at least 50 yards but no accurate working dates can be given. I would suggest that they were done by John Tebay around the 1830s as part of his adventures.

Brandlehow Mine

THE MAIN lode runs virtually N/S and hades 2 feet per fathom, varying in width from 2 feet to 6 feet, and containing a variety of minerals: galena/silver(9 oz per ton), cerussite, blende, baryte, gold, pyrite, manganese and copper. In the northern part of the mine, a branch is thrown off to the east and is as rich as the main vein. Numerous quartz stringers intersect the vein mostly at right angles and a 20 foot wide dyke of igneous rock running east/west contains galena and blende. A rather unique occurrence is that the vein in the northern part of the mine releases gallons of water which is impregnated with salt. This has been used medicinally, and an analysis was carried out in 1848 by Thomas Ransome, the findings of which are as follows:

Chloride of calcium	87.67
Chloride of magnesium	1.53
Chloride of sodium	110.23
Sulphate of magnesia	4.35
	203.78

This is the solid content found in an imperial pint, and it is interesting to note that the amount of chloride of calcium found is one of the largest recorded.

The mine is certainly very old and the first recorded extraction was in 1567 when 3 cwt of pure copper ore from Brandlehow was smelted by Daniel Hechstetter. The ore would have been taken by picking on the back of the vein, as here the ground cover is in places non-existent, and therefore the vein would have been easily spotted by the early miners. This first working on the Brandlehow vein would certainly have been around what is now known as Whitwells Level and the bell pits above.

In 1569 it is recorded that 6 kibbles of ore were taken from Fechtenbachs Nick in 'Brandelgil'. This stream falls directly down the steep eastern side of

Southernmost German open-work near Copperplate Mine, 1564. Caldbeck Mining Museum Collection.

Elizabethan trial at Copperplate Mine, 1564. Caldbeck Mining Museum Collection.

Elizabethan trial at Copperplate Mine 1564, underground section. Caldbeck Mining Museum Collection.

Entrance to upper trial at Copperplate Mine, 1564. Caldbeck Mining Museum Collection.

Copperplate Mine, coffin level on north drive circa 1568. Ian Hebson Collection

Open-work, Copperplate Mine, 1564. Caldbeck Mining Museum Collection.

Black Crag, original open work on surface circa 1825. Ian Hebson Collection

Black Crag Mine, level showing sump and old timber staging circa 1825.
Ian Hebson Collection

Top: Salt Well, Manesty. Caldbeck Mining Museum Collection.
Bottom: Site of shaft workings near Salt Well. Caldbeck Mining Museum Collection.

Top: Site of Manesty Mine showing calcified copper heap. Caldbeck Mining Museum Collection.
Bottom: Brandlehow Mine site today. Caldbeck Mining Museum Collection.

Top: Main waterwheel at Brandlehow Mine circa 1880. Caldbeck Mining Museum collection
Bottom: Brandlehow Mine after closure 1891. Caldbeck Mining Museum Collection

Top: Brandlehow Mine, Whitwells Level. Caldbeck Mining Museum Collection.
Bottom: Old Mine Manager's house, Brandlehow. Caldbeck Mining Museum Collection.

Brandlehow Mine, Salt Level. Stoped area rising up to Wood Level. Roy Fellows Collection

Brandlehow Mine, Salt Level. Head of manway. Roy Fellows Collection

Old Brandley Mine, open-stopes on Catbells. Caldbeck Mining Museum Collection.

John Tebay's trial at Old Brandley Mine. Caldbeck Mining Museum Collection.

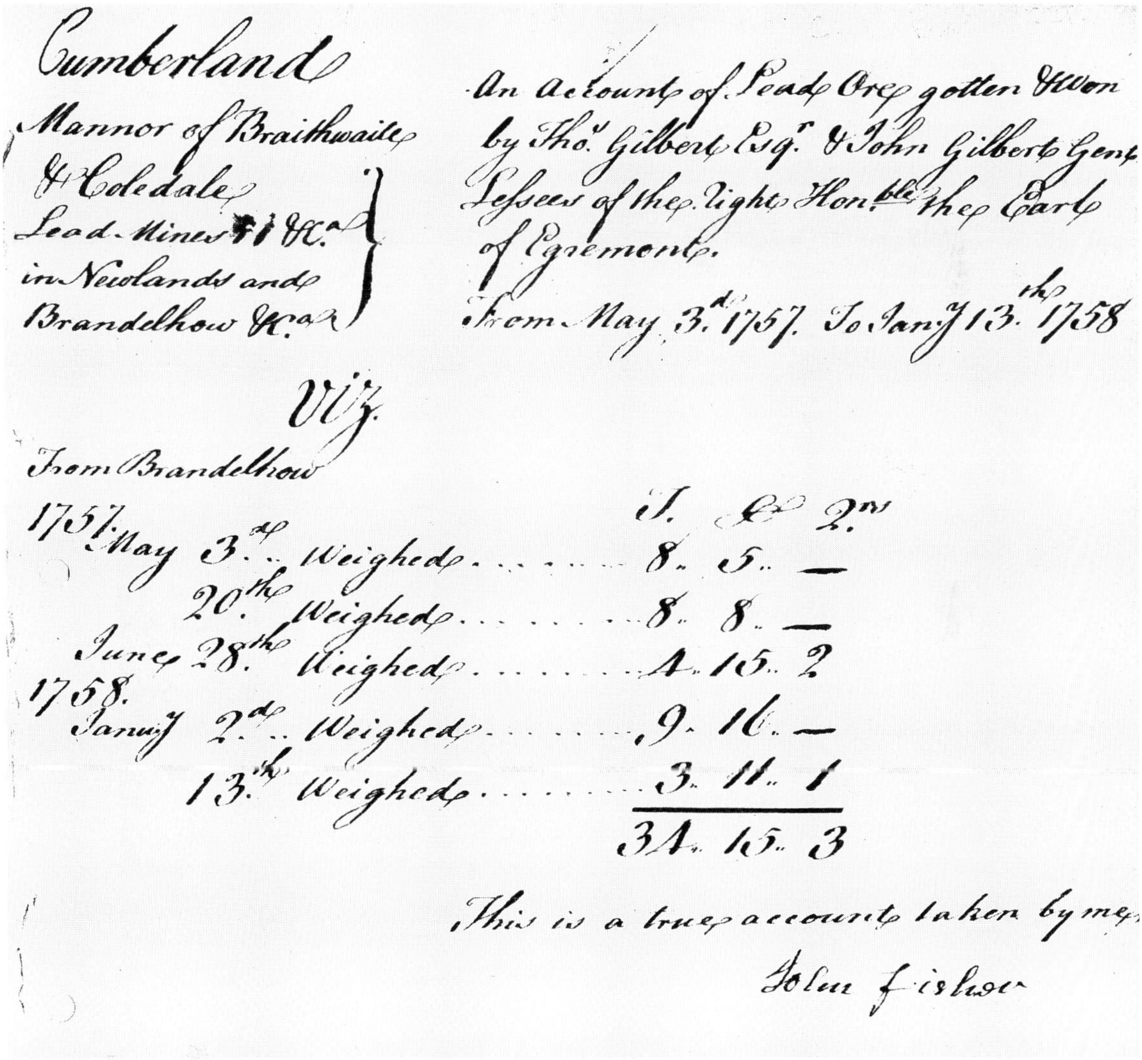

Cumberland

Mannor of Braithwaite & Coledale Lead Mines &c. in Newlands and Brandelhow &c.

An Account of Lead Ore gotten & Won by Tho.s Gilbert Esq.r & John Gilbert Gent. Lessees of the Right Hon.ble the Earl of Egremont.

From May 3.d 1757. To Jan.y 13.th 1758

Viz.

From Brandelhow

		T.	C.	Q.rs
1757. May 3.d	Weighed	8.	5.	—
20.th	Weighed	8.	8.	—
June 28.th	Weighed	4.	15.	2
1758. Jan.y 2.d	Weighed	9.	16.	—
13.th	Weighed	3.	11.	1
		34.	15.	3

This is a true account taken by me

John Fisher

Account of lead raised by the Gilberts at Brandlehow Mine 1758. Courtesy of C R O

Catbells and would have cut practically through the middle of the sett. Just above the mine is the location of this early working although unfortunately nothing now remains. Close by the stream however can be found the remains of the vein, and here the rock is streaked by mineralisation. Nearby are two old quarries, and it was presumably when the higher of the two was worked that Fechtenbachs Nick was obliterated.

During the early days of the tenure of the German miners, a great deal of building was going on, including the usual mine buildings such as smithies, stamp mills, dressing floors and of course, the great smelter at Brigham said to be at that time the largest in Europe. A jetty or landing stage, 'Midingstett' was built on the lake shore at Keswick, and goods and materials were constantly being transported over the water by boat from an area on the eastern shore of Derwentwater called Copperheap Bay. There was a great deal of wood at Brandlehow much of it birch, and along with quarry stone it was sent across to the Midingstett to be used in Keswick.

By 1571, we find great activity on Vicar's Island where were being erected small houses, a windmill, pig-sties, a pigeon-house, brewery and gardens. Again, material was being taken from Brandlehow to the island and as a great part of the work was taking place in winter, this was conveyed over the ice which now covered Derwentwater.

In spite of all this intense labour there were moments of relaxation, and in November 1571 Daniel Hechstetter celebrated his birthday by providing one quart of wine each for the 74 Germans and 36 quarts for the Englishmen who were working at the mines and the Smelthouses!

After the Germans' tenure, there was one early lease issued to Jon Scott who, between 1726 and 1729 raised 6 tons and 3 qrs of ore. Then in April 1754, a lease was agreed between the Earl of Egremont and Thomas and John Gilbert at a royalty payment of one eighth. In their first year the two men raised 60 tons 11 cwt 3 qrs for which they paid a royalty of £19 16s 0d and it appears they worked on until the 24th of November 1767. It is quite possible that these early adventurers were responsible for driving the first proper underground levels as they were experienced miners. These would have been Whitwells, driven directly under the ancient surface workings to undercut the western vein at depth and lower down and driven on the east vein, Wood Level. The entrance to this was cut in solid rock and was driven a few yards when a westerly crosscut was put in to intersect the west vein. The crosscut reached the vein after about 12 feet and this was then pursued parallel to the adit level and recorded on plans as Woods Level West; the adit level was then known as Wood Level East. Both these workings are old and were eventually connected by stope workings and an internal shaft all of which work was probably done prior to the arrival of John Tebay.

In 1819, John Tebay who had the lease on Old Brandley Mine, took over the Brandlehow lease and drove the Salt Level (not to be confused with the Salt Well). For those unfamiliar with the area, the vein has cut a saline spring which now runs out of the level, hence the name. The level was driven into solid rock just a few feet above the shores of Derwentwater. This was the lowest point a level could be driven and would succeed in de-watering all the upper workings. Here the miners pushed forward for 30 yards in a westerly direction and at this point the level strikes north. Just before the heading came under the steepening surface, a rise was put up for ventilation and was called Coates Shaft. Eventually this drive would continue firstly under the old Wood Level where the vein divides and then onwards under Whitwells.

To further prove the vein to the south, John Tebay sank a shaft (Old Shaft or Tebays Shaft) to a depth of 20 fathoms with levels off at 10 fathoms and at the shaft bottom. To pump the workings dry, a 34 foot waterwheel was erected and this was also the main hauling shaft. Just to the south, a small rise was put up from the 10 fathom level to surface and was laddered to provide an access shaft for the miners. A good bunch of lead ore was discovered in the southern drive but this success was short-lived although a considerable amount of stoping was done.

John Tebay pursued this venture with great vigour and whilst his other mining efforts were helping to support the ailing Brandlehow, his losses were mounting. Shaft work mining is expensive, pumping costs and effort are always a drain on resources, and everything below the adit level has to be handled at least three times whether it is rubbish coming out or equipment going in and down. In a last effort to survive, John wrote to Lord Egremont in March 1836 to ask for a reduction in his royalty payments from one eighth to one eleventh for lead and down to one twelfth for copper. It was hoped that on negotiating this new agreement he would have the ears of other investors but alas it was not to be, and with debts accruing (finally totalling £2,600) he decided to quit. During his seventeen year tenure he had spent upwards of £14,000 pounds on the development of his mines and now he was penniless.

A new company was formed in 1847 calling itself the Keswick Mining Company, and this was run by the mining engineer Samuel Merryweather and Messrs Langton and Richardson (also working Old Brandley). It was decided that the old shaft was badly sited and so a new engine shaft was sunk further north. A 30 foot waterwheel was erected for the initial pumping out of the shaft as it went down and, eventually passing the Salt Level horizon, the shaft arrived at the 30 fathom horizon. From here levels were driven out to extended the workings northwards. In doing this they cut many leads of water and it was soon discovered that the waterwheel was inadequate, which resulted in the purchase of a 26 hp steam engine to ensure a greater pumping capacity.

When John Tebay's men blasted the Salt Level forward it was cut to a very small size, just over 5 feet 7 inches high and 3 feet 6 inches wide and was not straight. The twists and turns made it impossible to rail out for wagons and consequently all the rubbish from this level up to now had been removed by wheelbarrow. The new engine shaft however would alter all that and now underground levels could be cut to a good size and laid with rails. All transportation of the lead ore and waste to the shaft stagings was now by wagons which could then be raised to the surface.

By 1853, around sixty men were employed at the mine and during this period extra buildings were erected to accommodate new machinery, and tramways were laid to remove the ore from the engine shaft. One branch led to the mill, whilst another took the waste to the lake edge where it was dumped. In 1854, the 20 Fathom Level working north was in a solid rib of ore about 10 inches thick; this was called the Salt Sump Stope and was worked up into the Salt Level and from here a rise called Dents Shaft (Salt Sump Shaft) was pushed out through to the surface. This success was short-lived however, and further development took place. The levels were pushed north in the vein a distance of 80 fathoms in the hope that the rich showing of galena would re-appear, but this was not to be. During the next 10 years, levels at 10, 20, 30 and 40 fathoms were driven north with occasional success and pockets of ore were found and duly stoped out. The 30 Fathom Level produced some very rich deposits particularly from Beauchers and Smiths stopes which were 160 yards north of the Engine Shaft and were stoped through to the 20 Fathom above; most of this section was producing half a ton of lead per fathom. These finds spurred the company on to more development work and the vigour with which the mine was being worked is indicated by the size of the workforce which, by 1857 totalled approximately seventy men. Of these, about a third worked on surface in the new washing and dressing plant and the rest were engaged in the actual development of the mine. The price of lead had risen to £14 0s 0d per ton and the company wanted to cut in on the profitability.

The Engine Shaft was sunk to a depth of 50 fathoms and main headings were again taken off, one from the shaft bottom on a northerly heading and another, also going north at the 40 fathom horizon. The 40 Fathom Level proved to be very sparse although odd pockets of lead were found. Apart from Mitchells stope, just off the shaft and Tysons which was found 70 yards north, virtually no deposits were found in the southern headings. The 50 Fathom Level was much richer, and in the area of the shaft bottom was a very rich orebody. The first 40 yards of this level were eventually stoped out to the 40 Fathom Level above, and was known as Atkinsons Stope. Although ore was being raised, the pumping and hauling costs were becoming excessive and the old engine was now working 24 hours a day, removing the 150 gallons of

"Henry Dickinson falls to his death" J Tyler.

water per minute flowing into the mine and which was increasing as the mine was opened out.

The search for lead continued by the re-opening and sinking of the old Tebay Shaft a further 10 fathoms, bringing its total depth to 30 fathoms. Levels were driven north from the 20 fathom station and the bottom of the shaft, and both these eventually connected with the main engine shaft which joined the two workings together. Here the ore from the southern workings could now be drawn out more efficiently, however, these were now well below the water-table and the vein being less than 50 yards from the edge of Derwentwater, the state of things underground can be well imagined. Mining conditions during these times were primitive enough but to have to contend with the influx of hundreds of gallons of salty water getting into cuts and eyes must have been testing indeed. This together with the acrid fumes from the exploding charges and the stench of tallow candle smoke hanging in stagnant air, would have tested the determination of the most tenacious miner.

A serious accident occurred on 13th of November 1857 when a young miner, Henry Dickinson was descending the ladders in the engine shaft. On arriving at the 40 Fathom Level, he was somehow struck by the kibble being lowered from above. Not seeing or hearing the descending object he was dashed against the ladder by it, so losing his grip. Poor Henry plunged headlong the 60 feet to the bottom of the shaft, where he received mortal fractures and died instantly. The other miners on the scene, Moses Mawson, John Dover, John Graves and Daniel Dunglinson all rushed to his aid but it was too late to save him. The following day, Saturday, an inquest was held at Jane Lowden's house at Mill Dam and coroner Henry Beale summoned twelve mine workers to attend. The verdict brought in was accidental death, and this was one of the few fatal mine accidents to occur in non-ferrous mining in the Lake District.

The 40 and 50 Fathom Levels were pursued north with all possible speed and the ore stoped out and winched to the surface. Once it had been sorted and crushed it was sold to Locke, Blackett and Co of Gallowgate, Newcastle on Tyne and another buyer, Shield Turnbull, at prices varying from £13 5s 6d to £15 5s 0d per ton.

During 1860, the Keswick Mining Company had a change of partners and now included Messrs Charles Dear, John Whitwell of Kendal, William James Dunsford, Edward John Ranken, James Postlethwaite of Brandlehow and Miles Farrer of Braithwaite and the royalties payable were one fifteenth value of ore raised. The partners made a management decision to abandon their other mining interests in the area to concentrate on Brandlehow. This, they believed, could become another Greenside or Coniston and consequently all their resources were channelled into the mine which was worked with great vigour. The area round the bottom of the shaft was still productive, and a rise

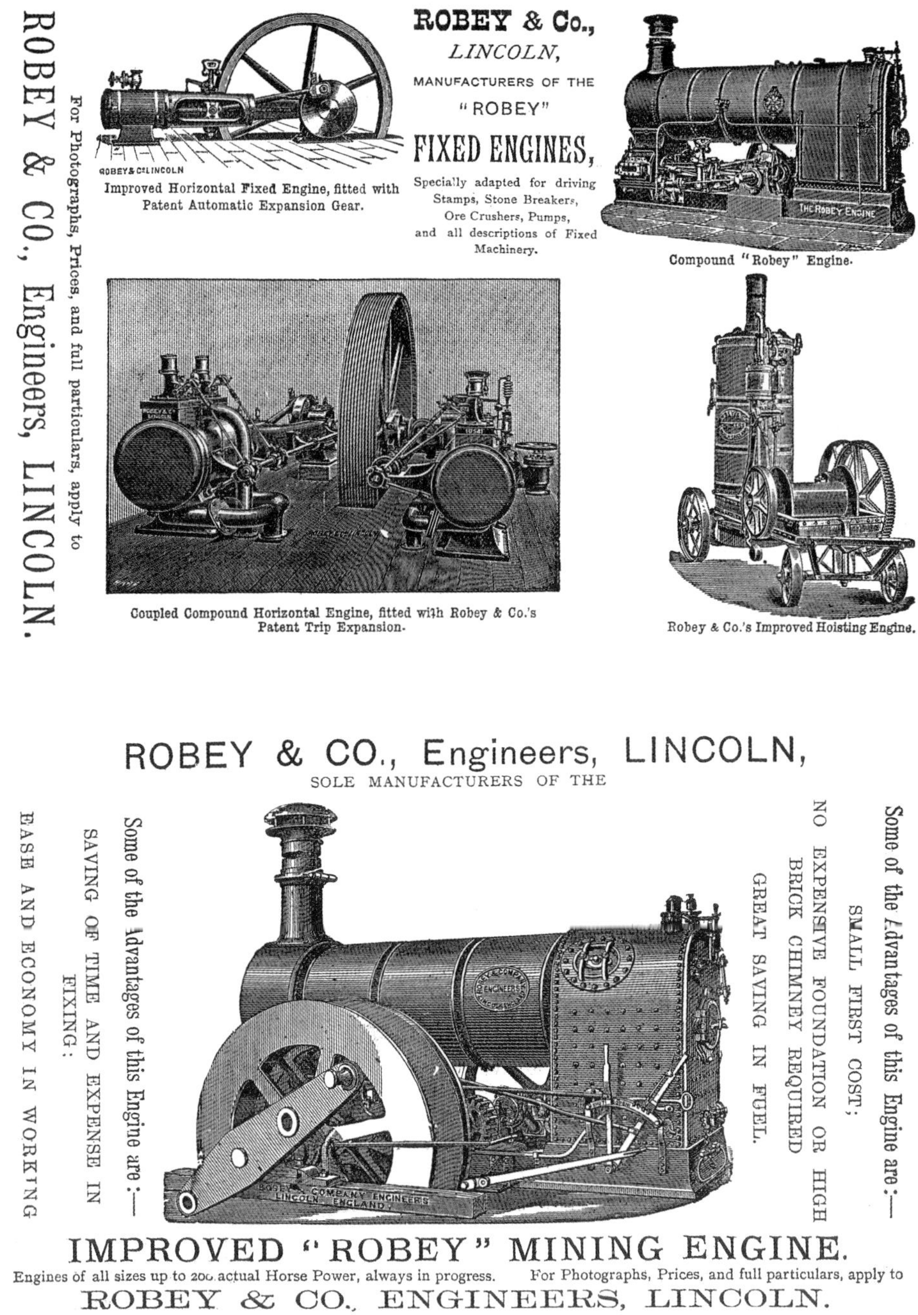

Advert for Robey, suppliers of mine machinery to Brandlehow Mine circa 1890. Caldbeck Mining Museum Collection.

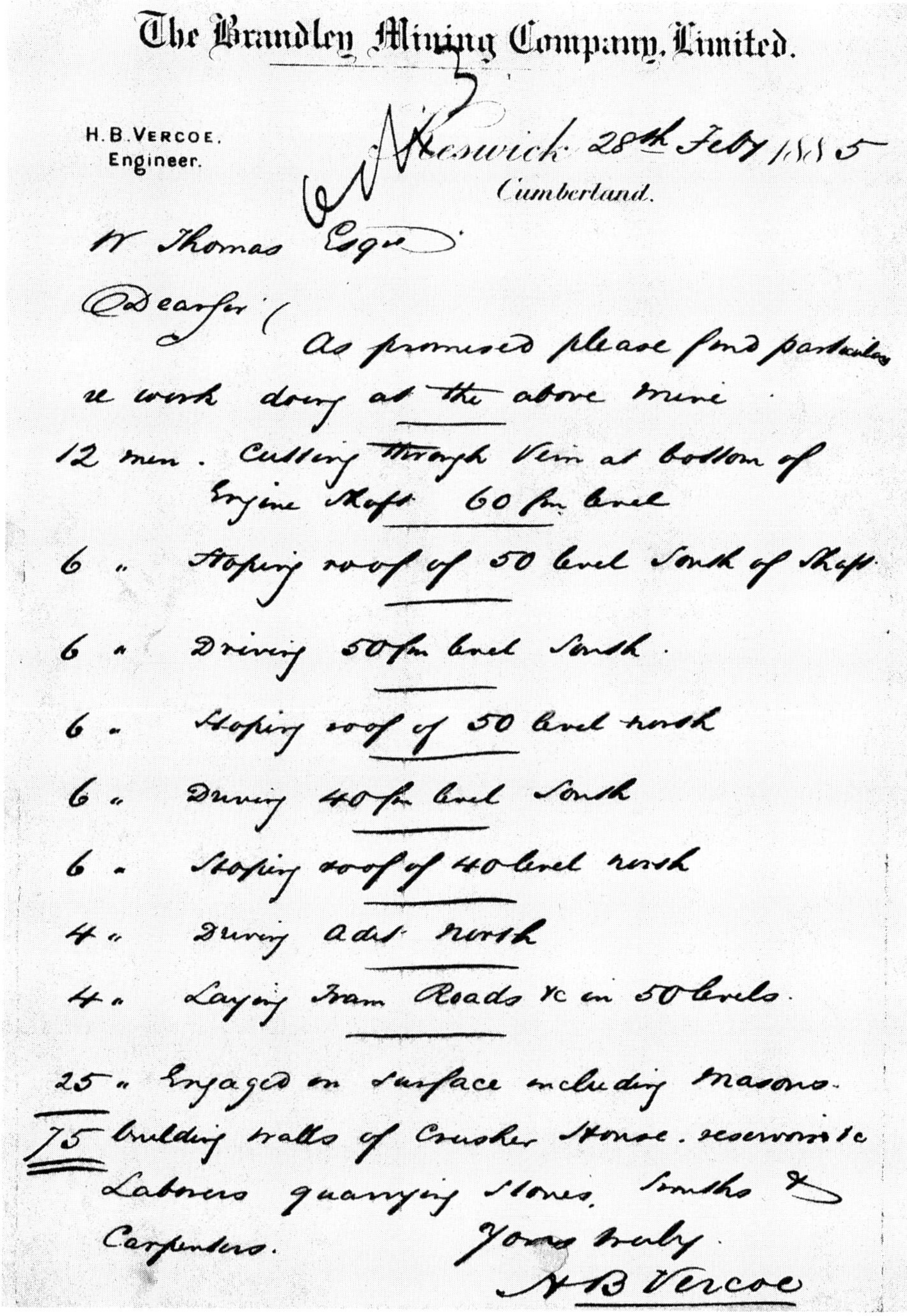
The Brandley Mining Company, Limited.

H. B. Vercoe, Engineer.

Keswick 28th Feby 1885
Cumberland.

W Thomas Esqr

Dear Sir

As promised please find particulars re work doing at the above mine.

12 men. Cutting through Vein at bottom of Engine Shaft 60 fm level

6 " Stoping roof of 50 level South of Shaft

6 " Driving 50 fm level South.

6 " Stoping roof of 50 level north

6 " Driving 40 fm level South

6 " Stoping roof of 40 level north

4 " Driving adit north

4 " Laying Tram Roads &c in 50 levels.

25 " Engaged on surface including Masons
75 building walls of Crusher House. reservoir &c Laborers quarrying stones, Smiths & Carpenters.

Yours truly

H B Vercoe

Distribution of workforce at Brandlehow Mine 1885. Courtesy of C R O was put up from the 50 Fathom to the 40 Fathom Level and named Whitwells Rise after one of the owners. A reasonable amount of lead was also retrieved from the adjoining stope. The 30 Fathom Level had now been driven a distance of over 240 yards and many areas stoped. These efforts were rewarded, and over three years the mine produced 290 tons of lead per year. This was sold to a variety of companies, a new customer being the Washington Chemical Co who were taking 28 tons per quarter on a regular basis.

Flooding was still a major problem as the mine had expanded both in depth and laterally, and the existing 26 hp engine just could not cope with the workload. The engine had been working non-stop since its installation and was now in urgent need of replacement. Pumping and hauling costs alone had soared to over £800 per year and so a call was made on the shareholders for more money, however the majority, having already lost money on the other mining leases owned by the company, were reluctant to provide more. This resulted in a lengthy dispute between shareholders and directors and in the meantime the mine was slowly drowning. By May 1862 the company had spent between £25,000 and £30,000 over the previous 15 years on Brandlehow and other sites. Most of this money had been provided by shareholders and yet, during this period, not one dividend had been paid. By 1863 the water had risen to the 30 Fathom Level and in desperation, a letter was sent by Charles Dear to Lord Egremont's agent hoping for something more than moral support. The reply was short and to the point:

"In view of your predicament, it is recommended by His Lordship that the expensive steam pumps should be sold and that water pumps be used. To do this, a new dam and water course could be built at a cost of £1,000. Should you convince the shareholders, the Lord of the Manor may waive his royalty payments for a short period whilst you once again become solvent."

By 1864 however, the dispute had not been resolved, no further money was available and the mine was virtually flooded to the collar. The fact of the mine not working was in breach of the conditions of the lease and on the 22nd of March 1865, the Directors were each delivered a letter by the hand of one W L Newby from The Right Honourable George, Lord Leconfield ordering them to quit possession of the mine by the 29th of September 1865.

The mine then remained closed until 1870 when the lease was taken up by Messrs H K Spark of Darlington and B Plummer who also had interests in the other mines of the sett, and a little exploration work was done. By 1874 nothing of any consequence had been achieved and by 1876 the mine was not working. In accordance with the lease therefore, the shaft collars were arched over.

It was during 1883 that an energetic mining engineer by the name of Henry Burrow Vercoe, son of an already well-established and respected mining engineer from Islay decided to take up the option on the mine, and his company was called the Brandley Mining Company. Henry at this time lived in Portinscale just outside Keswick, and about four miles from the mine. Development work was carried out during 1884 to facilitate a better hauling and pumping system, and a 50 hp Robey engine costing £560 was installed. This was housed, along with a smithy with two forges, a carpenter's shop and a bothy for the miners on the shore of Derwentwater. Two small quarries just above the mine were opened up to provide ready building materials and in doing this work the old German working, Fechtenbachs Nick was destroyed. A new spur road was put in from the north and a barracks built for the men just above where a new reservoir had been constructed. By this time, many of the older mine buildings had been pulled down, but an existing stone cottage was repaired and became the agent's accommodation.

Most of the mining activity was now centred around the Engine Shaft, and two waterwheels were erected, one of 30 foot diameter to assist with the crushing of the ore, and the other of 12 foot diameter which was used mainly for sawing wood.

The engine shaft continued to be sunk and at a depth of about 57 fathoms the vein displayed much promise being some 6 feet wide and containing a solid rib of galena 18 inches thick. Again it was the northern drive which proved fruitful while to the south the ground was poor and showed very little lead. It was decided that as soon as the shaft was down to 60 fathoms, levels again would be struck out both north and south and this work was pursued with great vigour. Both headings were in good ore and at last the mine seemed to have a secure future. By 1885, the mine was producing around 260 tons of lead ore per year and some indication of the size of the operation can be visualised by a breakdown of the sixty three strong workforce in February of that year. On the surface twenty five men were employed, some of them skilled masons building a new crusher house and a reservoir, whilst labourers toiled bringing in the stone. The shaft was now down to the 60 fathom horizon and here twelve men were driving in the vein. Above at the 50 Fathom Level south of the shaft, six men were driving forward into new ground, whilst north of the shaft a further six men were stoping in the roof and producing ore. As a result of this work, four men were busy laying tram roads. In the 40 Fathom south of the shaft, six men were driving the level forward in the search for ore-bearing ground and to the north of the shaft the roof was being stoped out. In the old Salt Level, four men were pushing the adit forward and ore was being raised. This was an encouraging situation and the scenes of work and general activity must indeed have gladdened the hearts of the owners.

Then, just when the mine appeared to be really working well, Henry Burrow Vercoe withdrew his expertise and support. Production slumped virtually right away, and during 1886 only 113 tons of ore were produced and the mine was allowed to flood! Henry was a very experienced mining engineer and it appears he quit while the going was good, but all was not lost and the lease was transferred to Messrs Jennings, White and Miller in the year of 1887. The mine was eventually pumped out by the 50 hp engine which had now become totally inadequate for pumping from the new lower horizon, and the new owners therefore purchased a more powerful unit. A new larger engine house was constructed for completion by December 1888 ready for the arrival of the replacement engine, which was a monster and although second-hand, it was more than up to the job. This was a 60 inch Cornish beam condensing engine with a 9 foot stroke; the two steel boilers were 30 feet by 6 feet and when fired up and in steam they would provide 350 hp. The engine shaft was now down to a depth of 75 fathoms and the water was lifted from here by the 13 inch by 14 inch pumps with ease. The Robey engine was now connected only to the winding drum for hauling up the kibbles on wire rope making for a more efficient operation. The ore, once raised, was sent to the newly modernised mill where it was crushed by 30 inch rollers then separated by three 3-compartment jigs, and the final separation was by two circular buddles. Other energy sources on the site were provided by three waterwheels, 30 feet by 3 feet, 22 feet by 2 feet and 6 feet by 1 foot.

By 1888, the workforce comprised thirty six men disposed as follows: thirteen on the shaft, eight mining, one shaftman and fourteen on surface. Despite the effort put in by the miners, a total of only 250 tons of ore was raised over the next three years, some of this going to the well established company of Walker Parker Ltd, Bagill and the rest to Sheldon Bush and Co of Bristol.

By the end of 1889, over two miles of underground tunnels had been hacked and blasted out to a depth of 75 fathoms, and no less than 1,700 feet of rises, winzes and shafts had been sunk. Despite all this effort, the workforce had now been reduced to a mere twenty two men and in order to save further money the pumps were stopped from working 24 hours a day. This of course resulted in the mine starting to flood, and by 1890 the new 75 Fathom Level was completely under water which was still rising up the Engine Shaft. By the end of the year the workforce had been reduced to ten men, all working the 60 Fathom north as now everything below here was flooded.

The frustration of deep mining is apparent, the costs as stated before are high; one must be getting ore and shareholders and investors will not wait forever. Despite all the miners' efforts and having to work in those appalling conditions 450 feet down, lead could not be found in sufficient quantities to sustain the operation. The workforce by 1891 was reduced to two old miners working in the Salt Level and the company, realising that the situation was now totally hopeless, had no alternative but to abandon the mine.

March 1892 saw the dismantling of all the mine equipment and the shafts sealed off in accordance with the terms of the lease. Brandlehow was closed forever and its secrets drowned in hundreds of feet of water.

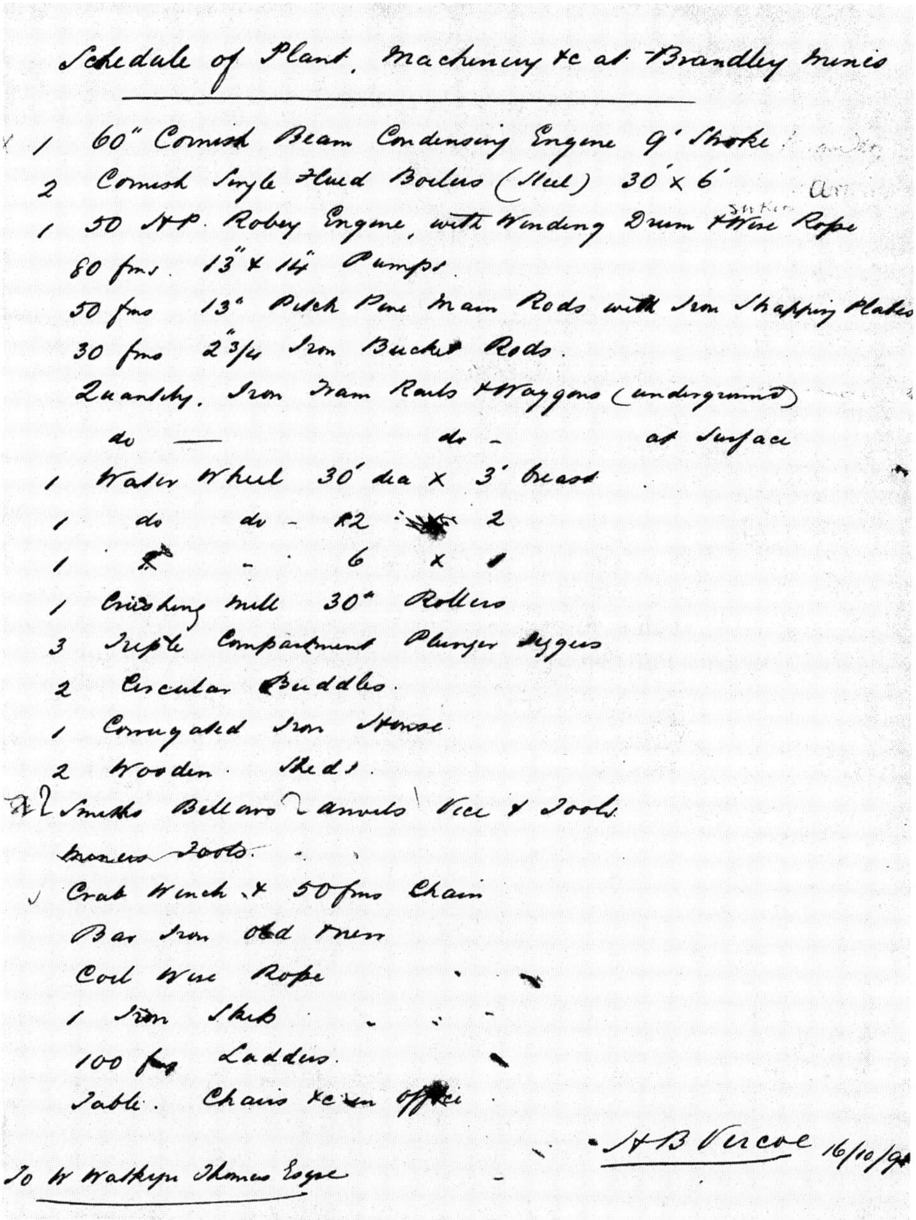

Schedule of Plant, Machinery &c at Brandley Mines

1 60" Cornish Beam Condensing Engine 9' Stroke
2 Cornish Single Flued Boilers (Steel) 30' x 6'
1 50 H.P. Robey Engine, with Winding Drum & Wire Rope
80 fms. 13" x 14" Pumps.
50 fms 13" Pitch Pine Main Rods with Iron Strapping Plates
30 fms 2¾" Iron Bucket Rods.
Quantity. Iron Tram Rails & Waggons (underground)
do — do — at Surface
1 Water Wheel 30' dia x 3' breast
1 do do – 22 2
1 – 6 x
1 Crushing mill 30" Rollers
3 Triple Compartment Plunger Jiggers
2 Circular Buddles.
1 Corrugated Iron House
2 Wooden Sheds.
2 Smiths Bellows, anvils Vice & Tools
Miners Tools.
Crab Winch & 50 fms Chain
Bar Iron Old men
Coil Wire Rope
1 Iron Stub
100 fms Ladders.
Table. Chairs &c in office.

H B Vercoe 16/10/91

To W Watkyn Thomas Esqre

Plant and machinery at Brandlehow Mine at closure 1891. Courtesy of C R O

Topography of Borrowdale Copper Mines

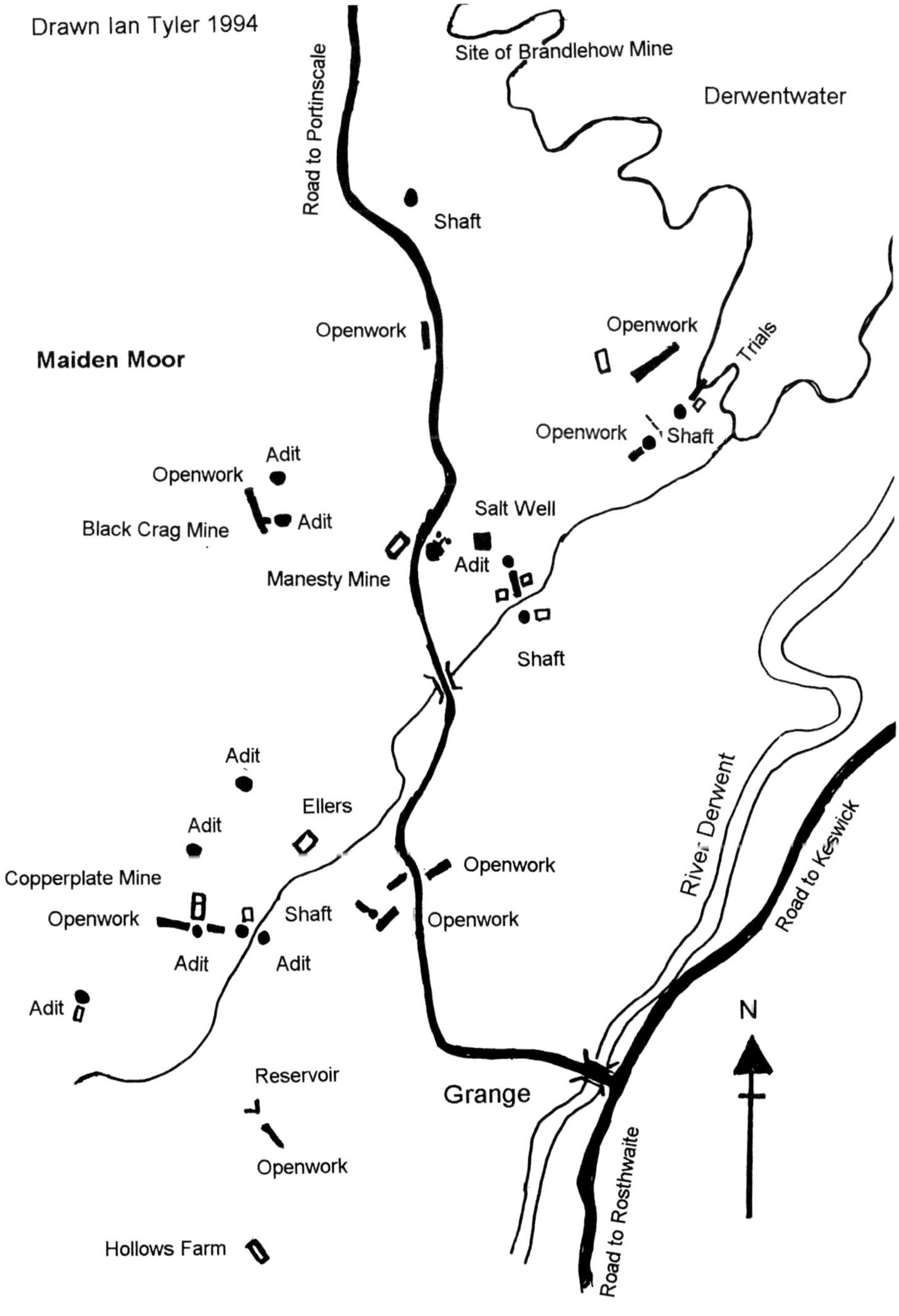

Brandlehow Mine Salt Level

Surveyed Roy Fellows 1995 Drawn by Ian Tyler

Scale 10mm = 20 metres

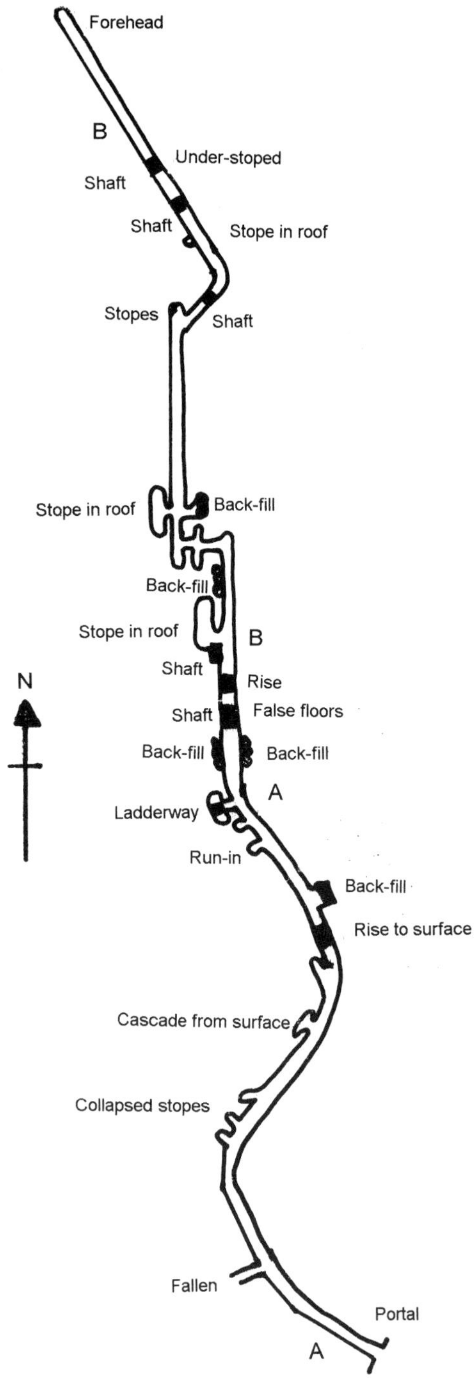

Level size: 4ft wide by 6ft high B B

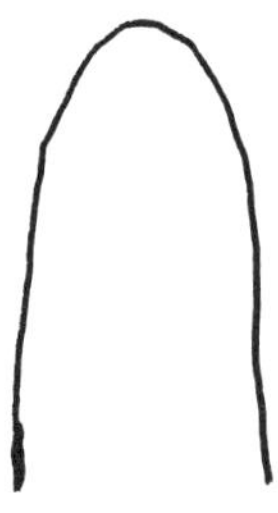

Level size: 3ft wide by 5ft 9ins high A A

Warning

Much of this level is under-stoped and flooded and can sump at the level entrance in wet weather

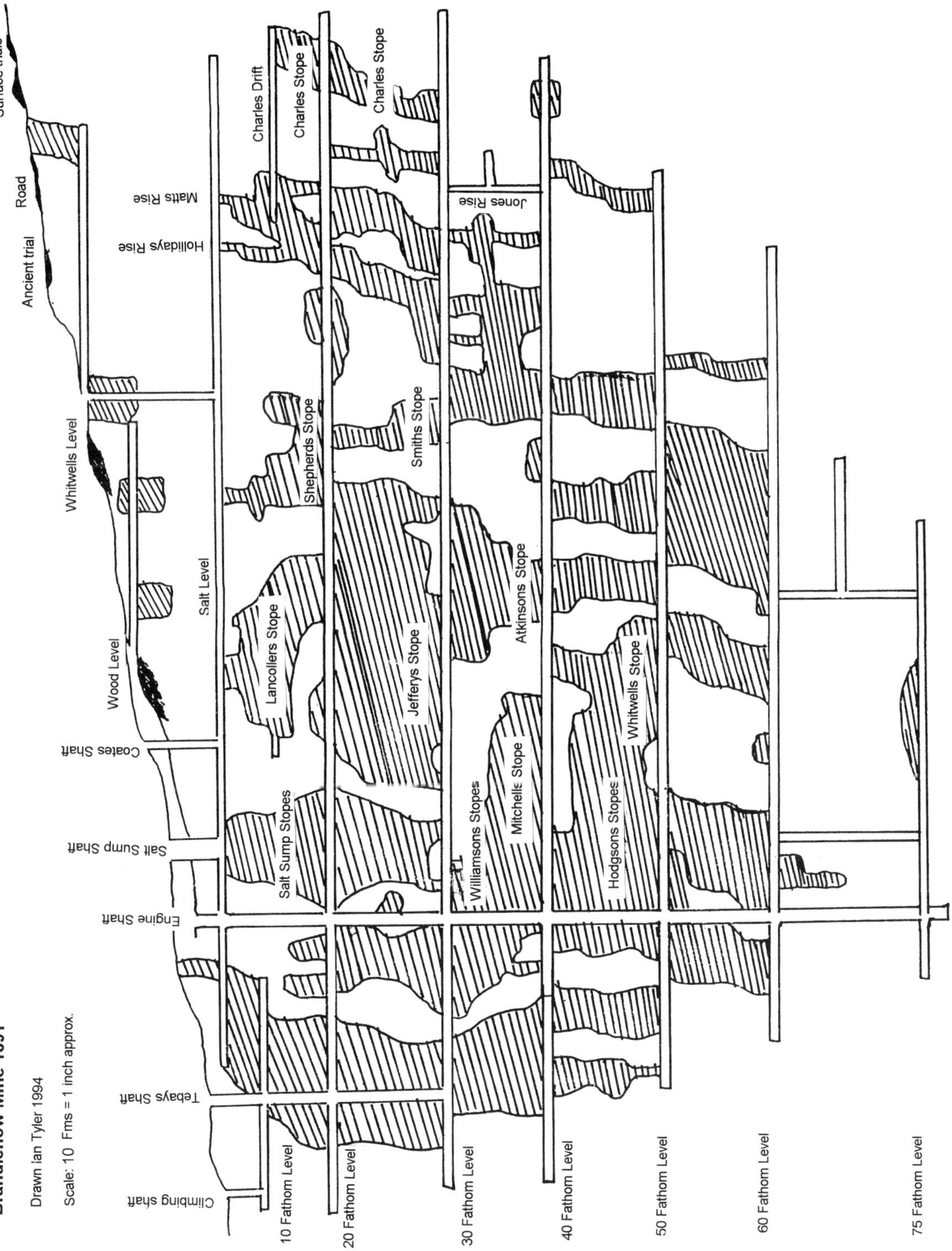

Brandlehow Mine 1891

Drawn Ian Tyler 1994

Scale: 10 Fms = 1 inch approx.

Old Brandley Mine

Drawn Ian Tyler 1995

Scale: 40 Fms = 1 inch

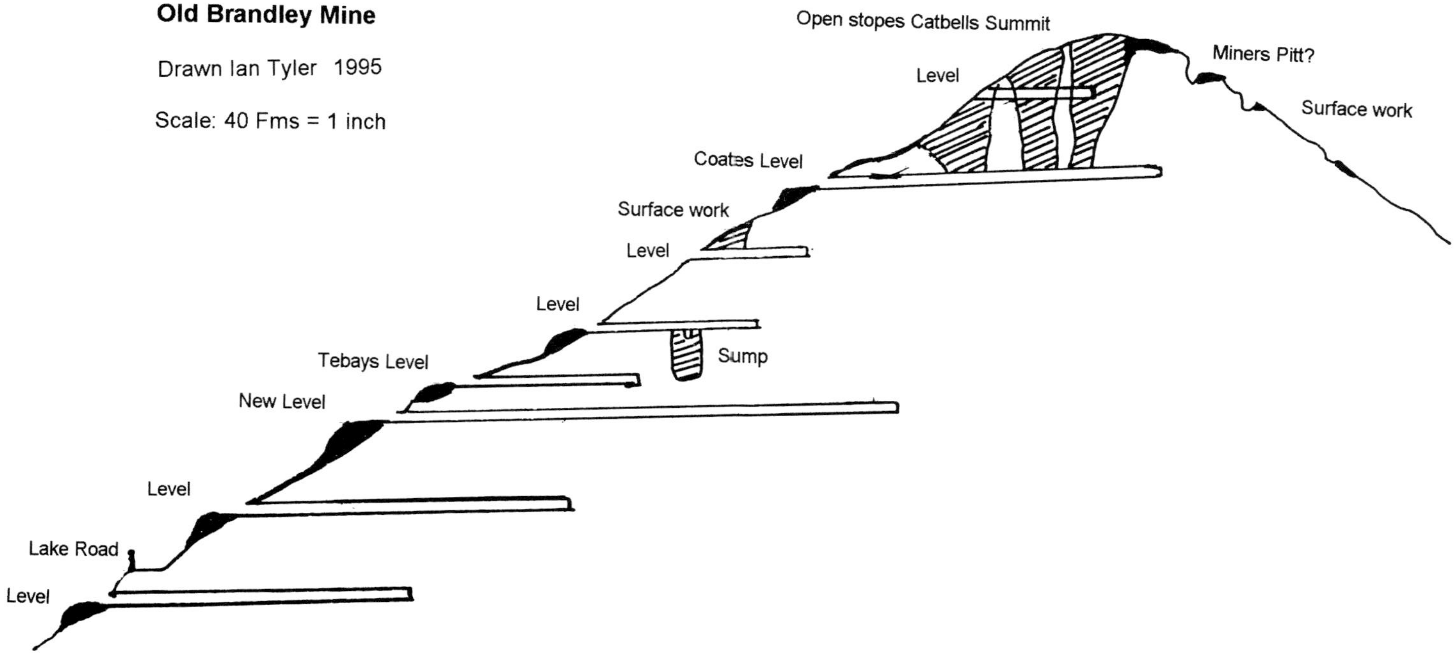

Miners at Brandlehow

1569	Fechtenbach	Miner
1726	Jon Scott	Miner
1754	Thomas Gilbert	Miner
1754	John Gilbert	Miner
1819	John Tebay	Owner/Miner
1847	Samuel Merryweather	Owner/Mining Engineer
1847	Mr Richardson	Owner
1847	Mr Langton	Owner
1850	Coates	Miner
1850	Lancollers	Miner
1850	Glynns	Miner
1850	Shepherd	Miner
1850	Bennett	Miner
1850	Holliday	Miner
1850	Beaucher	Miner
1850	Matt	Miner
1850	Charles	Miner
1850	Smith	Miner
1850	Cheney	Miner
1850	Tyson	Miner
1850	Mitchell	Miner
1850	Hodgeson	Miner
1850	Williamson	Miner
1850	Greenwood	Miner
1850	Tindales	Miner
1850	Tolmer	Miner
1850	Atkinsons	Miner
1850	Banners	Miner
1850	Stanley	Miner
1850	Hutchinson	Miner
1850	Conner	Miner
1857	Moses Mawson	Miner
1857	John Dover	Miner
1857	John Graves	Miner
1857	Henry Dickinson	Miner
1857	Daniel Dunglinson	Miner
1860	Charles Dear	Owner
1860	John Whitwell	Owner
1860	William James	Owner
1860	James Postlethwaite	Owner

1860	Edward Rankin	Owner
1860	William Dunsford	Owner
1860	Miles Farrer	Owner
1870	Hy King Spark	Owner
1870	B Plummer	Owner
1873	Thomas Davidson	Mine Manager
1883	Henry B Vercoe	Owner/Mining Engineer
1886	Mr Jennings	Owner
1886	Mr White	Owner
1886	Mr Millar	Owner
1887	Mr Sawrey	Owner

It is interesting to see that some of the miners who are listed above, have also been engaged at working in the Seathwaite Wad Mine. The workforce listed here would have no doubt been engaged to work at Brandley, Black Crag, Copperplate from the time of John Tebay onwards.

Miners at Copperplate

1567	Schopf	Miner
1567	Wurzer	Miner
1569	Wulff Hund	Miner
1571	W Hocholzer	
1571	Franz Dorn	
1571	Jacob Hofer	Miner
1571	Jorg Bachmair	Miner
1571	V Schlegel	Miner
1571	S Buechberger	Miner
1571	J Colmanstetter	Miner
1571	H Moser	Miner
1571	W Binder	Miner
1571	J Heisel	Miner
1820	John Tebay	Owner/Miner

Miners at Black Crag

1569	Wyllen Fisher	Miner
1569	Mathew Hodge	Miner

Borrowdale Production Figures

Brandlehow Mine

YEAR	LEAD-TONS	SILVER-OZ	£ VALUE
1567 *			
1726	6		90
1753	25		400
1754	60		1080
1755	59		1062
1756	63		945
1757	34		510
1758	43		645
1759	29		377
1762	9		126
1763	61		915
1766	11		165
1790	17		323
1808	5		165
1824	5		115
1825	15		405
1827	35		700
1828	64		1152
1829	29		464
1831	26		338
1833	13		169
1835	3		54
1837	10		200
1854	78		1794
1855	162		3726
1856	235		5640
1857	269		6187
1858	230	1840	4830
1860	222	1776	4884
1861	225	1802	4950
1862	212	1700	4240
1863	74	596	1480
1864	37	300	777
1865	4	30	80
1866	6	26	120
1885	265		2915
1886	113		1468

YEAR	LEAD-TONS	SILVER-OZ	£ VALUE
1888	89		1246
1888**			91
1889	80		1040
1890	80		1040

* 15673 cwt of Copper. ** 7 tons of Blende

The production figures for Brandlehow Mine in some cases were integrated with Yewthwaite, Barrow and Brandley consequently it has been impossible to identify the individual mine's output for its complete working period. However these figures have been compiled as accurately as possible.

Brandley & Skelgill

YEAR	LEAD-TONS	SILVER-OZ	£ VALUE
1651	21		
1654	9		
1657	4		
1701	35		630
1810	5		180
1833	96		1248
1834	54		918
1836	12		288
1843	5		80
1849	3		48
1850	50		850
1855	182		4186
1856	235		5640
1857	97		2231
1858	306		6426
1860	199		4378
1885	212	2070	2287
1886	85		1016
1888	70	682	776
1889	62	625	675
1890	62	385	702

The production figures for Brandley and Skelgill (Miners Pits) were in some cases integrated with Yewthaite, Brandlehow and Barrow consequently it has been impossible to identify the individual mine's output for its complete working period. However these figures have been compiled as accurately as possible.

THE WAD MINE

Black Lead Mine, Borrowdale, Cumberland

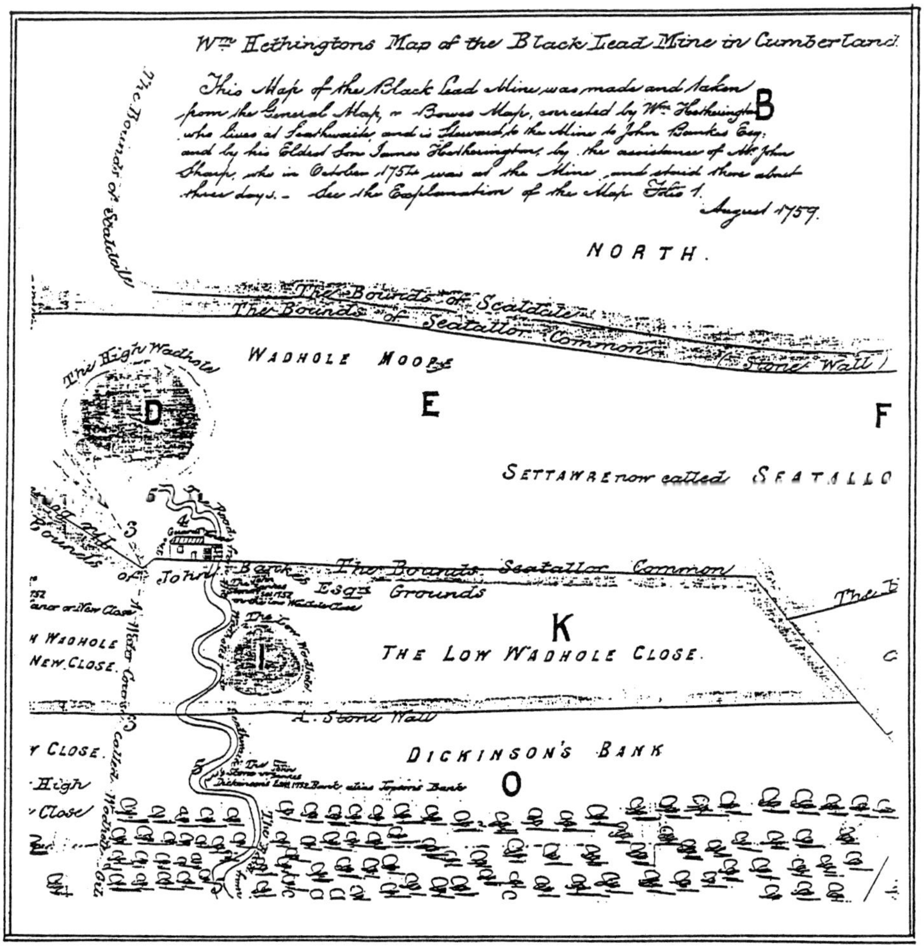

Map of the Black Lead Mine by Wm Hetherington 1759. Courtesy of the National Trust.

A Word About Wad

GRAPHITE OF the quality found in Borrowdale was considered to be the purest in the world, and although wad has been found in other countries such as Czechoslovakia, Bavaria and Ceylon in much larger quantities it has always inferior to the deposit at Seathwaite.

The wad was found in sops which in basic terms are blobbish, irregular shaped masses varying in size from a few inches to deposits many feet in mass. The miners cut pipes or shafts in an effort to locate the wad and it was soon realised that in one pipe there could be numerous sops. In some cases the pipes were bisected by stages; between Gilberts Stage and Gills Stage for example there were at least twenty four.

Once the mining got under way it was soon realised that the wad varied vastly in type. There was "Flote Wad" found by trenching and varying in quality; "Sludge Wad" was found in vein crossings and was soft and flaky and had the appearance of pulverent wad; "Glaze of Wad" was a very bright, thin coating found in pipe stuff, vein stuff and sometimes on the skirts of naked rock; "Waddy Clay" was steatite vein stuff, much glazed with wad which, through exposure in the stage or pipe, had decayed; "Bullets of Wad" were small masses of wad. The "Sops" were the large masses to which the main efforts of mining were directed. There were many different grades and these have been indicated in the production figures.

Many veins were located and recorded by the mining engineer John Farey in 1818, and they amount to a total number of around one hundred and seventy. These were listed in an effort to formulate some method of locating the sops, but on completion of his work it appears that little or no conclusive evidence pointed to any one vein or another being the cause of the wad. Suffice it to say that following the large veins made the breaking of new ground somewhat easier.

Wad is a unique substance inasmuch as, unlike other mineral ores, there is no need for a sophisticated dressing plant, a washing and separating floor being all that is required. It also does not de-grade down so that it can be left and stored in any conditions. It is virtually indestructible and can withstand a temperature of 3,367 degrees centigrade before it becomes sublime (vaporises) and will only melt under pressure; on the hardness scale it is 1 and its specific gravity is 2.2. Consequently, its uses in industry are very varied from making the finest drawing pencils, crucibles in the smelting industry, moulds for casting metals, as a lubricant or simply grate blacking. It is also employed in the electronics industry and in nuclear technology, where it is used in reactors since it effectively slows down neutrons, absorbing them only slightly.

Because of its pure quality, the price at its height during the 1830s rose to around 45/- per lb or £5,000 per ton making it the most valuable substance extracted from the Cumbrian earth. By reason of this, claims were made of wad strikes all over the place, one of these being at Bannerdale Crags not far from Mungrisdale, back of Skiddaw. Here a small level has been driven a few yards on a black, smudgy substance. This work was most likely done by a Mr Crozier who was working the lead mines during the 1870, although nothing has been recorded regarding the wad removed.

Another and more interesting trial was at Watermillock near Ullswater. Here there was supposed to have been a mine actually backing onto a small mill making pencils. Other recorded graphite finds have been in Rebecca Quarry in Dalton-in-Furness, Bowscale Tarn, Dale Head Mine, Wanthwaite Mine and Shap Granite Quarry.

Then there is the tale of two miners in 1860 working in the night at Dead Beck high on the back of Bakestall Fell. It was reported that the men worked the mine at night by the light of a lantern, and after retrieving enough of the wad before day-break, they would cover over the entrance to evade discovery as they had no lease to work......a story as dark and mysterious as wad itself!

Into the Wad Mine

AT ABOUT 8.00 am, the car sped along the eastern side of Derwentwater, the gentle mound of Catbells reflected in the calm water, the summer sky clear and all looking well for a superb day underground. Passing through Grange and by the majesty of Castle Crag, the old Volvo purred up the winding road through the area of Borrowdale described as the 'loveliest square mile in Lakeland'. However, many of the thousands of people who pass this way have little or no idea that this was the heart of the northern slate industry, and also the site of the most unusual and valuable mined substance in the Lake District....wad. Known also as graphite, plumbago or black lead, fortunes were founded on this shiny, dark grey treasure. As I steered the car down into the blind valley of Seathwaite, the line of pinky-brown spoil heaps could be seen, dotted on the shoulder of the fell to the west.

I arrived at the white-washed farms and houses known collectively as Seathwaite, where little has changed in hundreds of years. The largest of the farms is the home of the Edmondson family, who have kept hill sheep here for generations. The head of the valley is overshadowed by the massive north face of Great End, a favourite haunt for winter ice climbers, and this is also a main stepping off point for Great Gable and Scafell Pike.

The weather in this place can be so appalling that the area has featured in Barbour jacket advertisements and understandably so, for this little hamlet has the distinction of being the wettest place in England. Today however, it seemed I was being treated to the best of Lakeland weather. No sooner had I parked and started to change, than my fellow mine explorers arrived. Today we were going to abseil through the mine from Gills Stage to the lowest exit point, Gilberts Level, a vertical distance of some 400 feet. This incredible journey would take us into the oldest workings, dating from the 14th Century to the late 1800's.

We started to unpack the gear, and soon tangled masses of rope, dirty overalls and scraped helmets, rubber boots, industrial gloves, harnesses and hardware decked the area around the cars. Finally everything was sorted out and packed into tackle bags and we set off for our destination.

The atmosphere and antiquity of the place is evoked the moment you walk through the old cobbled courtyard from the farm, and you are immediately aware of the great history here, and that you are walking in the footsteps of the earliest of travellers. Here is one of the oldest pack-horse routes in the Lake District, the way the pedlars came hawking their wares and maybe exchanging goods for bits of the strange black stone called wad. Perhaps it was those itinerant tradesmen who supplied the monks of Furness with this graphic aid, all those hundreds of years ago.

Crossing the River Derwent by the bridge, the remains of the old ford can be clearly seen, and here in bygone days, the heavily laden wagons of wad would have splashed through the river on the way to the warehouse in Keswick. In those early times, this would have been virtually a full day's trek. Heading north one passes the old saw mill, plant and dispatch area of the last company to work the mine, now heavily overgrown and further along is a plantation of conifers, discreetly hiding Robsons Level and its huge spoil heap. This was the lowest level to be driven, and one of the last to be worked, its once fortified entrance now a pile of rubble. Passing through the gate, keen eyes will spot the new boundary stone for the wad mine, the original having been vandalised. Just past the wood, one picks up the old miners' original zigzag path, which was the route taken by everyone going to the mine, and each turn will take you to the different workings or adits on this steep ascent. The second level you arrive at is Gilberts level, where the ruins of the portal buildings are still in evidence. This was the main drawing level for many years, and the vast spoil heap testifies to its importance. In fact, this is the level we will exit from some hours from now. Dave kindly offers to go down the level and check that the internal shaft exit is clear, soon re-appearing rather wetter than he was. We started up the next section, passing the original boundary stone which is actually a huge piece of Honister slate, inscribed with the date 1752 and the name J Bankes Esquire. From here the climb becomes steeper and the talking stops, as each of us strains under the weight of the gear. Following the track one soon comes to an area of ruined buildings which were the old hand-sorting and dressing floors, and are now only just discernible under oceans of spoil. This is the Old Mens working attributed to the 1560's, and is the site of the first proper underground trial.

The heavy rope bag was passed over again and again, as the never ending path wound its way upwards, and soon the lush plateau of Fareys Stage was reached, an excellent viewpoint and an ideal spot for a rest. Now there was time to wonder and muse over the theory that it was here that the first wad was discovered. Legend has it that an ash tree was uprooted in a violent storm and so exposed the wad.

We now moved up the final 140 feet or so to Gills stage, where the spoil plateau here once again provides a wonderful spot from which to soak up the beauty of the area. On arrival, the bags were dumped quickly and unceremoniously on the ground, and the ever stunning view of the northern and eastern fells spread before us. It had taken us just over an hour to climb up to our starting point for the mine trip. After a short break, we strolled a few feet above to look at the old fortified entrance of Harrisons Stage, which is situated just beneath the formidable boundary wall, this being 6 or 7 feet high and stoutly made, and a clear indication that it was built to keep out more than sheep. Just south-west of here hidden in the bracken, is the site of another boundary stone. Above the wall, a whole series of workings extends many feet up onto Seatoller Fell, and continues for nearly a quarter of a mile almost as far as Gillercombe. Some of these isolated trials have been found to have copper mineral on the dumps. Slightly to the north of the highest trial, can be detected a substantial angled track down to the top of Honister Pass, no doubt an old route from the wad mine to Honister and Buttermere.

Well, it was now time to go and the three of us donned our gear and prepared to set off through the system, checking carefully to see that nothing was left behind, because the next time we would step out into daylight would be some four hours later and 400 feet lower. First, we were to explore the labyrinth of passages and workings off Gills stage, a maze-planner's delight. This area had been a very rich part of the mine where many pipes and sops had intertwined and the miners, following the wad, have left a number of very intricate passages.

To ensure that we were starting our through trip from the highest point, we decided to investigate Harrisons Stage and the bottom of Gortons Stage. This can only be achieved by some tricky climbing up a 20 foot rise down which pour gallons of icy cold water, making for a thoroughly soaking start to the route. Now, suitably baptised, we could begin our descent and so, rope well secured, we dropped down the first dark shaft.

Our journey through and into the history of the wad mine had begun....

1 A Hidden Gleam of Grey

The date of the very first wad working or its actual location will never be ascertained for sure, for there are at least three alternative locations for its original extraction. One problem in positively identifying the first site, is that wad is not found in vertical or horizontal veins, but in sops and pipes. This means quite simply, that the usual method of hushing or trenching to establish a longitudinal vein, would not ensure success as it would in normal prospecting. It is fair to say however, that there is some evidence of hushing and trenching above the boundary wall on Seatoller Common. Below the wall there are also some mysterious grooves, but whether these are natural or man made is difficult to determine.

The ground cover on parts of the fell is very shallow, and the excessive rain fall in this area could, no doubt, have exposed areas of wad through natural erosion. This would have stood out as a dark grey, metallic mass, and would have been totally different to the neighbouring rock. Inevitably, such an exposed area would have fallen under the eye of some wandering shepherd finding that the substance marked his hands with a waxen, grey smudge, difficult to remove in water and ideal for sheep marking. Eventually, one supposes, he would have shown his find to others, but these early workings certainly pre-date any organised local metalliferous mining. This area of the Lake District was very poorly inhabited at the time, and was a wild and desolate place, the land infertile and the weather predominantly bad. It can therefore be surmised that the wad was found purely by accident, and not by a trial by an organised mining operation.

Bearing these theories in mind, I would propose that the likeliest original sites were:

1) The area directly above the wall on Seatoller Common, referred to as the High Wadhole Moor, where Gortons (Goatons) and Woodmans Pipes both break to surface. Here, the bedrock is exposed, cut by more than one stream, and the wad could have easily been seen. The site is very old and pre-dates many of the lower workings, and there is also some early documentation to substantiate this.

2) The favoured site is that of Bills Stage, which is in fact, the head of the Grand Pipe, the biggest single wad pipe, measuring 8 feet in width and some 280 feet in depth. Local folk-lore has it that the top of the pipe was discovered when an ash tree was uprooted in a violent storm, exposing the wad. However, none of this area directly below surface in the actual upper reaches of the Grand Pipe exhibits any clear form of early working, apart from a grassy

mound where the wad pipe breaks surface. Below the surface in the top sections, there is no evidence of hand-chipping but it is likely that this would have been eroded by subsequent working.

3) Below Fareys Stage, the Grand Pipe curls down and is cut by the Old Mens Stage. This is a hand-chipped coffin level driven in the days prior to gunpowder, and not far in from the entrance there is a small wad sop curving back towards the surface. This is now choked with rubbish, but here again, the possibility exists that this could have been the first working.

As I have said, the earliest positive dates of discovery are vague, but originally, the Manor belonged to the monks of Furness Abbey who were a Cistercian order and had been given the lands by one Alice de Rumelli. Their huge abbey on the outskirts of Barrow in Furness, was constructed in about 1127 of massive red sandstone blocks, and would have taken many years to complete.

Borudale (Borrowdale), as it was known by the Norsemen who settled in the valley, is an old Nordic name meaning 'the valley of the fortress', this no doubt referring to Castle Crag, standing silent guard on the valley. Many small valley hamlets have names originating from those early Nordic settlers. Thwaite is the old Norse for clearing, thus giving us Thornthwaite, 'the clearing amongst the thorn trees', Stonethwaite, 'the clearing in the stones' and Rosthwaite, more romantically, 'the clearing in the rose thorns'. One thing for sure is, that the valley in those early days was a hostile, barren wilderness, an entanglement of undergrowth, woodland and boulders intermingled with thousands of years of rotting vegetation. But the early Viking settlers cleared the ground to make their homes and develop the land.

The lands of Borrowdale were granted to Furness Abbey by Alice de Rumelli in 1209 in return for £150 and 10 marks in lieu of two horses. In the monastery records, dating back to 1412 are two large and ancient volumes known as the Coucher Books, which bear drawn guidelines to assist the scribe. It is believed that these were inscribed with wad, although no reference is actually made of it being used. The first real documentary evidence is a report dated 1540, recording a profit of 6/8d for 'cawke stone' in Borrowdale, and a report in 1542 makes further mention. These records were made after the dissolution of the monasteries in 1537, when lands were subsequently returned to the Crown and King Henry VIII. During the thirty third year of Henry's reign, a John Fyssher with his son Lancelot were bailiffs for the King in Borrowdale. In this wild place, however, where the policing of the land and observation of proper boundaries would have been difficult, the probable lack of any reasonable law and order would have given rise to the early adventurers' efforts.

A gentleman by the name of Walter Graham of Netherby, Border riever and leader of the Graham Clan, was in possession of lands in Borrowdale, Watendlath and Stonethwaite, and apparently had some early dealings with the Borrowdale mines, supplying wood from the Watendlath and Stonethwaite woods. However, in 1606, along with most of the Graham family, he was deported to Ireland during James the First's determined efforts to 'break the Border'.

The only other clue to the mine's early beginnings, was the discovery in Nether Wasdale in 1865, of some counterfeit coin moulds found hidden under a cairn of stones. The moulds, in two halves, were of pure graphite, each weighing 5oz and with the capacity for making three different coins: a groat, a half groat and a penny. These were all common coins of the reign of King Henry VII in about 1500. An assessment of the date of the moulds has been put at between 1500-1509. This would certainly prove that the mine in some shape or form was working sometime during that period. Remember, that even though the area was remote, the road through the pass via Sty Head leads directly down to Wasdale and Nether Wasdale, and hence to the coast and the western sea ports. Here, the illicit coins could have been easily transported to London and other ports in the south, where they could have been distributed with the utmost ease.

No doubt, eventually, as the word spread of this remarkable new marking stone, pieces of the magic wad filtered through to London and other areas of commerce, merchants soon realising its potential. However it may have happened, enough interest was generated, and two Royal Commissioners were sent to Borrowdale on the 26th of August, 1555. One can perhaps imagine the feelings of Thomas Legh and Nicholas Bardsey, having to leave their fine residences and the fashionable court of London, to journey the hundreds of miles by sea and road to the desolation of Borrowdale, to look for the site of the wad. It was a long sea journey from the port of London to Newcastle, then by whatever means available overland by Hadrians Wall to Carlisle, a dreary and dismal journey if the weather had deteriorated at this late time of the year. Then the last lap through to Keswick, at that time little more than a hamlet, and the final weary ride through the wilderness of the Borrowdale valley. It was certainly some months before their report was made. They also visited the Salt Well in Manesty at Borrowdale, to which they put a rent of 2/- per annum. The report recommended a rent of 13s 4d for the Wad Mine and it also stated that the Upper Wadhole on Seatoller Common was in fact flooded, and that this occurred regularly and it had to be de-watered to get the wad. This description fits the locations of Gortons and Woodmans Pipes, and no other workings are referred to. A further observation was, that the locals 'colour their sheep with wad in the Common of Seatower'. It appears also that the locals paid the Lord of the Manor 1d for breaking the ground, and apparently this had been the custom for years.

Wad was not unknown at this time, and the German Austrian border town of Passau had mined it for many years, but this was not of the pure quality of the Borrowdale material, and its commercial uses were for crucibles, pottery and foundry castings. The first writing stylus had been introduced by 1565.

Convinced by the Royal commissioners' report that the mine was worth working, a gentleman by the name of Ambrose Dormer of Ascot in Great Milton, Oxfordshire, the son of Sir Michael Dormer, an ex-Mayor of London 1541/42, was granted a 21 year lease on the property in December 1555. Dormer died eleven years after this and the site was later occupied by Roger Robinson, who took a lease in 1578 at a rent of 15s 4d per annum. This was replaced by another 21 year lease to Matthew Buck, on the 22nd of October 1594. It is to this gentleman that the first real enterprise can be attributed, and now we have some indication as to the amount of ground being worked. The area of the Upper Wadhole was being mined, as was the Lower Wadhole which was the top of the Grand Pipe. A barn owned by William Braithwaite in Seathwaite was being used to store the wad, and Matthew Buck had 7 tons of dressed wad in store valued at £13 0s 0d per ton. By 1597, the value of wad had risen to £13 6s 8d, and there was also some inferior wad valued at £5 6s 8d per ton. Sometime during his short tenure, it appears that Matthew Buck died and a John Hudson went on to work the Upper Wadhole. In 1597, a case was brought against Hudson and under-sheriff Richard Tolson, both of whom had seized, by writ, half of the dead Buck's store of wad. The plaintiffs were William Gale and his wife, Buck's widow. It was alleged that the Crown 'had not the right' to let more than the Lower Wadhole, the upper one, on Seatoller Common being for the freeholders' use, and it was found in fact that Matthew Buck had falsified the Robinson lease by adding an 's' to the word 'wadhole'. The court found for the plaintiffs who were awarded £3 6s 8d costs, and Tolson and Hudson were fined £5 0s 0d each. In the future, the tenants were to be allowed to dig in the Upper Wadhole and to 'take so much wadd as will only serve for the markinge or smuttinge of their sheepe and other their necessary use as they have done and not to sell the same or to dispose of it in any other sort'.

So far, the German miners, experts in copper mining and well established in Keswick, Newlands and in Borrowdale itself, had not acquainted themselves with this mine, however, this was soon to change.

2 The German Connection

The Company of Mines Royal was initiated in 1564 with the advent of the German miners, and took some four years to establish as a fully operational company. It was, by this time, well established in the Lake District particularly in the areas of Keswick, Borrowdale and Newlands. Interest in the wad mine did not manifest itself until 1607, and it was not in fact the Mines Royal company which showed the interest but Daniel Hechstetter the younger and his family, whose dealings in the wad mine were on a purely personal level.

The original indenture given by Queen Elizabeth I was for the exploration for copper, lead, silver, gold, quick-silver minerals, rubies and pearls; in fact, the freedom really to extract any mineral at all which was considered of value. This was based initially on the high price of copper, and the acceptance by German technologists to contract to refine coins, under the direction of William Cecil, Lord Burleigh. In order to carry out this, they were given dispensation to dig and search unhindered in the counties of Cumberland, Westmorland, Lancaster, Cornwall, Devon, Gloucester, Worcester and Wales. The Queen in return, was entitled to a royalty of one tenth of gold and silver, 2/- for every cwt of copper, or 1/20th during the first five years and after this period, 1/15th or 2/6d per cwt. Precious stones, emeralds and pearls were to be offered to the Queen, and any rights to tin or lead.

Thomas Thurland, Master of the Savoy in London, had an agreement drawn up dated the 16th of July 1561, to mine with a Johan Steinberger, but the final draft was left unsigned and it was evidently never followed up. In 1563, Daniel Hechstetter paid his first visit to England, and he and Thomas Thurland together with others, were granted permission to survey for minerals. Daniel had served his apprenticeship as a mining engineer in the Rauros Valley in East Tyrol, and later became an agent for David Haug of the Hans Langnauer Co of Augsburg. This was a very large company of general merchants with interests in mining. At Schwatz, near Innsbruck in the Tyrol, they were mining for silver, copper and iron, and the company had also recently taken over some mining interests from the great house of Fugger. This was a large organization which had copper mines in Neusohl in Hungary. It is interesting to see that even in those far off days, mining was an international business.

Daniel returned to England with the company's agent Hans Loner in June 1564, bringing with him twelve miners. The prospecting went well, and more men came over to England to work in the Keswick area. Daniel returned to Germany after nearly two years away, to visit his wife Radagunda and their six children. On his eventual return to Keswick in October 1566, he was appalled to learn that one of his workmen had been brutally murdered. The account of this is somewhat vague, but the miner involved, Leonard Stoultz was set upon by local ruffians led by one Fisher. During the fierce struggle which ensued, Leonard put up a brave fight but his arm was severely damaged by the son of John Awood and, unable thus to defend himself properly, he was beaten to death. Despite this unfortunate happening, the local dales folk finally realised what prosperity was being brought into the area, and gradually the German miners were accepted and, indeed, many of them married local girls and never returned to their home country.

From the initial days of exploration, mines were operating at Borrowdale, Stoneycroft, Fornside, Buttermere, Grasmere, Newlands and Caldbeck, and a smelter had been constructed at Brigham near Keswick. Indeed, all this had been achieved by 1568, when the Company of the Mines Royal was incorporated. The company did, during 1569, purchase Vicar Island (now Derwent Island) on Derwentwater for the sum of £60 0s 0d from one John Williamson, and some of the Germans moved to the island. When Daniel came to settle finally in Cumbria with his wife Radagunda and their large family in 1572, they lived in the Master's house in Keswick, previous incumbents of which had been Thomas Thurland and then Daniel Ulstatt. During the following years, the German miners continued to develop their operation, and generally integrate into the life style of the English. It is something of a myth that all the Germans and their entourage actually resided on the island, as it only covers an area of 4,700 square yards.

After Matthew Buck's tenure, the lease on the wad mine was acquired in 1606 by two gentlemen by the names of Edward Boraston and Thomas Fanshaw. The rent for the mine at this time is recorded as being 15s 4d. Little is known of their activities, but nothing much could have been done in the way of development in this short time, as the lease was transferred in 1607 to Daniel and Emanuel Hechstetter, John Masefield, an armourer from London and Mr John Williamson, who were to hold the lease for varying periods each until 1634.

Daniel Hechstetter the Elder, the mining engineer and steward who had set up the Company of Mines Royal in 1564, died in 1581, and was survived by his widow and ten children. Two of his sons, Emanuel aged 25 and Daniel aged 19, had been taught their craft well by their father, and the two brothers were now running the Company of the Mines Royal in the British Isles.

During the year of 1613, James the First of England granted the land of the Manor of Borrowdale containing five hamlets, to James Whitmore and Jonas Verdon but without the Salt Well, which had been included in previous contracts. They in turn, sold various parcels of this land to many of the original tenants, and some land was also purchased by Sir Wilfred Lawson. This was an extremely complicated series of conveyancing and eventually became known as The Great Deed of Borrowdale, dated the 28th November 1614. The lands affecting the wad mine were taken up by Charles Hudson of Botherbeck (Borrowdale), Jonas Verdon, William Lamplugh, a local gent and Daniel Hechstetter of Rosthwaite with no less than thirty two others. None of these land transactions affected the Hechstetter mining lease, as they had already obtained the rights to work the mine. During their tenure, the mine was not exploited constantly, but was mined only sporadically and indeed, this was to be the norm for many years. Unfortunately, Emanuel did not see the fruits of his investment as he died on the 26th August 1614, and was succeeded in the venture by his eldest son Joseph, who inherited his share. The workings during this period were confined to the High Wadhole in the area high on Seatoller Common. The Low Wadhole was the area around where the Grand Pipe comes to surface. The mining operation of course gave work to other local tradesmen, and we see that in 1617, local carrier John Williamson collected 1 ton of wad to deliver to Thomas Butler, this given free of charge in lieu of a delivery which had been sent the previous year, but was not up to the quality expected. Anthony Teyllor and Martin Zuckmantell were both employed at the mine, and had also worked on Vicar Island. It appears that over the last few years their main employment had been washing, cleaning, weighing and packing the wad prior to its dispatch and, for a three week period during 1619, they were paid 9/- and 7/- respectively.

The spoil surrounding the collar of the Low Wadhole indicates that it would have been no more than 40 feet deep before it was realised that the constant de-watering operation, by jackroll and bucket every day, was a time consuming and laborious task before any extraction of graphite could begin. Many of the early reports indicate that the Low Wadhole was always flooded and often not working, as was the situation with the Upper Wadhole. The early adventurers simply had not the skill to drive a crosscut, but the German miners had, and with their technology, a crosscut to gain access to the graphite pipe and eventually drain the sump, was a logical solution. The workmen, now under the guidance and expertise of the Germans, were soon sinking in the sole of the Grand Pipe and starting to drive the new adit, whilst others were removing wad from the higher pits on Seatoller Common.

This new adit, known as the Old Mens Stage, is a superb hand-chipped level extending about 80 yards through to the Grand Pipe. Gunpowder was not unknown to the Germans, for as early as 1571 a barrel of the explosive had been supplied to them at Keswick. This however, was apparently for the use of firearms either for hunting or possibly protection, but evidently not for blasting, as there is no reference anywhere in the considerable records available, to suggest its use in local mining at this time. The driving was carried out by seasoned miners, probably seconded from some of the Mines Royal operations. Thomas Kalcher, an experienced pickman was just one of these men, having worked at Coniston and Newlands, and who had been taught the trade by his father Steffan, a Goldscope miner.

By 1620, the level was still under construction but incomplete, the miners literally chipping the rock away inch by inch. The level, cut in the traditional coffin shape, was about 5 feet 7 inches high and 2 feet wide. The driving of 36 fathoms to intersect the wad pipe was costing £10 0s 0d per fathom, a total of some £360 to complete. During this period, the operation was under the control of Daniel and Joseph Hechstetter, who enjoyed the profit of £827 11s 7d each, and the other two partners, Mr Masefield and Mr Williamson, who each received £413 15s 9d.

Customers for the graphite during this period were H Stamler of Stade, Nr Hamburg, who was in fact a cousin to the Hechstetters, Messrs Butlers, a company of merchants operating out of Newcastle on Tyne and Messrs Essington of London. This last company of merchants was quick to realise the importance of the Borrowdale find. They endeavoured to obtain an agreement from the company for them to be the sole supplier for a period of five years from 1620/1625, which agreement was eventually ratified. During the year of 1622, the moiety of William Lamplugh and Charles Hudson was acquired by Sir John Bankes and his father in law, Ralph Hawtrey. A member of a local family, Sir John was born in Keswick in 1589 and had qualified as a lawyer in London.

Vicar's Isle was now not only a home for some of the Germans, but was also an isolated area where the wad could be stored for safe keeping before its transportation to Newcastle. Graphite was now reasonably well known although its actual extraction was limited, as trading locations had not yet been established world-wide, neither had its many applications been yet envisaged. However, an early form of crude pencil was referred to by Conrad Gesner in Zurich in 1565 and graphite had been used for drawing in the Michaelangelo School of Art in Florence since 1580.

Sometime after the Hechstetter brothers took over, Daniel's son Francis bought a sixth share from John Masefield, whilst in 1625, Joseph sold a sixth of a share which was half his holding to Sir John Bankes, a London lawyer for £150 0s 0d. This gentleman was his brother in law, for Joseph had married Sir John's sister some years earlier. It was not the first dealing Sir John Bankes had had with the wad mine, for three years earlier, in March 1622, he had acquired a parcel of land from William Lamplugh and Ralph Hawtrey

One of the last transactions before the Hechstetters sold up was to supply Jonathon, one of their cousins, with half a ton of wad. Daniel and Joseph Hechstetter sold all their holdings for around £1,000 0s 0d to Messrs Birkett, Gawen Helm, who had been their London agent, and three other investors, Helm acting as agent and banker for the partners. The new adventurers worked the mine with great vigour, and produced 60 tons of wad in 1631, for which they were paid £24 10s 0d per ton.

DATE	TONS	CWT	£	s	d	PURCHASER
1607?	37	10	1,110	0	0	
1607?	40	00	1,280	0	0	STAMLER HAMBURG
1619	5	00	135	10	0	BUTLER NEWCASTLE
1619	5	00	85	0	0	EWER LONDON
1619	5	00	85	0	0*	ESSINGTON LONDON
1620	40	00	1,470	0	0	JOHNSON & ESSINGTON LONDON
1620	20	00	85	0	0	JOHNSON & ESSINGTON LONDON
1620	8	10	36	0	0*	ESSINGTON LONDON
1631	40	00}	1,470	0	0	ALLON LONDON
	20	00}				
1631		10	6	15	0*	JONATHON
TOTAL	221	10	5,763	5	0	

* Estimated figure. The wad mined at this time was graded great and small. This accounts for the vast differences in price per ton. The approximate cost of setting up these early mining operations and driving the adit was £2,475.

By this time the crosscut had now reached the Grand Pipe, and here the wad was virtually a solid mass. The miners were now working up into the grey, gleaming wad towards the base of the sump and down into the sole with great vigour. No doubt the miners had little knowledge of the fortunes they were making for these early owners.

During September 1632, yet another alteration to the lease was effected when the following gentlemen bought into the lease: Robert Jopson, William Braithwaite, John Birkett and John Fisher, and the lease was for no less than 3,000 years!

By 1634, most of the Hechstetters' affairs had been wound up in Keswick. Daniel, now aged 71, went to the peace and quiet of the fen country to stay with his relative Roger Hechstetter, a clergyman in Soham, Nr Cambridge, and on the 21st of May 1638, Daniel died. His death signified the end of at least two generations of the Hechstetter family's mining activities. They had brought wealth and prosperity, and a singular expertise to one of the wildest parts of the Lake District. They had taught the English how to mine, how to tunnel and break the hard rock to win wad, copper and lead, and how to dress and smelt the ores. This was certainly a major turning point in British hard rock mining, but now we were on our own..... the Germans had gone.

The Wad Mine from Seathwaite hamlet. Caldbeck Mining Museum Collection.

Seathwaite Wad Mine, head of Grand Pipe at surface where a small ash tree still grows. Caldbeck Mining Museum Collection.

Seathwaite Wad Mine, Old Mens Level circa 1625. Roy Fellows Collection

Seathwaite Wad Mine, Old Mens Level circa 1625. Ian Hebson Collection.

Top: Graphite moulds with counterfeit coins and examples of unfinished coins. Courtesy of Tullie House
Bottom: Graphite moulds found at Nether Wasdale for the manufacture of counterfeit coins of Henry VII circa 1500. Courtesy of Tullie House

Sir John Bankes, Lord Chief Justice, 1589 - 1644. Kingston Lacy Archive.

Sir Ralph Bankes, ?1631 - 1677. Yale Centre for British Art.

3 The Great Bankes Family

During 1638, Mr Hawtrey, one of the early shareholders, died and his share was purchased by Sir John Bankes, which now meant that he had control of the whole of the moiety.

The workings on Seatoller Common were now identifiable as a definite mine site, rather than a rough area pock marked by trials of no significance. Now, proper adits were visible from the hamlet below as the mine continued to work and operate successfully, and graphite was swiftly becoming a very marketable product. Although not unique, the Borrowdale product was in fact by now, known as the purest graphite in the world! Consequently, the periods of extracting the wad were restricted, by which policy its scarcity was enhanced and this resulted in maintaining an inflated price. Would be merchants were selected carefully, to ensure that the distribution was tightly controlled. One of these distributors was Messrs Robert Ellison and Ralph Lomax of Newcastle on Tyne who, on the 14th of July 1642, negotiated a deal for 20 tons of wad costing £400 0s 0d, to be supplied in three different grades. So tough however were the bargaining tactics used, that this merchant company sent a letter to the mine owners, Sir John Bankes and Charles Hudson informing them that another mine was producing wad, and that the samples they had seen were first class. They advised that they were not reliant solely on the Borrowdale wad, and were naturally looking for a more favourable price. The ruse (for so it was) totally failed to sway the mine owners and in fact, resulted in an increased price of £25 0s 0d per ton!

By now, Civil War was looming, and these were to be dark days for the Bankes family who were ardent Royalists. To add to the family's problems, Sir John Bankes died on the 24th December 1644, in Christ Church College, Oxford and was survived by his wife and two sons Ralph and John Bankes. Lady Bankes took over her husband's estate and interest in the mine and appears to have been a woman of substance, apparently acquitting herself well in the business dealings. She also fared well in rebuffing no less than two sieges by the Roundheads at her family seat of Corfe Castle in Dorset, finally surrendering no doubt, for the sake of her family. The lands were confiscated by Cromwell, but, despite being a proud Royalist, she remained unharmed and unintimidated. After paying a substantial fine, she was able to regain her lands and castle, and allowed to continue her life unhindered

The reading of Sir Johns Bankes' will was, as can be imagined, a long and protracted affair, for he had been a man of substance and his estate was large, but in his generosity he did not forget the people of Keswick. Just prior to his death, he had purchased land in Keswick from a George Brown, comprising an orchard on which was a tenement. This was presumably in disrepair, for he required it to be pulled down, anything of value to be saved and put to good use in the construction of a poor house on the site. He also gave £200 0s 0d for its construction, and a further £30 0s 0d a year for the next three years. The poor house was demolished in 1890 to make way for the Post Office which still stands on the site.

DATE	TONS	CWT	GRADE	£	s	d	MERCHANTS
1642	20	0	?	400	0	0	R ELLISON, R LOMAX, NEWCASTLE
1646	50	0	?	900	0	0	S BOULTON, J BRETT, LONDON
1646	30	0	?	300	0	0	
1655	50	0	SUPERIOR	900	0	0*	R & B ELLISON, NEWCASTLE
1655	17	0	INFERIOR	350	0	0*	J BROWN, LONDON
1663	6	0	LARGE }				
1663	9	0	SECOND }				R & B ELLISON,
1663	18	0	THIRD }	1,600	0	0	NEWCASTLE &
1663	33	0	FOURTH }				S BOULTON, LONDON
1663	4	0	ROUGH }				
1671	6	0	LARGE	600	0	0	
1671	6	0	SECOND	270	0	0	DAVID LELONG,
1671	6	0	THIRD }	480	0	0	LONDON
1671	6	0	FOURTH }				
1671	30	0	FIFTH	450	0	0	
TOTAL	301	0		6,250	0	0	

* Estimated figure.

The value of the product was plain to see, and prospectors were anxiously searching remote hills, ravines and other mining fields for a trace of the elusive wad, and hopefully their fortunes. A strike was recorded in Coniston at a place called Mealy Gill in 1658, where two short trial tunnels had been driven just below a waterfall. The mine was known as the Boot Polish mine, and apparently a small mill was constructed on the banks of Church Beck where the wad could be dressed, but this was swept away in a flood. There is also the mention of a wad trial in Tilberthwaite Gill, and there are two places which appear to be man-made, and where possible trials could have been attempted. Both these areas contain rock strata that is very dark and shaly, and which, in a decomposed state could be mistaken for wad. However, it appears that nothing came of it.

A query arose about the lease during May 1661, concerning Sir William Carleton and his 21 year entitlement. As early as this date, people who had land in Borrowdale assumed that if they had land tracts within the wad mine area, this gave them a right to the profits which were apparent. During this period, the mine agent appears to have been one Roger Griggs who evidently had neither the authority nor the legal knowledge to deal with the query. In this case he referred the lease to the Dean of Carlisle, who was well known to Sir Ralph Bankes, for ratification but he, in turn, declined to undertake the instruction as it had not been sent with the authority of Sir Ralph. Griggs therefore arranged to dispatch the lease to London to avoid further loss of time. Nothing more seems to have been heard of this enquiry and one must therefore assume that the gentleman, although possibly owning land in the valley, had no mining right at all.

The High Wad Moor was at this present time working, but the men were driving in very hard rock and progress was slow. The adit they were driving was to de-water a surface shaft which, once completed, would help in the production of more wad. It was essential therefore, that more men be employed for dressing and mining. Also more money was needed to fund the operation, so Mr Griggs wrote to Sir Ralph, acknowledging £20 0s 0d already received and requesting a further £50 0s 0d to pay the men etc. The weather, he said, was good and he recommended that the mine be started to work with all speed. By 1664, however, poor Griggs had become a sick man, possibly some of it stress related, although the mine had produced £1,528 2s 9d worth of wad which was good, steady business. Mr Griggs had been promised a fourth share for his toils in running the operation. Money for expenses and wages came sporadically from Sir Ralph in London, but no sooner had another £50 0s 0d arrived than a further sum was required. This resulted, on more than one occasion, in poor old Griggs having to fend off the creditors by dipping into his own finances to support the operation. So frustrated was he, that he even sent his son Francis to London during April bearing a receipt for £6 18s 6d for money expended, and also to collect his fourth share in the profits.

The place where the wad was being extracted at this time is not indicated, but it is reasonable to assume that the poorer grades were coming from the Higher Wadhole. Probably some of the tips would have been re-worked also for the easy pickings. It is recorded that in 1667, the High Wad Mine was re-opened by Sir Ralph Bankes and the higher grades from underground were almost all still at the Grand Pipe working. It was during this period that a further change occurred in the lease, John Hudson acquiring John Birkett's share on the 11th of October 1669.

It is interesting to note that all the merchants were either from Newcastle or London, presumably because of the size of the ports there. The contracts with

"Pony train carrying the wad" J Tyler

merchant companies for the periods of the last workings of 1642, 1644, 1655, 1663 and 1671 had nearly all carried stringent covenants. In 1655 for instance, the arrangement was that the mine was not to be re-opened or worked for the next 7 years. This meant, of course that the merchants could charge virtually what they wanted for the wad. A penalty clause was also inserted, that should the mine owners sell any wad during the agreement period, they would pay a penalty of £20 0s 0d per cwt. As they had produced during that year 67 tons of wad, this would have meant a cash penalty being levied against the company of £26,800 had they actually sold the year's production. The wad trade was still being developed, and as more uses were being found for the material, more grades were being offered into the market, not all industries requiring the very highest quality.

One very serious problem which had manifested itself was that of theft. It was becoming a regular occurrence, both from the mine itself and during transportation. This was of course, a direct result of the escalating value of the product and presented the mining company with a problem hitherto unknown in local mining. Once the wad had been extracted and put into barrels, it suddenly became a liability until it was safely with the recipient. The company, having sold the product prior to it leaving the mine and anxious to be relieved of the problem during transportation, declared to the merchants and carriers, that all responsibility was theirs once the company had delivered the wad to Keswick.

The trade routes taken during this period would probably have been via Carlisle to Newcastle, then by sea to either London or Europe. Another and more simple route would have been by mule to Ravenglass via Sty Head Pass, but there is no mention of this. When one starts to consider the size of a mule train of say a 5 ton load, assuming that the mules could each carry two barrels weighing approximately 70 lb each, this could mean a train of 80 mules or two trips of 40! Even if carts were used with oxen or horses, it would take at least four carts. Alternative routes to the east coast could have been by way of Penrith, Appleby, Barnard Castle and Durham. The journey by sea was of course much safer and quicker unless inclement weather struck, but on land the load was a target for every footpad from Keswick to London, a journey of some 286 miles and not only that, but the costs were nearly double.

In 1677, Sir Ralph Bankes died, and the following year his son and heir John Bankes of Kingston Hall in the County of Dorset inherited his father's moiety, valued at £100 0s 0d, the other being owned by Mr John Hudson and valued the same. Young Mr Bankes, to ensure that his mine was not interfered with nor his money embezzled, employed a Mr Joseph Beck to look after his interests and estate affairs.

Much of the black lead was being sold to the established merchants in London and Newcastle, however, there was at this time one merchant in

Scotland, a Mr Geddy of Galloway, who had paid £500 in advance for wad with a promise of a further purchase of £500. After this contract was signed, the mine would be closed for a period of five years. The amount of wad to be supplied was an assortment of five grades weighing a total of 67 tons. Of the fifth and lowest grade, 120 lb per cwt was to be sent, the extra 8 lb being a bonus on such a large order, and the graphite was to be taken over the next sixteen months. The mine agent arranged for the quantity of graphite to be mined and the first of it dispatched, and the second order also to be made ready. Mr Geddy was, unfortunately, not true to his word and the wad, now prepared and ready for carriage, was an immediate liability to the company. Despite several letters insisting payment be made as agreed, Mr Geddy was not forthcoming, explaining that a sea passage was too risky at this time of the year as the seas were rough and dangerous. Consequently, the wad had to be sealed in the mine for safety, much to the consternation of the owners.

By 1683, the first real 'lead' pencil was produced, using either cedar wood or deal for the casing round the graphite, and although crude, demand soon began to increase. Although wad had been found in abundance on the Continent, the quality of the Borrowdale material was superlative, and hence, it was now winning world-wide acclaim.

4 Vagabonds, Rogues and Thieves

Towards the end of the 17th Century, the mine came under part ownership of John Shepherd of Bettys Town, Co Meath who had invested £200, which entitled him to a fourth share along with the Bankes family. This new lease was drawn up on the 18th of August 1697.

With the further exploitation of the mine, uses of wad were extended, some of them appearing rather bizarre. For instance, in the medical profession it was crushed down and used to help the colic, and a concoction for relieving the pain of kidney stones was a potion made from wad in mulled white wine. More realistic uses were mixing with grease for wagon axles, lubricating pulley wheels and block and tackle on ships' rigging, dyeing cloth and blacking felt hats. As usual, anything to do with armaments seems to have been essential, and wad was no exception. It was ideal for musket and cannon ball moulds, for working into gun barrels as a rust preventative, for crucibles in the foundries, and of course, for coin moulds. Despite all these new and varied uses, it seems that little was happening at the mine itself, although a suitable stockpile was available. The mine was supposedly re-opened by John Bankes in 1710, although it was rumoured that the mine had been working 'unofficially' as it were, and a substantial deposit had been found below the Old Mens Level in the Grand Pipe. This was known as the Third Sop and was at a position about 155 feet down in the Grand Pipe. During 1713, Gortons was once again being worked on Seatoller Common.

On the 14th of July 1714, John Bankes died and the passing of this important and powerful partner led to a series of petty disputes about ownership of lands, mineral rights and payments which came to a head during 1717. Eventually, it was left to the courts to sort out, the main problem being that so many leases for land were exchanged almost on a yearly basis, and small parcels of land sold off or bequeathed. As stated before, many of the purchasers and beneficiaries thought that because a lease referred to Seathwaite or Borrowdale, they automatically had claim to the wad mine or part thereof. An example of this appears in one particular case brought by a descendant of John Jopson. It appears that Jopson had been associated with the mine in 1656 and had, prior to his death in 1715, sold the shares he had in the mine itself but retained the land. The various papers had been scrutinised by the lawyers to prove the entitlement, and had now been treated to the customary tardiness of the law, the case dragging on until being thrown out two years later.

The trade with London had now been well established and during 1715, a bargain was struck to supply two London ironmongers, John Baker and Edmund Brown, with 40 tons of graphite at £70 0s 0d per ton. The agreement was that a quarter of the price was to be paid up front and the balance on delivery, the cost of which would be incurred by the purchaser, and the total consignment of wad to be collected within six months. Then the mine had to remain closed and no further wad sold for seven years. It appears the final agreement was for 38 tons at the £70 0s 0d per ton rate making a total of £2,660, and a penalty clause to the company of £5,600 for failure to deliver or breaking the contract. Likewise, should the merchants fail to clear their account by the agreed date, the company would be at liberty to open the mine and trade freely.

The Upper Wadholes were again worked with vigour during 1735, and had been extended, now consisting of at least five or six shafts, some of which were drained by short adits. The most adventurous of these was a level just above a wall or hedge on the north side of the upper reaches of Wadhole Gill. The level entrance was stone walled, with a small hut for the storage of tools and to afford the miners a little protection from the weather. Here, the level was being driven on through hard rock to gain what would be later known as Gortons and Woodmans Pipes which had been worked earlier from the surface. Two brothers called Gorton were driving the level, which was eventually named for them, and they were ably assisted by a local miner by the name of Hugh Workman. The driving forward of Gortons level was basically a straight forward mining operation, and the three men were all experienced and used to the privations. It is therefore some what surprising, that after working at the mine for a short time and whilst driving the level, they suddenly decided to down tools and quit. It could have been the atrocious weather, the rude conditions or the stark remoteness of the area of course, or even intimidation by the locals, there is no way of knowing. Records show however, that it was only the smooth talking of the mine bosses which brought them round and so the work continued. It has been suggested that the Gorton family hailed from Gunnerside, and that they had also been involved with the Tilberthwaite copper mine back in 1717.

August 1735 saw another agreement made by John Shepherd, his son William Shepherd of Drogheda, Ireland and John Bankes to supply Messrs Samuel Sandeford and John Lancashire, both colourmen (dyers) of Budge Row, London with 2,130 lb of assorted graphite for which they paid £377 15s 0d in cash. No agreement was required to close the mine as the total amount required was insufficient to negotiate a long term bargain, and although another delivery was taken by them, this was for only a few pounds.

The mine had been worked intermittently for 300 years, and by now it was quite extensive as one can imagine, and up to this time the recorded output was around 560 tons. It should also be borne in mind that the workforce here generally consisted of only about a dozen men. The wad, when found as stones or lumps of various size, appears to have been fairly easy to extract. Washing and grading of the wad was all that was required, so no elaborate dressing floors were necessary.

The main problem still was security, and now the price for wad was about to spiral upwards and make certain people rich beyond their wildest dreams. Never before or since has any substance been mined in Cumbria of equal value. For example, a miner's wage in 1671 was about 15s 0d per week, and wad was fetching £100 0s 0d per ton rising to £1,344 0s 0d per ton by 1761.

The jaws of Borrowdale are rugged and craggy, small oaks and larch trees clinging desperately to the lower valley slopes, making travel difficult along the small trading roads; to get from Seathwaite to Keswick was a good day's journey. This quiet backwater had now become an area for vagabonds, rogues and thieves, who would stop at virtually nothing to get their hands on the precious wad. Because of the terrain and the wildness of the land, it was virtually impossible to police or protect, and it was mainly at night that the gangs came to plunder and rob the mine dumps of any graphite they could find. Their lanterns could be seen twinkling in the night skies high on the fell, 1,000 feet above the dwellings at Seathwaite. The robbers knew the fells well, and as soon as they heard dogs being unleashed, they could make good their escape over to Honister, or towards smugglers' routes like Moses Trod around Great Gable. The wet, spongy ground around the base of Gillercombe would confuse the dogs, and the thieves would soon be long gone with their precious booty.

The illicit wad would turn up in the hostelries and ale-houses of Keswick, creating a thriving black market. (It is thought that this expression derives from the dealing in stolen black lead). One of these ale-houses, the George Hotel, still stands but in those ancient times it was called the George and Dragon. It is supposedly the oldest hostelry in the town and the place where the Elizabethan miners dealt their copper transactions. Another tavern of that time was The Grapes, now no longer in existence. This was situated on the main street in Keswick near the market place and in the mid 1800s became the premises of A Gatey, Drapers. Although during this period Keswick town was still fairly small, it had numerous little back ways and alleys in which there were many dives and low pot-houses where this illegal trade would have been plied. Here, in smoky, candle-lit back rooms, amongst flea-ridden dogs and muttering, gin-soaked hags, the thieves sold the wad to Jewish dealers, who would trade in any commodity for a quick profit. These transactions were secret and very lucrative and created a greater source of revenue than could be earned honestly. It is reported that one smuggler, Black Sal, turned her attentions to the wad mine rather than plying her normal trade of liquor smuggling. From her filthy, rat-infested hovel at Rosthwaite she would creep along to the mine workings under cover of darkness, scurrying up through the wooded area on Dickinson Bank. Once at the mine she would scrat the surface of the outdoor washing areas for her few pounds of wad, and when her small leather bag was full Sal would return to her hiding place beside the river Derwent, where she kept her hoard of wad hidden. Sadly for her, one day of intense rain swelled the river to such a depth that it swept her stash of wad away and shortly after this, whilst out scavenging one dark and windy night, Black Sal met a savage death at the jaws of a pack of wolf hounds.

It is estimated that at least £1,000 per year was being made by organised raids, so it is not surprising that many were tempted when the average wage was around £25 0s 0d per year. One report indicates that at least forty lanterns could be seen dotted about the workings one night, which illustrates the magnitude of the black market, even in these early days.

Some people, however, were rather more enterprising and were intent on obtaining the valuable wad on a more long term basis and from right under the noses of the owners. During January 1739, William Hetherington, a miner from Keswick and his associate John Martin of Newbiggin applied for a lease to mine for copper within the confines of Seatoller Common. This was granted, and they each paid £25 0s 0d and started working high on the fell. Here the men worked diligently, driving at least three levels, and a little copper was encountered although not enough for commercial use. Disgruntled at the poor prospects, they decided to quit and filled in two of the workings. Prior to the lease taken out in 1739, William Hetherington had taken an option on another lease years before in September 1736 which in fact, he had never bothered to exploit. It may have been his intention to sell it on as the wad business boomed. This tract of land was situated much lower down the fell in a place called Daniel Jopsons New Close, below the boundary wall and just south of Wadhole Gill and virtually opposite the Low Wadhole and the Grand Pipe. It was here that he and Martin commenced driving a level in search of copper, and the usual small stone hut was built at the level entrance for tools and shelter. The level was blasted forward in hard rock for a distance of 10 yards, at which point it divided, one branch carrying on as an innocent copper trial, whilst the other tunnel meandered off for a distance of 25 yards..... towards Gortons Sop which was already well established. The first section of the level was very heavily and cosmetically timbered, and it was behind this timbering that a secret door concealed the right hand tunnel. So well disguised was this, that Hetherington would leave the main level entrance wide open for anyone to venture inside, to show that he seemed only to be working for copper. However, his audacious attitude was his undoing when a Mr James Spedding of Whitehaven, steward to Sir James Lowther, was sent to dial the mine, no doubt on the authority of the mine owners. Mr Spedding was being assisted by Charles Bowman, a miner working at the wad mine, who spotted nodules of wad on the level floor. For years Hetherington had been suspected of being involved in the night raids and the smuggling of wad, but nothing had ever been proved against him. Suspicions had been aroused though, by the amount of tools and lanterns in his hut, far more than would be required for just two men and it was suspected that these were left there for the raiders to use, particularly in the robbing of the Upper Wadhole just a few hundred feet up the fell. After his discovery, it seems likely that Hetherington went to ground with other members of the bandit fraternity. The information regarding his very clever underground operation was not collated until 1750 and it seems it was a little later when he was actually caught and sent to stand trial at Carlisle.

Meanwhile, the year of 1745 had seen another substantial find of graphite in Gortons Level, and this was called Bowes Sop after the agent James Bowes, the other agent at that time being one Gowan Youdale. The sop was discovered in the south-west end of the level, and produced thirteen casks of quality graphite. This was transported from the mine by pack mule, oddly, as it seemed at the time, under cover of darkness to a barn at Chapel House near Rosthwaite, Mr Bowes' residence. By the following morning however, the wad had mysteriously disappeared and was never seen again!

During this period, when wad was fetching 7/9d per lb, the mine was repeatedly under threat and one day in August 1750, John White, a local man employed as a guard, discovered that plans were afoot to raid the mine and gain entry at all costs. White waited anxiously at the guardhouse, the windows tightly shuttered and the door securely bolted, his musket and pistols charged and ready. Suddenly the silent night air was shattered by a battering at the door, and a mob too great for John to handle on his own, surrounded the house. A loud, rough voice called to him that if he did not sit tight he would be put to death, and the gang then went off into the night and rifled the mine. The rogues apparently returned with the wad to Hetherington's house, two miles from the mine. John White was then given a friendly warning a day or two later by a Mr Nichols, that another raid was imminent and suggested for his own safety that he should keep away from the mine at night. With this information in mind, John White decided to go to guard the mine with extra men, and enlisted the help of six young fellows including one of the Jopson boys. Sure enough, the mine was attacked that night by nine men armed with pistols and muskets, and a fearsome exchange of shots ensued as the gang attacked the guardhouse. This was situated between the High Wadhole and Low Wadhole Closes in the lea of the hill just below Gortons Stage, but overlooking the Low Wadhole (in fact, near the site of the later Harrisons Stage). The raiders got onto the roof where they tore the slates off with their bare hands, and having made a big enough hole, they proceeded to fire into the room below wounding one of the men. It was during this vicious exchange that one of the gang was mortally wounded, and so taken aback were the villains at the ferocity of the retaliation that they fled. The man killed was Daniel

"Attack through the roof, 1750" J Tyler

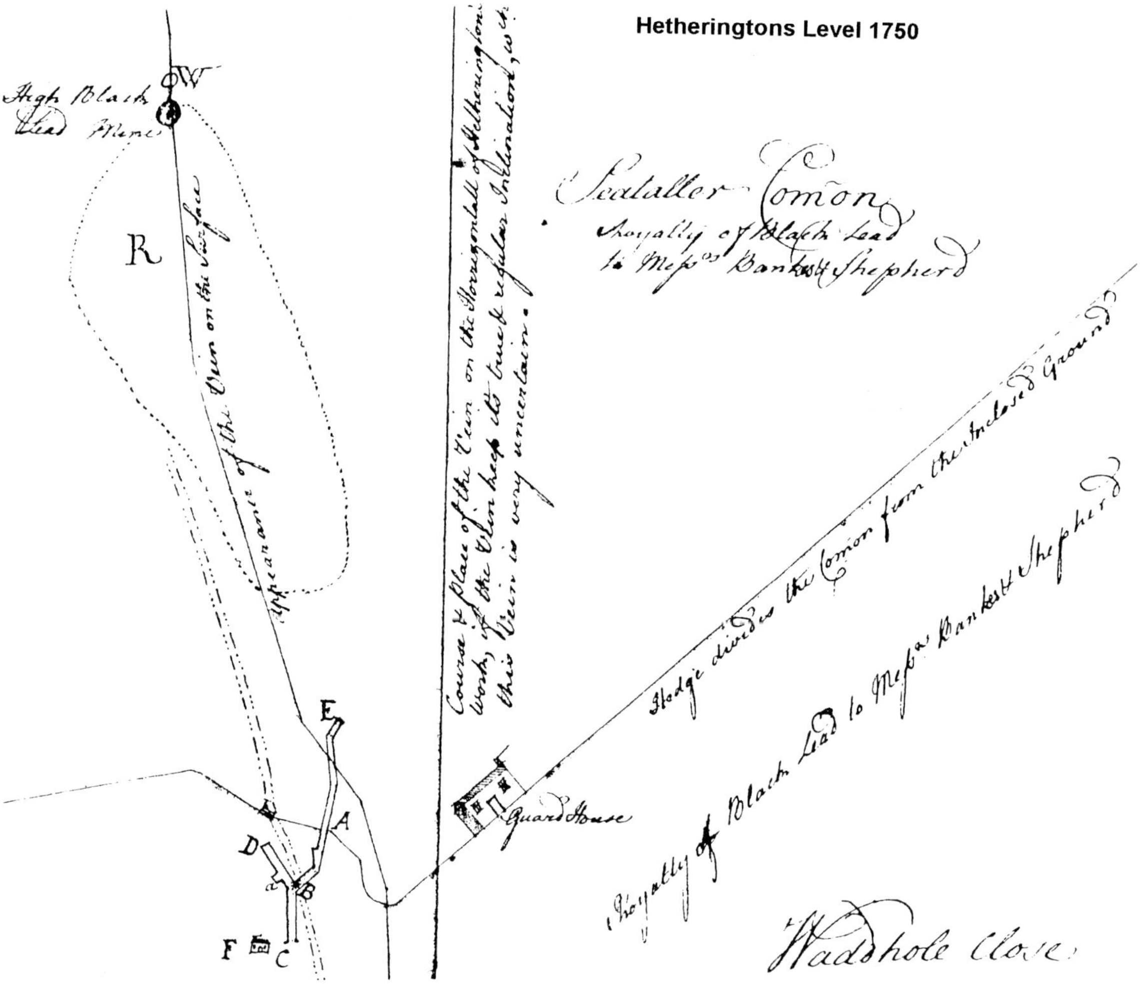

CBDAE	*Hetherington's works*
B to E	*The secret part of Hetherington's work*
C to D	*Hetherington '...never secreted his work but left it open.*
C to A	*Hetherington '...framed his work with timber as if to support the level but was for the purpose to hide a false door.'*
B	*Communication between the open and secret part of his work.*
F	*A small hut where one man kept watch whilst another worked the secret passage.*
W	*A place lately opened by pilferers.*

William Hetherington's secret level 1750. Courtesy of C R O.

Wright, the gang leader, and his bleeding body was found 70 yards from the house. Such was the severity of the attack suffered by the guards, that they absconded in fear of their lives not only from the ruffians and rogues, but from the law of the land, and made for the Coniston area to look for work. It was the all powerful Henry Bankes who vouched for their innocence in the matter and assured them of a complete pardon. Wright's killing had indeed been a regrettable incident, but had been brought about by his own greed.

The raids on the mine continued, and the sheer value of the wad was now inflaming people to violent attacks, risking their own lives at the same time in an effort to get at the treasure. Once more, on the 20th of October in the same year, the mine was again viciously attacked and the guardhouse badly damaged. However on this occasion the thieves left empty handed although repairs had to be carried out to the value of 15/-, with more work done on security of the house costing £2 11s 1d. The guarding of the mine had now become a dangerous occupation, and surrounded by wild moorland as it was, the house was an easy target. Here the guards were isolated and probably for the most part scared out of their wits, knowing that the robbers would stop at nothing to steal the 'black gold'.

It was during this period that a case was finally brought against William Hetherington, and as a result he was convicted and did time in the infamous Carlisle Gaol. It must be surmised that Hetherington decided that the life of a villain was not for him, he was after all a pretty good miner! On his release, it seems that Mr Bankes wished to help him towards rehabilitation and so he employed William at the wad mine.....a case of 'set a thief to catch a thief' perhaps! It would be obvious that through his previous involvement with the criminal fraternity, the knowledge he had gained could be turned to the company's advantage. It was hoped that by using his intelligence, the security of the mine and the surrounding land could be greatly strengthened. In short, William had become a 'mole' and it was now up to him to ensure that the pilfering and the night raids were brought to a halt. In a letter to Mr Sharp, Mr Henry Bankes' agent in London, he makes a detailed statement implicating several men. Corruption was rife and William was aware that most of the current workforce was dishonest. This did not only apply to the ordinary workers, and he knew for sure that James Spedding, Littledale, Simpson, Dawson, Scott, Levie, White, Fisher, Bowman and even James Bowes were on the take. Bowes was certainly disposing of wad illicitly in the ale-houses of Cockermouth, and he was working jointly with Dawson at whose house he regularly stayed for nights on end. He would then travel by horse to Cockermouth to peddle the wad, where he sold the poor quality for an exorbitant 6/- per lb. The recipients in one instance complained that the price was extortionate and that 4/- was reasonable. Bowes' attitude was one of swaggering bravado and he laughed in their faces and told them to take it or leave it. Even young John Jopson, son of that respectable Borrowdale farming family, was found in possession of stolen wad whilst trying to sell it in Keswick. These were hard men in desperate times and in these remote lands, to accuse some one openly could result in violent retribution, and in his letter William asks Mr Sharp to keep this to himself for the moment. It appears also that the 'coat and two shirts' which every poor person of the parish received each year under the will of Judge Bankes in 1642, were now no longer forthcoming, although the amount of money available for the Poor House was £60 per year. It looks as though William certainly had his work cut out for him.

All the raids up to now had taken place at the higher workings, and at the Grand Pipe the Third Sop was still being worked along with further development. By virtue of this, it was nigh impossible to gain illegal entry, not to mention the fact that unless regular de-watering took place the shaft was flooded to the Old Mens Stage. One of William Hetherington's first trials was to supervise the opening of a new level called Jopsons Level which is directly in Wadhole Gill and just below the guardhouse. This was driven forward a distance of 20 yards before being given up, after only a small amount of wad was recovered. Attentions were then transferred back up to the High Wad Moor where a further shaft was sunk under the instructions of William Hetherington which was subsequently named after him and from which a few casks of wad were extracted.

The attacks on the mine still did not cease, and to some degree the robbers had become even bolder, and an attack in broad daylight brought home to the owners the vulnerability of situation for everyone. On this occasion, Charles Bowman and a fellow miner were engaged in digging a surface shaft into a sop on Seatoller Fell when the villains arrived. The two men, outnumbered and unarmed, were brutally attacked with cudgels and thrown into the shaft. The ruffians looted any of the wad they could find and made off, leaving the two poor men trapped in the shaft. Eventually, tired, cold and bleeding they managed to escape and raise the alarm. This outrage must have been the last straw, and as a result of this incursion onto his property, Henry Bankes MP of Boswells Court, Lincolns Inn, London started to lobby for stronger laws to deal with these acts of terrorism within his territory. Eventually, through his tenacity, in 1752 an Act of Parliament was passed to deal exclusively with the theft of wad. The penalties were now harsh indeed, and illegal entry into the mine or the theft of wad could incur a public flogging, a year's hard labour or seven years deportation.

Shortly after the Act was passed, the company erected five large engraved boundary stones, standing some 4 feet high and brought from Honister Quarry. These were placed strategically on the fell, informing people that to pass the stones would bring them into trespass. The highest stone is situated

200 yards south-west of Harrisons Stage, above the wall on Seatoller Fell and inscribed Shepherd 1752. A second stone was erected just a few yards north-east of the guardhouse at what is now Harrisons Stage. A third stone was sited due south of Wadhole Gill and inscribed J Bankes Esquire 1752, and a fourth stone is to be seen slightly above what is now Gilberts Stage, just above the pack horse route to the High Wad Mine. The fifth stone was placed beside the path leading from the ford.

John Bankes marker stone, 1752, near Gilberts Stage. Caldbeck Mining Museum Collection.

John Shepherd stone, 1752, Seatoller Fell. Caldbeck Mining Museum Collection.

Top: Beck House, Seathwaite. home of the Dixon family. Caldeck Mining Museum Collection.
Bottom: High House, Seathwaite, home of Joseph Glover. Courtesy of the 'K'-Farers Rambling Club.

Top: Joseph Jopson's house, Thornythwaite. S Bland Collection.
Bottom: Chapel House, J W Harrison's house. David Felton Collection.

Top: The George Hotel, Keswick. Caldbeck Mining Museum Collection.
Bottom: The Miners Arms, Rosthwaite, now the Royal Oak. Neil Dowie Collection.

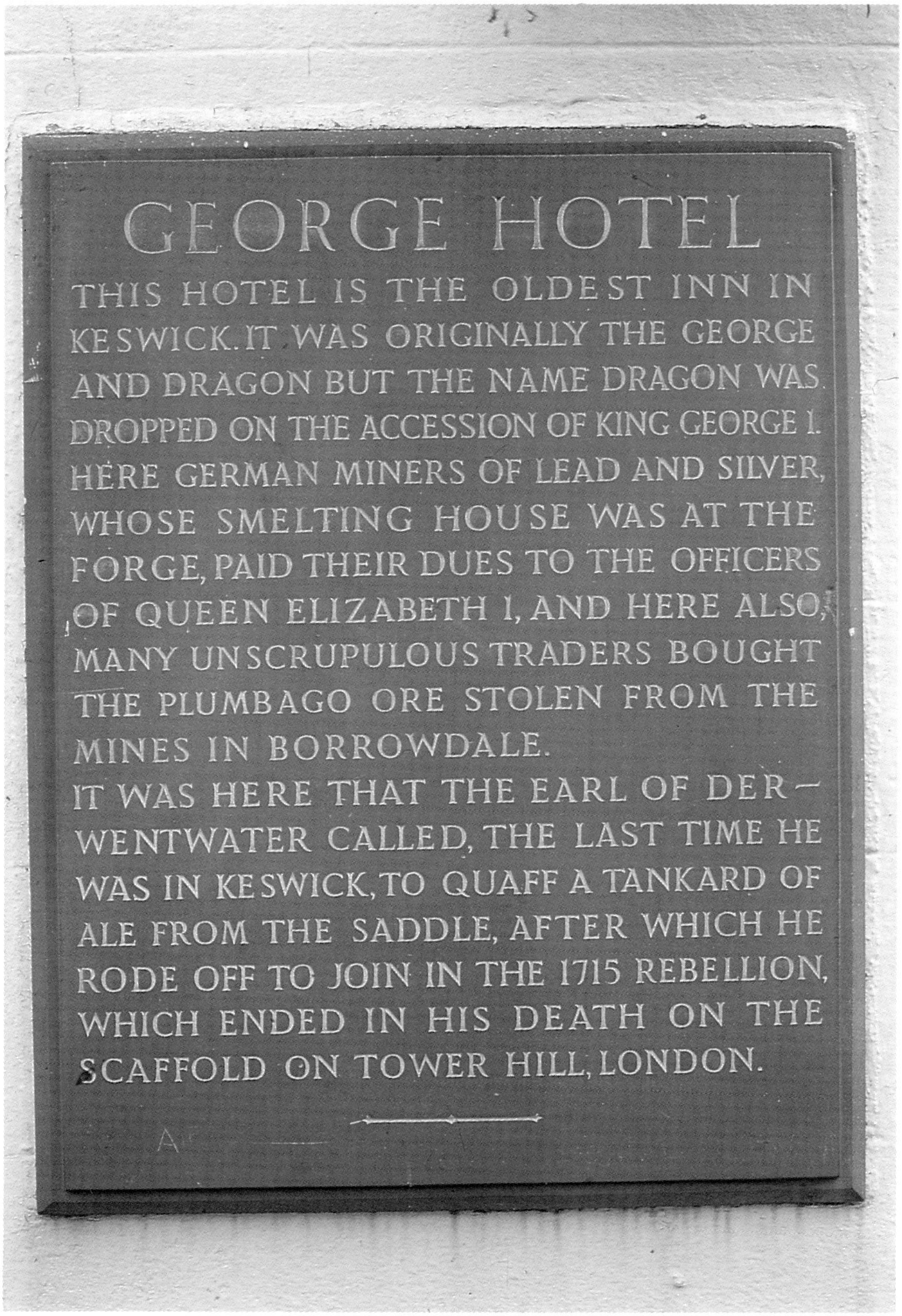

Plaque outside the George Hotel, Keswick. Caldbeck Mining Museum Collection.

5 The Manesty Gang

William Hetherington was promoted to the position of mine steward on the 19th of October 1754 and, now a convert to law and order, he was to do his best to vindicate his new position. William was asked with the aid of his son James to provide an accurate surface plan of the wad mine, and this he did, basing it in an old map drawn by James Bowes.

The Old Mens Level, which had been closed for many years, was re-opened in September 1754 under the instructions of John Shepherd who held the Upper Wadhole moiety. The Lower Wadhole was under the control of Mr Bankes, and the wad gained from this lower area was generally of a better quality. John Shepherd decided to expose the pipe via the Old Mens Level thus gaining access, hopefully, into the lower depths of the pipe and workings. His men commenced work shovelling the spoil which was now inconveniently blocking the access, and after a day's toil had uncovered the stone walls of the entrance, perched on top of which were large flat stones forming a stable roof for a natural bunning to form. The entrance was narrow and the level had of course, been cut into solid rock. The men eased their way forward, and after about 70 yards the level split in two, the right hand branch continuing a few yards to a blind heading and the left revealing the Grand Pipe, stretching upwards of 90 feet to the surface. The pipe in the sole of the level was a black abyss gaping at their feet, and lanterns and tallow did little to pierce the darkness. A small shaft of light could be seen filtering in from the surface, enough to illuminate, on the wall to the left a vivid green secondary deposit revealing an exposed copper vein. Shepherd cursed, throwing a rock down the pipe in front to test the depth, and to his surprise he heard it strike the bottom with a resounding boom. It seemed his luck was in, ladders and rope were swiftly brought and a descent was made of about 27 feet (now known as Waltons Stage) where the bottom of the pipe was reached. Here, the men scratched about and managed to find a few pounds of graphite, but the adventure was short lived. Work was interrupted by a visit by a Mr Bankes' personal representative, John Sharp of London. He informed Shepherd in no uncertain terms to get off Mr Bankes' property, as he was trespassing and stealing. He pointed out that the Old Mens Level was three yards outside his moiety, the boundary being clearly defined by the old boundary wall and confirming beyond doubt that the level was definitely within Mr Bankes' sett. John Shepherd argued that the boundaries had been inaccurately marked out, and that on a vertical plain the wad hole was his, but Sharp was adamant, and saw to it personally that Shepherd and his men were escorted from the property. He then supervised the back filling of the level before returning to London, the whole incident having taken just five days.

It may well have been this easily gained access into the Old Mens Level which occasioned a further incident at the mine in the same year. With a complete disregard for the new laws, John White, erstwhile mine guard, his two brothers and one, Joseph Medcalfe broke into the mine for the purpose of stealing wad. Unfortunately for them, they were spotted by John Braithwaite who lived in Seathwaite, and as they fled he trailed them and raised the alarm. Eventually, John White was caught and he was taken to Carlisle Gaol where he was held until 1755. His bail stood at £500 but was never paid, so he rotted at His Majesty's pleasure for a further year. The other three were never seen or heard of again, and it was rumoured that they made good their escape out of the county.

The 28th of February 1758 saw a major change once again in the structure of the lease when John Shepherd extended participation in his lease to the following shareholders: William Bankes of Lincolnshire, Robert Banks Hodgkinson of Westminster, George Perrott of Lincoln's Inn, Middlesex, Thomas Lloyd, Daniel Fox, Gascoigne Fredrick of the Inner Temple, London, Robert Bill of Farley, Staffs, Gent, Charles Bill of Fetter Lane London, Gent, Rev John Bill of Draycott, Staffs, John Rhoydes of Rochdale, Gent, Thomas Gilbert of the Inner Temple, London and John Gilbert of Alverton, Staffs who all entered an agreement to last for 99 years.

The mine, during 1760 was again thriving and eight miners were gainfully employed. They were now being supervised by no less than six overseers, and miners were searched on coming out of the mine at the end of each shift to prevent any pilferage. The only guardhouse or substantial building on the site was at the later named Harrisons stage, and it was to this place that the miners were brought and searched. The mine was now being guarded night and day, such was the security required to ensure the safety of the company's assets. The development of the upper workings continued under Messrs Wallerby and Francis Bill, and during this same year, Gortons Level was again re-opened under the direction of a Mr Allen, a miner from Derbyshire. He and his men were responsible for clearing the level and finding another large sop in another part of what was what was already known as Gortons Pipe. This came out to surface in High Wadhole Close and was cleared to a depth of 50 feet, revealing a large volume of wad weighing around 7 tons and worth in total about £3,000.

A further shaft was sunk at the High Wadhole Close by William Hetherington no more than a few yards from the existing three shafts and wad obtained, and it was William who was given the job of driving Gortons Level on to bisect them and so de-water them.

The success of the upper working continued and in 1765 attention was turned again to the easier pickings at the Upper Wadhole, to a place just a few yards away from Gortons, called Wilgoose Shaft. Here the men sunk down 60 feet and again struck lucky raising 96 cwt of wad. Happy with the new find, the men put in a binding 18 feet from the surface and then completely back filled to secure it. The success of recent years consolidated the reserves of mined wad, and the stores were once again full when the mine closed for its next seven years period. This of course, was in conjunction with the usual agreement with the London and Newcastle merchants, and ensured that the price would be maintained.

The graphite industry was, as we know, already established in Europe and also in some other parts of the world. Graphite was available from Mexico, this being better than the Spanish product, which was very pyritic. It was also brought from the East Indies but was the poorer quality, and New England was, by this time, a known producer. Consequently, efforts were made by other companies to expand their share of the market and introduce their graphite into Britain, especially when the Borrowdale mine was closed, in an effort to squeeze into the market. One such shipment from Rotterdam, of 43 cwt 11 lb of graphite was cargo on the ship Queen Charlotte, arriving in the Port of London during December. The wad was in lumps of 8 lb down to 3 oz and dust. It was a good colour, although very brittle and unfit for quality pencils, but it could be made into reed pencils and sold on the London streets by Jews. Her Majesty's Customs took the wad to Henry Bankes' warehouse where he inspected it and found that the quality was much inferior to that of the Borrowdale wad, its only similarity being in the colour. Henry considered it only fit for crucibles and blacking grates.

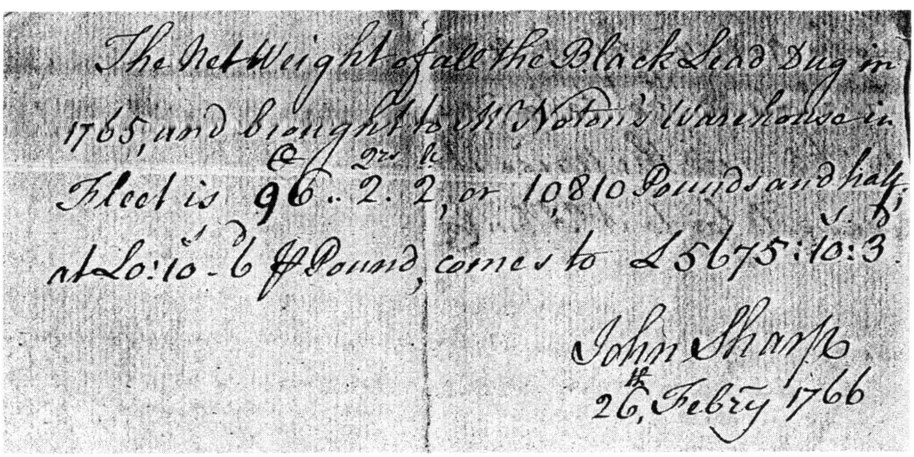

The Net Weight of all the Black Lead Dug in 1765, and brought to Mr Noton's Warehouse in Fleet is 96..2..2, or 10810 Pounds and half, at £0:10-6 ₱ Pound, comes to £5675:10:3

John Sharpe
26, Febry 1766

Record of Wad dug in 1765 and held in Mr Noton's warehouse. Courtesy of D R O.

One of these warehouses in London was a Mr Noton's in Fleet who, during this year of 1765 had brought in 10,810 lb at 10/6d per lb, a total value of £5675 10s 3d wholesale, most of which was sold to a Mr Albin Cox. From

THE

PRICES OF THE BLACK LEAD,

AND OTHER

Conditions to be obſerved by the Purchaſers, on Thurſday the 30th Day of January, 1766.

The Whole has been divided, with as much Care as the Proprietors were able, into two Sorts:

The Caſks No. 1. are the beſt Sort, and to be Sold for Seventeen Shillings per Pound.

The Caſks No. 2. are the ſecond Sort, and to be Sold at Eight Shillings per Pound.

No leſs a Quantity than two Caſks, one of each Sort, to be Sold in each Lot.

Each Perſon who ſhall be a Purchaſer, to make a Depoſit upon buying, at the Rate of Five Shillings in Twenty Shillings, for what he ſhall purchaſe; and the Lead to be taken away in Three Days after the Sale, between the Hours of Eleven and Two in the Afternoon; and the Remainder of the Money to be paid at the ſame Time: And in caſe the Lead ſhall not be taken away, and the Money paid within that Time, the Depoſit of Fiv Shillings in Twenty Shillings, ſhall be forfeited; and the Proprietors at Liberty to ſell the ſaid Black Lead or Wad, to any other Perſon.

The Proprietors engage not to open the Black Lead Mine, in leſs than Four Years from April 1765; that being the proper Time of the Year for beginning to open the Works.

Each Perſon at the Time of View, ſhall be at Liberty to have one Caſk of each Sort at his own Choice, out of the whole Quantity brought forth and opened.

At the Time of Sale, the Purchaſer ſhall be at Liberty to chooſe any two Caſks, one of each Sort; which if he buys, he ſhall immediately either pay the whole Money for, and take the Caſks away, or pay the Depoſit, and mark them with his own Name; and which are to be taken away within three Days, under the Forfeiture before-mentioned.

Where any Perſon buys or refuſes a Lot, the next Purchaſer ſhall be called; and he, and every other Purchaſer, ſhall in like Manner take his Turn; to the Intent that all Perſons who deal in this Commodity, may become Purchaſers at a reaſonable Price from the firſt Hands; and that the greateſt Impartiality may be ſhewn to all Perſons.

Conditions of purchase of Black Lead 1766. Courtesy of D R O.

Extracted from the LONDON GAZETTE of the 11th of December, 1770.

St. James's, December 11, 1770.

WHEREAS it has been humbly repreſented to the KING, That a Number of deſperate Men, armed with Fire Arms, whoſe Names are at preſent unknown, did on the 13th Day of *October*, and on the 20th Day of *November* laſt, break open the GUARD HOUSE, erected at the Entrance of the BLACK LEAD MINE, near *Seathwait*, in the County of *Cumberland*, and did forcibly enter into a Part of the ſaid Mine, with Intent to take and carry away Black Lead from thence, and did alſo threaten the Lives of the Perſons who had the Care of the ſaid Mines. His Majeſty, for the better diſcovering and bringing to Juſtice the Perſons concerned in the ſaid Offences, is hereby pleaſed to Promiſe his moſt Gracious Pardon to any one of them who ſhall diſcover his Accomplice or Accomplices therein, ſo that he or they may be apprehended and convicted thereof.

WEYMOUTH.

And as a farther Encouragement, the PROPRIETORS of the ſaid BLACK LEAD MINE, do hereby Promiſe a Reward of FIFTY POUNDS to any Perſon or Perſons making ſuch Diſcovery as aforeſaid, to be paid on the Conviction of any one or more of the Offenders. by Mr Thomas Webster at Cockermouth in Cumberland Attorney at Law.

Reward poster 1770. Courtesy of D R O.

these warehouses, sales were made on a regular basis, one such on the 30th of January 1766, where best sort No 1 was selling at 17/- per lb and sort No 2 at 8/- per lb. The wad was sold in casks, and the minimum purchase was of two casks, one of each quality. A deposit of a quarter of the price was required, the casks to be removed within three days, otherwise the deposit was forfeit.

John Bankes, in 1765, purchased one of the few houses in Seathwaite from John Braithwaite who at this time owned most of the property. The rest was owned by Daniel Jopson of Thornythwaite, his eldest son John of Seathwaite and Jonathon Jopson also of Seathwaite. Between them they owned at least three of the other houses, all having been recently purchased from John Braithwaite. Daniel had lived in the valley for many years, and he and his family had been involved in land ownership and the mine and also, regrettably, some clandestine operations.

It was during this closed period, in February 1766 that William Hetherington died. Also during this year, John Harrison was commissioned to draw plans for a mine steward's house at Seathwaite, which was completed during 1767. The house, known as Beck Cottage faced west and therefore provided a very good view of the wad mine.(This house still stands behind Seathwaite Farm and is now called Raingauge Cottage).

In 1768, one of the first attacks on the Low Wad mine took place by an organised gang, the ringleaders being John Raven and Bridgett Birkett, both of Manesty. Others involved in the raid were Joseph Middlefield, Simon Graham, Thomas Temple, Joseph Birkin and Andrew Henderson, all of whom hailed from various parts of Cumbria. On information received from informants, a list of over twenty five names was given to the agents. Many of these people were interviewed, most pleading total innocence, and finally agents Dixon and Willgoose applied, on behalf of Mr Bankes, for warrants for the arrest of the those named above. Literally dozens of people were interviewed by the two men in their attempt to acquire sworn affidavits from supposed witnesses. Their search took them to Cockermouth, Keswick, Under Skiddaw, Penrith and Buttermere in their efforts to bring the thieves to justice. The work of employing the various lawyers and the physical effort of writing dozens of letters to them and riding with the witnesses to various places to have the affidavits sworn was indeed a full- time job in itself.

The first major breakthrough came during December 1768, when the stolen wad was discovered at Gillercombe, a remote and craggy area high up on the fell and S/W of the mine, by agents Thomas Dixon and John Jopson. After recovering it they put it back into the mine for safety. The mine owners, anxious to publicise their displeasure, placed no fewer than ten adverts in various news sheets asking for information and offering rewards. Also, two hundred 'wanted' posters were printed for the price of 4/-. In order to increase security, Charles Norman visited local towns and villages to recruit men specifically to guard the mine. Initially the pay was to be 1/- to 1/6d a night, however, this was considered too little considering the dangerous nature of the work and the pay was increased to 6/-, which was in fact more than some of the best miners could earn. One of the new guards, Thomas Green from Buttermere was on the higher rate and it was he who caught Bridgett Birkett, whilst Isaac Martin apprehended Andrew Henderson who was taken into custody in Cockermouth to await bail. In October 1769, Temple, Birkin and Middlefield had also been caught. Joshua Lincock, who was the lawyer for the prosecution of the thieves, was busy compiling his case, when John Raven, who had been apprehended early on and was being held in custody in Carlisle Goal somehow made good his escape, much to the consternation of the mine owners.

6 *Progress and Security*

It was decided at this time, to engage someone to replace William Hetherington, and agent Thomas Dixon's son William who was a wad dresser, was promoted to the position. He was to continue the family's association with the mine along with his father and later his son and grandson, for many years. A further senior appointment at a local level was made during May 1769, introducing William Wakerley (Wackersley/Wickersley) as the senior agent reporting directly to Mr John Bankes. He was to be paid a guinea a week plus travelling expenses and an annual retaining fee. His immediate subordinates at the mine would be Charles Norman and Thomas Dixon, who were paid 10/- per week plus £10 0s 0d per year for holding the position of stewards. Other agents were Robert Jopson and John Youdale, a foreman.

The Upper Wadhole in 1769 was still leased by John Shepherd, whose agent was Francis Bill and his two inspectors/stewards were William Allen and John Wren. The Upper Wadhole was on Seatoller Common and as such, was part of the common land of the people of Seatoller. This was a grazing area for sheep, cows and horses, although these grazings were not the best. There are large areas of grass but of poor quality suitable only for sheep, and it was these lands which, over many years had been contested by local commoners for their right to dig for wad.

At this time, a regular delivery of malt and hops was made to Seathwaite from Jonathon Wood for which he charged in the region of £4 19s 6d. This was for pay-days and other celebrations. Ale was brewed here in one of the cottages which would have served as a pot-house for the local men, miners, farm labourers, slaters and such. In those days, the ale was brewed in the kitchen and brought through to the main room where the men would sit in the inglenook relaxing after a hard day's work. It is not difficult to imagine the scene, lit dimly by candles or oil-lamp, a peat fire in the grate and the men seated on wooden stools or settles discussing the day's doings in their respective trades; the farm boys with straw still in their hair and the wad miners with a subtle, greyish sheen to their skin. What tales those dalesmen must have told whilst in their cups!

The security of the mine was still uppermost in the thoughts of the directors, and they were also aware that if the mine was to continue successfully, new ground would have to be gained. Too much time had been spent foraging around the ancient workings, which were now becoming worked out. But, highest on the list of priorities was security, and they decided on the simple yet logical course of erecting another substantial guardhouse. William Wakerley was instructed to organize the building of this directly over the entrance of the Old Mens Level. Work commenced immediately, and an old miner was brought up to the site to verify the exact position of the level entrance, as this was now under acres of spoil. Some of this would have been deliberately put there when the mine was closed after the unauthorised intrusion by Mr Shepherd. The old timer was paid 1/- for his knowledge and, the position of the adit now verified, work started with the labourers clearing the spoil to the bedrock and eventually revealing the level entrance. The men employed on this job were Edward Watson, John Dixon, Matthias Vicar and Solomon Benson who were paid between 1/6d and 1/8d per day for their 62 days toil. An area of flat ground was cleared on the steep hillside to accommodate the single storey house, which was to be 40 feet by 22 feet in dimension. The house was of local stone construction and built by three masons, Jonathon Piell, John Jackson and Joseph Crossthwaite who were paid 2/- or 2/2d per day and who collectively spent 44 working days on the job. The roof was of slate as were the floor flags. These were brought by cart from Yewcrag Quarry, Honister under the guidance of Solomon Benson who was paid a total of £1 16s 0d for this work. The roof was put on by three slaters, Joseph Norman, Henry Crossthwaite and Charles Norman who also did some rendering. They spent a total of 13 days on site. Thomas Cockin glazed the windows and the carpentry work was done by John Hunter. All the window shutters and doors were of oak construction.

To prevent any unauthorised access, the level entrance was kept totally sealed until the whole of the house was completed. The smithy, which was an integral part of the house was in fact, built directly over the portal. Once the guardhouse was finished, the backfilled level was cleared, the date the 22nd of May 1769. This work was done by Samuel Matthew and Thomas Flint, both miners, and for their two days work they were paid 4/- each. As an added precaution, to gain entry to the mine one had to descend through a trapdoor in the floor of the smithy. This was again to ensure that miners and labourers working the level, could not secrete any wad. They were also aware that they would be bodily searched by the agent who was always at the mine twenty four hours a day. Adjacent to the smithy was a common-room which served as the kitchen and bedroom, and beyond this was a storeroom, where the newly raised wad was stored and weighed on a brand new set of scales, recently purchased for the purpose from Richard Reeves for the price of £4 2s 0d. This house was a much larger construction than the small lodge above, near the Common.

Now again, as years before, all was ready for exploration into the level, and as the miners edged forward by the light of the flickering tallow, they noted the confinement of the tunnel. It was very small, in places no more than 5 feet high and 20 inches wide, far too narrow for the use of a wheelbarrow. The level twisted its way for just over 60 yards to the Grand Pipe. The miners also saw that level had been hand-chipped, no gunpowder having been used to blast the level forward and of course it was in the shape of a coffin. Indeed, they were in the Old Mens Level driven by the German miners some 200 years before, and which had only very briefly been opened in 1754 by Mr Shepherd. The miners were pleased to see that the level although small, was in sound condition and would require little in the way of timbering, although some work would be required to allow the modern operation to proceed with wheelbarrows! It was noted by the agents and approved by the four inspectors, that the level should be heightened and widened for the "wheelers". However, the sight which greeted them at the end of the level at its intersection with the Grand Pipe itself, was disappointing. The pipe was filled to the collar with rubbish, water and rocks, and the tallow flickered in the draught coming from above as the miners surveyed the problem.

It is important to remember that Fareys Stage had not at this time been driven, and the only access to the Grand Pipe was from surface (Bills Stage), and was a 90 foot steep incline down to the Old Mens Level. The ancients had chipped their way downwards to way below this point. The agents, now satisfied with the security of the Old Mens Level with its trap door entrance and doors, decided on a further measure to prevent unauthorised access, and this was to literally block off the Grand Pipe from the surface. A binding was set into the Grand Pipe, 40 feet from the pipe collar. This was constructed of stout oak timbers set close and spanning the pipe, on top of which were placed large stones to a depth of 15 feet. These were placed in such a manner that they allowed a good passage of air. With the binding completed and positioned, it would be difficult to reach and virtually impossible to destroy, and consequently would be a very effective deterrent for would be robbers. It would also provide protection by preventing any surface debris falling down the pipe onto the miners working below. The installation of the binding was completed by the end of July, having been supervised by a miner called John Gibson, and was consequently known as Gibsons Binding.

The next job for the miners was to commence clearing the water and debris from the flooded pipe, and again, the job was given to John Gibson and another miner Robert Smith, at a price negotiated of 6/9d a fathom. The pipe depth was unknown as all previous records and plans had vanished, so the work was commenced literally blind. Water of course was a problem, as it streamed down the pipe from surface through the binding and into the sump. One of the carpenter's first jobs was to divert the water by means of trunking, and feed the water into the level and so away from the sump. The water of course, when arriving at day would eventually be used for the washing of wad. The work was very hard, having to windlass the heavy kibbles up to the level. The pipe was cleared to a depth of 48 feet which was the position called Dixons Stage, and was below the area that John Shepherd had descended years before. The work had taken three weeks of hard graft, but this was just the beginning and their efforts were rewarded as here a sop of wad was discovered and as a bonus, much of what was thought to be waste rock filling the pipe was seen to be reasonable grade wad. This resulted in the material from the sump being washed and dressed to ensure nothing was lost. This responsible job was done by John Youdale and William Dixon who were the wad dressers. The wad sop was called Wakerleys Sop after the agent, and from it a total of 183 casks of wad was mined. A sludgy wad was found near to this point, and William Wakerley, pleased at his find, saw fit to give this low grade paste to the local shepherds for marking their sheep, for that was all it was good for! The miners kept on clearing the pipe and as they went deeper, more sops of wad were found. Some of the low grades were simply left in situ, but the top grade was mined out and lifted to the security of the guardhouse. The sump continued down and down, varying in width from 6 feet to 12 feet and the miners were convinced time and again that they had finally reached the bottom of the pipe. As they cleared what they thought were the last of the rocks, they found their shovels were uncovering more timber. The men toiled on and eventually managed to prise up one of the timbers. By the wavering flame of a tallow candle clutched in a grimy hand, could be seen their reflections in a black, stagnant pool in the dim, yellow light. This was not the bottom but a binding, and so the water was plumbed and found to go down another 24 feet. The sump was now airless, and it stank from the stagnating water beneath. Each time an attempt was made to raise the water or a dislodged rock fell down to disturb it, the sickly smell of rotten eggs prevailed upon the air (hydrogen sulphide). The miners complained bitterly that working here was now intolerable and that air would have to be pumped down somehow, as the conditions were untenable.

Over the next few weeks deal air-pipes arrived, supplied by Crispin Clark and were fixed to the sump wall, but even with the air-trunking working was virtually impossible, for as the clearing work continued downwards the sides of the sump became increasingly unstable. Also, areas of the shaft were now pinching in and the miners were having to drill and blast these areas out to maintain a reasonable diameter. This totally exacerbated the situation, the hot sticky atmosphere combined with the sulphurous fumes now being compounded by the acrid powder reek, which took a full three days to clear after each blast. The miners were also afraid for their lives, as the crumbling rock in an unstable section was so precarious that they refused to work beneath it, until it had all been properly shuttered in a secure manner. The shaft was cleared down now a total of 120 feet below the Old Mens Level (position now known as Temperleys Stage or Old Mens 4th Sop) and was still going down. The raising of the water and rubble had to be by stages as the pipe was steeply inclined and therefore kibbles could not be windlassed straight up. At intervals wooden platforms had to be wedged into the pipe and the kibbles lifted from one to another.

The local ale-houses were alive with rumours as people gossiped about the doings 'up at t'wad 'oles'. Discussions took place as to the probabilities of the miners reaching the bottom of the Grand Pipe, and the crack was that they were now de-watering the ancient sump sunk 200 years before, and would continue for at least another 50 feet. However, this was something they would not find out this year as by October 1769, the agents and stewards, well satisfied with the progress made decided to seal the mine up as winter was again approaching.

To ensure the total security of the mine, Gibsons Binding was back-filled to the surface, and the pipe was allowed to refill with water to the collar at the Old Mens Level. As an added precaution, the level was back filled for a distance of 20 yards, and the work of sealing the mine took a mere four days.

This same year was to be particularly remembered by Mr William Wakerley, as the productivity of the mine had produced 183 firkins of wad, 86 of best and 97 of second best weighing 6 tons 5 cwt 95 lb. This was for many years, the highest recorded in a year's opening. Not all this wad could be stored in the house, and so it was kept within the confines of the mine, usually on one of the lower bindings or stagings, until it was ready to be transported to Keswick by various carters. Solomon Benson was paid £1 1s 0d and Joseph Crossthwaite £2 18s 0d for taking it to Keswick, from where it was taken on to Kendal by Thomas Jackson at a cost of £9 3s 0d.

Further to the excellent production figures, it appeared also that pilfering had been dramatically reduced, which could possibly be attributed to the fact that the only way of entry to the mine was now via the mine guardhouse, into the Old Mens Level. (The Grand Pipe at this time was still not bisected through to day by Fareys Stage). A further factor was that during this period, the mine was working 24 hours a day, the men working 3 shifts of 8 hours each. The owners also had established a further security rule, that at least two of the agents must sleep and stay at the mine guardhouse during the working period.

Wad was stored either underground or in the mine house, and as soon as 30 firkins had been cleaned and sorted it was transported to Keswick, then on to Kendal and so to London. The charge for this was 1©d per lb, and each firkin barrel weighed about 78 lb. The barrels were marked with a '1' for best wad, or '2' for second sort, and were all first weighed empty to ascertain that the exact weight of wad was recorded for sale. Each barrel was craftsman made and had two heavy steel hoops top and bottom for strength to ensure the safe transport of the wad on its final journey to the merchants.

7 The Freeholders Fight

The recent mining activities had once again attracted the interest of the thieves, with new ground being opened up and easy pickings to be had from the tips. Also, with mining now concentrating for the time being on the Low Wadhole the Seatoller Fell workings were left virtually unprotected. Despite the legislation and its consequences, the thieves remained undeterred and access was probably gained through the upper workings by means of ropes, as many of the interconnecting pipes were angled and could easily be scaled. The entrances to the disused workings were of course backfilled, but this would not discourage determined men. The activity of the smugglers is confirmed by a letter to the company from John Harris of Lodore stating that he was woken every night by the sounds of carts rumbling and creaking down the track past his house from the mine, and demanding to know what the company intended to do about it. Also, he states that as a commoner of Seatoller Fell, he has a right to know why his land has been sold by the stewards of the mine to a certain group of men, namely Bowman, Scott and Hodgson, to mine for wad.

In answer to this question it appears that a meeting had been held in December 1769 in Keswick, attended by Mr W Langholm, John Jopson of Seathwaite, Joseph Fisher and John Braithwaite of Seatoller, Thomas Gasgarth of Keswick and two attorneys. The meeting was held ostensibly to discuss the rights of the freeholders to dig on the Wadhole Moor (Seatoller Fell), for wad or any other mineral on this land. It seems that both Joshua Scott of Keswick and John Hodgson had apparently already signed a bond with Mr C Hudson to dig, and Charles Bowman of Buttermere held the necessary papers. What legality this arrangement had is not clear, but one can assume that money had changed hands and some formal document had already been signed.

During 1770, a William de Cracy, an attorney of some note was asked to try and unravel the problems of the freeholders. His brief conclusion was the question of the deeds and their construction, and the boundaries. This would be a moot point of law, and until it was resolved no action could be taken against the so called trespassers.

There were some however, to whom the law or such legalities meant nothing as once again, on a night in 1771, the quiet of the Borrowdale valley was shattered by the sounds of explosions as entry was gained to the mine. The work swiftly done, the robbers melted away into the night. Three men were eventually brought before the courts, but the case could not be proven and in March 1772 they were all acquitted. After the hearing, they retired to the nearest pot-house to brag to the locals of their escape from justice, and further laughed and mocked the mine agents when they appeared, presumably to drown their sorrows.

By now, very large amounts of money were being earned in the wad mine, and naturally, the local freeholders, still convinced that they had been cheated out of their rights, informed the company that they would exercise their God-given right as freeholders to dig for black lead on Seatoller Common, regardless of the consequences. Numerous letters were sent to the mine owners during this period not only from the freeholders' lawyers, but individual representations were also made. The company decided to try and finally settle the matter and took on the services of a surveyor by the name of T Richardson who, assisted by John Harrison of Chapel House, Rosthwaite was to draw a plan of the whole area, and establish where exactly the proper boundaries lay. The work commenced in winter time and the ground had a deep covering of snow which had been laying now for some weeks. The two men pursued their task diligently, but the conditions were appalling and the most they could work on some days was a bare three hours. Day after day the men trudged up the steep bank carrying their heavy equipment the mile up the hill to continue the work. One day, however, the weather got the better of them and they decided they could no longer carry on. Frozen to the marrow, Harrison descended the fell and then trudged back the two miles to his home at Rosthwaite, his clothes by now literally frozen to him. He had to stand on the hearth in front of a roaring fire for some time before he could remove them, and three hours passed before he felt comfortable again. Eventually though, the map was completed and was then contested on the 23rd of March 1772, by the all powerful Lord Egremont who made a claim that the boundaries to the wad mine which adjoined his property were inaccurate, and that the mine was on his land. The case for Lord Egremont's claim seems not to have been pursued with any diligence by his lawyers, and one must therefore assume that they were perhaps just testing the water.

During this period, amounts of wad were discovered on the now deserted Vicar Island (known later as Derwent Island). This was possibly the time when 'wad fever' was at its height, and prospectors were coming up with crazy ideas. This latest find had them actually considering the possibility of draining the lake to reveal the source of this new wad bonanza. Thankfully there was a simple explanation for its presence, it being the remains of the German occupation 150 years before.

Despite the previous problems and penalties for stealing wad, the illicit trade still persisted. One of the black market dealers was a Joseph Fisher of Keswick who, during 1773 had obtained wad to the value of £1,000 and disposed of it in London, thus enabling him to clear some of his debts from a failed business. A further incident concerned a previous miner called Miller, from Staffordshire who had been dismissed from the mine for theft. His stolen cache, however, was left hidden in a remote part of the mine, and with two or three others, he tried to regain access to retrieve his stash later. Whether or not he succeeded in his plan is unclear, although some time later, a parcel of wad was discovered on its way to Dublin to a John Atkinson who, it was suspected, was actually the alias of Miller. The wad was supposed to have come from the Plumburn Mine in Ayrshire! It was returned and inspected by a Dr Woodward, who confirmed it to be best Borrowdale graphite and the company had no record anyway of supplying wad to a John Atkinson. Dr Woodward had already seen samples from Sweden, New England, Virginia, Germany and Fife, Scotland, the largest sample, weighing 14 lb, being from Virginia. None of these sources produced the pure quality of Borrowdale, most of it being very crumbly.

In the meantime, the cause of the freeholders and their right to dig for wad was still being championed by the attorney Mr Bowman. He had researched the great leases and documents of 1602, 1707, 1727 and the 1614 agreement of William Whitmore and Jonas Verdon. His case was simple and in essence was as follows: the area of dispute was Seatoller Common which, on various legal documents, was referred to as the Forest of Seatoller or Seatoller Fell and also as stinted pasture. Because the freeholders had been given the right to the land for grazing, the question was why did they not also have the right to any wad found, and possible royalties from wad already drawn. The contention was that this right had been stolen from them, and it was the clever and unscrupulous lawyers who were preventing them from having their just rights. The freeholders' attorney had dispatched a further letter on the 26th of December 1775 to John Lanson of Cannon Row, Westminster, attorney to the Bankes family, to further plead the case of the freeholders. The claim in essence was now that much of the common land had been disturbed and this had cost them valuable grazing. Obviously, this case was weak but worth a try, however the claim seems to have left the opposition totally unimpressed.

The suggestion was then made by the Bankes' lawyer that the freeholders should actually sell their right to the Seatoller Hole with all the mines, minerals, royalties, privileges etc excepting the herbage and turf for fuel, and it seems that this was accepted. At long last, after so many years of frustration and struggle, a solution had been arrived at whereby the local people felt that they had finally got some kind of compensation for the years of trespass which they had honestly felt had been perpetrated upon them.

8 *The Dandy Wad Stealer*

With the re-opening of the mine, and the clearing of the Grand Pipe, the laborious task of de-watering began again. The initial work was relatively easy but on arriving at the lowest point of the previous clearing, the job of removing the solidified mass once again commenced. The miners continued down through the debris for another 38 feet and then in June 1778, there was a massive find. The Great Opening Sop at 168 feet down from the Old Mens Level was discovered and it was at this point that the true bottom of the Grand Pipe was reached. The miner credited with locating this pipe was John Morris and the amount produced was a staggering 417 casks of a very high grade wad. This would have been worth around £43,000 but, unfortunately, most of it was stolen during its passage to London.

The depth to which the Grand Pipe had been sunk was amazing, and although it had been smaller in diameter when originally cut, this had been an incredible feat of mining by the old men. The pipe had now been widened to make it easier for the de-watering process and the lifting of the material, but the owners had seen the problems at first hand. The time involved to de-water, let alone the hauling up of the wad etc was both costly and time consuming

In 1778, an underground survey was made of the upper mine by Thomas Kent and Thomas Temperley, two miners from Lancashire. This shows that Gortons Level had been driven west a distance of 60 yards, and intersected by three surface shafts. The first, Gortons was 25 yards in, the second, known as Willgoose shaft was on a short easterly crosscut and the next, on the main drive and near the forfield (forehead) was known as New Shaft. Just 10 yards further up the hill was another shaft, which working was known as High Shaft. Higher up the fell were the workings known as Pipehead Sop and Woodmans Sop, and it appears all these had been discovered by trenching (hushing). These old workings and trenchings were backfilled so as not to leave land disturbance and present a danger to cattle, no doubt to also placate the freeholders.

The present method of dressing the graphite was by the use of bucking hammers on large stones or iron plates, but this was considered to be slow and inefficient, so it was decided to engage a millwright. The man employed was James Morris who was brought up from Lancashire, and it is mentioned that he had a small horse-operated mill for crushing the graphite and was soon affectionately known as 'The Blue Miller'. Another of his jobs was to reduce the very coarse wad into powder which was then dumped into the gill so depriving any would-be thieves of profiting by it.

Travellers and explorers were few in this area of the Lake District, but the mine was visited about this time by a young William Wilberforce, later famous for his work in the abolishment of slavery

In 1788, the mine agents were Mr J Wilson, Mr J W Harrison, James Hurst, Thomas Burry, Thomas and William Dixon and Robert Jopson but in spite of all this supervision, the mine was struck by a series of thefts. Wad to the value of £300 was pilfered by miner Joseph Bank, in whom, unfortunately, agent Robert Jopson had placed great confidence, even making him his occasional deputy. Agent Thomas Dixon caused a search to be carried out and the miners were brought into the guardhouse and unceremoniously ordered to strip. Their clothes were searched and pockets turned out and to Dixon's surprise, four men were found to have graphite in their possession: miner Jonathon Hind, and Edward Watson, John Fletcher and George Tyson, three labourers who were employed to draw water from the mine. The agents appear to have been somewhat negligent over the matter of security, each apparently relying on the others to search the miners on a regular basis. Although being dismissed from their employment, it is not known whether any legal action was taken against the thieves. In the September of that year, the mine was sealed by a binding about 60 feet below the Old Mens Level at Deans Stage, and the coarse or small wad, which at this time had not been dressed or casked, was thrown down onto it to remain secured under that depth of water until the next opening of the mine, which took place the following year.

During this year, Georges Hole was sunk on the northern side of the Old Mens Stage near to the Grand Pipe in an effort to find more wad, but this proved barren. Bullets of wad however, were found in Bonnys Drift a new development just off Harrisons Pipe and which at this time was the lowest section of the Grand Pipe, 168 feet below the Old Mens Level. The agents at this time, were all experienced miners and were J W Harrison, Thomas Dixon, Robert Jopson, John Gibson, William Dixon and Benjamin Gregory, of whom we shall hear more later. It was John Gibson who had discovered the bullets of wad in Bonnys Drift, and his experienced eyes noticed the different rock strata in the dirt and grime of the new heading. It was another vein, later to be called the Germans Vein and was to be a very significant find.

The problem facing the owners was that of raising material from this great depth, not to mention the water which was constantly having also to be lifted. Therefore the possibility was considered of driving a major crosscut to undercut the bottom of the Grand Pipe. This of course would cost money, and a long barren drive of this size would take years. So, despite strong recommendations by the agents, and although it had already been driven a few yards, the famous Gilberts Level, for so it was to be, was going to have to wait for the time being.

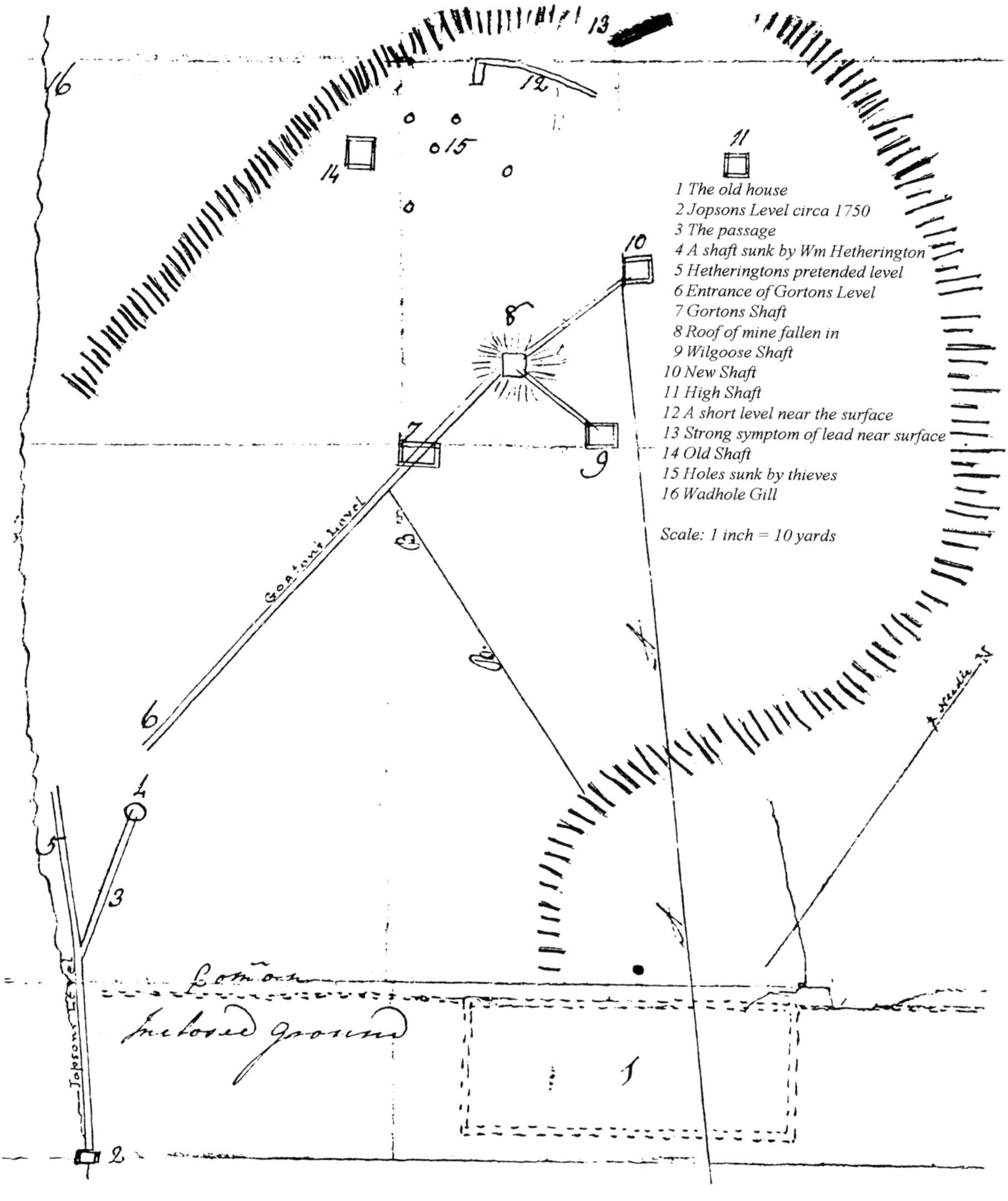

Plan of High Wad Mine by J W Harrison 1789. Courtesy of D R O.

Meanwhile, working Quayfoot quarry near Grange in 1790, Joseph Harris of Castle Lodge, Borrowdale was surprised to find a bullet of pure graphite encased in a solid clog of slate. It was this type of find which no doubt prompted the company directors to have one last look at the High Wadhole instead of prospecting lower down the fell. The new level that was planned was to be driven west to undercut Gortons Level on Seatoller Fell, and would be known as Harrisons Level. The portal of the level was at OD 1260 feet and just below the boundary wall, the year 1791 and the level was driven forward in solid hard rock by J W Harrison and his partner Benjamin Gregory. The level was named after Harrison in accordance with the tradition in Lake District mining of naming various workings, veins etc for the men who discovered or drove them. A substantial house was constructed over the mouth of the level entrance, much of the material for this house being re-cycled from the house over the entrance of the Old Mens Stage.

Eventually, Harrisons Level bisected the lower reaches of Gortons pipe and other miners, Bill Dean, Richard Dean, Thomas Jamieson, J Furness and William Charlton came and worked here, extending the drive north and so discovering Deans Sop. However, no others were to be found and the driving of Harrisons was virtually a failure. The company had also perhaps been rather too quick to pull down the mine house at the Old Mens Level. This was still accessible, although backfilled and with two stout doors placed inbye as an added security precaution.

These poor results now spurred the directors on to reconsider the much grander scheme of a level to undercut all the workings from a much lower depth. Sometime during 1791, Mr J Foulkes did the ground surveying for the new level and with his assistant, he clambered the fell, hammering heavy stakes into the ground, the first just outside Harrisons Level and another at the site of the North Needle Stone

At the same time, in an effort to exploit the middle mine, the Old Mens Level was re-opened and driven forward beyond the Grand Pipe, and this was now known as Kents Drift. Deep down in the Grand Pipe itself work was continuing in an area now known as Temperleys Stage and Bonnys Stage with great vigour.

Meanwhile, in 1792 a few minor shock waves were sent around the wad dealers of the area when it was found that a gentleman by the name of Conte had devised a method of producing artificial graphite. This process however, would take years to perfect, and Keswick and the wad mine could still look forward to many more years of work and prosperity.

In 1793, a few years prior to the Napoleonic Wars, Parliament voted to increase the size of His Majesty's Navy and land armaments but this decision was to have little effect on wad production. A new method of casting had been developed using 'dry sand' moulding, and although this obviated the necessity for more wad, the war did mean increased production from the Lake District copper and lead mines.

It was around this time that a Captain Budworth visited the mine. An early pioneer of fell-walking, he had seen action and had in fact, lost an arm whilst serving with the Royal Manchester Volunteers. His passion was now rambling the fells, in particular those around Buttermere, and it is to Captain Budworth's writings that the fate of Mary Robinson, the Beauty of Buttermere can be attributed.

The wad produced during this particular period reflects the lack of material readily available, only 5 tons of poor grade being produced. The only saving grace was that there were reasonably high reserves of good quality wad, hidden away in the deep recesses of the mine. In order to maintain this cache, development work continued and now the mine was regularly visited by various tradesmen. Beside the guardhouse was a stone hut for the peat, and this was delivered by sled at 3½d per load and came in 30 loads at a time. John Wakefield was supplying gunpowder at this time which was actually stored in the guardhouse! Michael Clark supplied timber, whilst Daniel Crossthwaite brought stationery. Another regular and necessary victualling was the various spirits supplied by Robert Jopson for £7 16s 0d. The miners were paid a daily rate of between 1/6d and 3/-. By comparison, the carriers seem to have fared better: George Ellis was paid £21 15s 0d for transportation of wad, and John Simpson £10 7s 2d for carriage of the same.

The workforce at the mine in 1793 consisted of seven miners who were working in the Old Mens 4th Sop, This area was at the bottom of the Grand Pipe in the lowest part of the mine and was now being ventilated by tin air pipes. The price of wad was around £3,360 a ton or 30/- per lb. The biggest recipient of wad during this period was a Mr W Cane of Westminster, London and various grades of Firsts, Seconds and Points were being dispatched to him.

In 1794, old Thomas Dixon died, for so long a steward at the 'Black Lead Mine' as it was called in the early days. Thomas had lived all his life at Seathwaite as had his wife who had pre-deceased him by a year. He had led an honest, hard-working life asking little but to do a good day's work for a fair wage, and had brought his son William up to follow in his footsteps at the mine. The Dixons were one of the oldest families in the valley and had had an association with the mine which went back to the very early days, and was to continue for many years to come.

Theft was again becoming a major problem at the mine and the surrounding area. The Seatoller Fell workings were still being exploited in 1796 when a rogue and villain, Willy Woodman known as the 'Dandy Wad-Stealer' had, by his nocturnal adventures on the High Wad Moor, broken into a vein or sop, which became known as Woodmans Pipe. With glee, Willy plundered the wad night after night up on the high fell, secreting his treasure away along with the mice in the holes in the walls of his mean lodgings. On certain days, he emerged from his impecunious mode and became the 'Dandy', all frayed ribbons and tarnished buckles and made his way to Keswick Town. Here, in the taverns, Willy held his clandestine meetings with the buyers, long-nosed, thin-fingered Jews who counted out the silver pennies onto the greasy, drink stained tables. Then Willy pursued his dissolute, reckless ways around the town seeking his pleasure in drinking, wenching and cards, until the early morning found him stealing a lift on the back of a cart away back down the valley. Eventually, Willy's escapades finally came to light and his days as the 'Dandy Wad-Stealer' were over. The company placed a watchman out on the fell day and night, until the two agents William Charlton and Joseph Saint could totally secure the pipe and remove all the wad which eventually came to 24 casks of best and 6 casks of coarse.

Those old miners were nomadic people, going where the work was, and so the workforce altered from time to time, some drifting to the local quarries or lead mines, which did not have the long periods of controlled closure. Men came from all parts of the country for work, and an off-comer from Derbyshire, Anthony Wright had started at the mine three years previously as a miner and dresser. He was now living at Hollows Farm in Borrowdale, and had married a cousin of William Dixon. Over the years he had befriended the two agents, Joseph Saint and William Charlton with whom he spent many a night at the Harrisons Level guardhouse. The friendship was strong enough for Wright to have been given the job as a guard. It was this trust that he had been working towards, for now he was locked in the mine house when the external doors were secured. During the night, Wright was able to pass the wad out up the chimney to his confederates whilst Charlton or Saint slept, most likely under the influence of drink. In 1796 also, Wright even had the luck to discover a wad sop on the Common near to Woodmans Pipe and this was actually named Wrights Trial! As Anthony Wright continued to work at the mine for some time, it seems evident that his criminal activities did not come to light until a later date.

Some of the last trials made during 1798 involved the complete re-opening of Gortons Stage, which had again been backfilled for security. This was inspected by the agent William Charlton who, after a few yards of driving, discovered a wad pipe just beyond Gortons Pipe. William was a man of high spirits and was so cheered by his discovery, that he fired off the guardhouse blunderbuss for fun and earned himself a strong reprimand for wasting gunpowder! Some of his fellow agents however, appear to have been just as crazy and amused by loud reports. A favourite pastime was to drill a series of six or seven shot holes in the surface crags near to Harrisons Level; these were then loosely charged and fired in fast repetition. These firings became known as 'The Rock Cannon' and when management heard about it, the men were again taken to task for wasting the company's gunpowder.

Perhaps these incidents brought home more clearly to the management the situation which now obtained. The upper wad area was finished, scratched bare, the men and agents were bored, and because of this lackadaisical attitude the pilfering was back. The mine had to be secured and the men put to meaningful work. After much discussion, the decision was finally made to drive a new low level to de-water and aerate the mine. The level would be driven from a point OD 810 feet at an already convenient junction with the zigzag track, and just below the Bankes marker stone. Also, at this point the bedrock was actually exposed to the surface. The other plus factor for this venture was that it would mean that all wad could be transferred internally, thus creating greater security. This was a bold gamble and the problems were of course mainly financial for, being one of the longest crosscuts ever to be undertaken in Lake District mining at this time, the costs would be enormous. The rock in this particular area of the mine was extremely hard, and the project would mean three years of barren production with the best men driving the level.

The decision made, the drive was to be called Gilberts Day Level, and the result would hopefully create a wealth and prosperity not seen in Keswick since the coming of the German miners in the 1560s. Indeed, Keswick was going to be firmly put back on the industrial map

9 The Great Gilberts Level

Gilberts Level was commenced on the 23rd of April 1798 and was to be driven virtually dead straight in a northerly heading according to the surveyor, and at 200 yards in it would intersect the Grand Pipe. The level was cut to 6 feet high and 4 feet 6 inches wide. The driving was hard going, and miner Anthony Wright was paid 31/6d per yard for his 50 yards of tortuous progress. His total revenue for the job was £78 15s 0d. To help ventilation, a water blast shaft was put up to surface 30 yards in from day. The final 170 yards driven into the hillside was, surprisingly, completed in just under two years. The level was laid with angle iron rail at a gauge of 24 inches and it appears that this level was the first to be railed out, all the others being mined and mucked out by the use of wheelbarrows. The two years of blasting the level forward was a hectic time, and some of the driving was through very hard ground containing pyrites. This quickly blunted the 'noggers', and unfortunately, at one point in time, caused a bad accident. Joseph Bragg was stemming a drill hole with an iron stemmer and, hitting pyrite, created a spark which resulted in a premature explosion, severely injuring his leg. The stench of tallow candles, the reek of spent gunpowder and the sweat of men and horses had been an ever present daily odour until at last, on the 10th of June 1800 the last section of the level came underneath the Grand Pipe.

On completion of the driving, security once more became a priority, and a substantial guardhouse was built totally encompassing the adit mouth. It took nearly two months to build, was constructed of local stone under a slate roof, the materials coming from the nearby quarries, and was completed in August 1800. The house was used also as an office by William Dixon, the mine superintendent who was now paid 10/6d a week. The house was two storeys high, the ground floor consisting of two large rooms, a smithy and a peat store. On the first floor were the wad room, two bedrooms, the search room, agents' sitting room and the wad dressing room. The overall dimensions were 24 feet wide by 48 feet long, not including the peat store. Outside, a small privy was made to the north of the house and serviced by a little gill known now as Privy Gill. In front of the house, two washing tubs were built using water directly from the mine adit. William Dixon or another agent had to inspect every tub brought from the mine for the quality of its content and also had the ignominious task of searching the miners at the end of every shift, and although many of the men had been there for years, none of them was above suspicion. The completion of the level must have been a great relief to the company, the Grand Pipe having been successfully bisected, and all credit must have gone of course, to the surveyor. His calculations were spot on, and looking back from the bottom of the pipe, the glimmer of daylight can be seen in the distance.

Soon the men would commence rising up in the black, glistening wad of the Grand Pipe, and this would of course, eventually de-water the mine and in turn ventilate the whole section from the top. The security of the mine was greatly enhanced because all the material could, theoretically, be passed down the Grand Pipe and eventually out of Gilberts Level.

It is interesting to compare these techniques with those of metalliferous mining. At Seathwaite, levels cut into the hillside followed a fault vein for easier driving in much the same way, but whereas this would bring the metal miners to the ore, it was not the case in wad mining. The sops were completely random, and there could be three in a row or two side by side or whatever, with absolutely no indication of what they were coming to. Although the driving through the barren ground was just as difficult as in other types of hard rock mining, the actual extraction of the wad was much easier and probably with less dust. However, the greasy colouration would contaminate clothes, hands and tools, and to remove this must have been a real problem.

In 1800, in the forehead of Gilberts Level, a sop of wad was found which became known as Benjamins Pipe and, under the direction of William Dixon, was sunk 42 feet down. In the August of this year, the miners working the 40 feet upwards from Gilberts Level, broke through into Harrisons Pipe bottom in the sole of the Grand Pipe. This immediately de-watered the upper part of the mine whilst, possibly more importantly, ventilating the whole system through which the wind now literally howled. This was a great moment and the miners had worked hard, and no doubt there would have been some rejoicing in the pot-house that night.

On the re-opening of the mine proper on the 6th of November 1800, a further investigation was made of the Old Mens deads in the area of the Grand Pipe, and 109 casks of wad were made up. No less than 395 more were recovered from Wilsons and Dixons Pipes weighing in at 63,348 lb of neat grade, and a further 580 casks weighing 78,726 lb were brought to surface. This vast amount of wad was produced over the few years following and was certainly the most lucrative period of the operation so far.

One of the major discoveries was a further find in Dixons Pipe off Dixons Stage. This was intersected just beyond the Grand Pipe and had been named after the loyal steward William Dixon. By April 1801, the workforce had increased to twelve, and the extra manpower is reflected in the overall increased productivity. Miners like Robert Richardson were buying tools, an expensive item indeed from the average wage, at £5 0s 7½d. The development continued and gunpowder was purchased from John Wakefield in March 1802, for £28 10s 6d. A further consignment was bought in June for £12 4s 5d and candles for £7 12s 7d. It appears that not all wad was taken down to the stores by mule, and the ancient method of sledging was sometimes used, ten trips at 3½d producing a revenue of 2/11d.

In July 1802, came the big discovery of Ridgeways Sop off the Grand Pipe, named after the discoverer Mark Ridgeway and worked by him, Benjamin Gregory and William Dixon. This area had already been worked by the ancients years before and surprisingly the sop had been missed. The best graphite was carried to the guardhouse in leather bags, whilst the coarse was thrown down the Grand Pipe.

About this time, some pieces of wad were found by Benjamin Gregory and James Hurst whilst they were walking on Seatoller Common. They duly noted the spot, keeping the information to themselves, and approached local pencil manufacturer John Ladyman, to see if he was interested, but no reference can be found as to whether or not this option was ever taken up. It was some time later that Benjamin Gregory told Mr Dixon of this find, perhaps as a way to cover up his own illicit trail.

There was a massive find in February 1803 in the aforementioned Germans Vein in the Grand Opening Sop, where a lump of wad weighing 168 lb was discovered. This being of course too big for a cask, it was broken up and a piece weighing 87 lb was sent to London. Other large lumps weighing 64 lb and 61 lb, plus twelve others weighing between 31 lb and 57 lb were recovered from this sop. Such was the size of it, that the miners drove 6 yards in solid graphite just using picks.

The four year period to the end of 1803 had produced tons of wad, and some of the most productive pipes would reveal new sops in years to come. The total weight of graphite raised was something like 142,074 lb valued at about £106,300. The expenditure had only been £3,802 including the driving of Gilberts Level and the building of the mine house, and this had resulted in a staggering £102,498 profit!

With the glut however had come carelessness, and much of the material which had been thrown down the Grand Pipe and Harrisons, had been left and was now festering in dirty solidified heaps. This contamination of the wad meant that it had to be washed and separated outside at the temporary washing tables. The heaps left at the foot of Harrisons Sop on Fredricks Stage and on Gilberts were areas frequented by the miners on their regular journey up into the mine. The sheer fact that they had to clamber over it created an obvious security risk. The ground between Dixons and Ridgeways Stages had been an area of intense mining and inadvertently a horse or jaumb of rock had been created, and as wad was removed the huge wedge of rock became more and more undercut. This was situated directly above the ladderway between Gilberts and Ridgeways, and as time went by it became something of a Sword of Damocles until it was eventually blasted out much later in December 1819, and the rubbish trammed out of Gilberts.

"Black Market" *J Tyler*

Over the last hundred years the mine had aroused much interest, and had been visited by various eminent people, such as Bishop Nicholson, a local scholar and historian from Carlisle, the poet Thomas Gray, celebrated French mining engineer Gabriel Jars and Charles Hatchett, well known mineralogist. The most recent visitor was Mr John Mawe of the Strand, London who was an important mineralogist and miner. Visitors, however, were not actually welcomed as, following their visits, articles of interest were printed in various papers expounding on the workings and the mining methods used, although they were always requested not to. In consequence, although one might have thought that interest from these clever and professional people would have been welcomed, in fact it served only to aggravate the company.

Another interesting find occurred once again in slate, when quarryman Jonathon Thompson was working Castle Crag quarry. On cleaving a slate, he split a bullet of embedded wad clean in two, leaving half in each slate. This was not the first time wad had been found in this quarry, for some years earlier when Thompson and his men were removing some old slate waste, they had discovered old iron tools and a quantity of good quality wad. One piece had been fashioned flat like a button with a hole in the middle. It was well known that the smugglers often hid their ill-gotten gains for later collection, and they were known also to dress the wad in order to obtain the best price.

One known smuggler of this period was an ex-miner by the name of Stephen Wright, half brother to Anthony, who had been spotted in London selling wad to Lewis Lazarus, a Jewish merchant. London at that time was a seething, bustling, clamouring stew of humanity, mostly conducting its life outdoors on the streets. Furtive buying and selling went on in doorways, under arches and in low taverns and cellars, the haunts of the criminal fraternity. And here, in the company of the Jew, Wright was recognised by a finger missing from one hand! The sighting was reported to Mr Dixon, who was of the opinion that Wright was selling from a cache of wad stolen some time earlier, and which was possibly part of his half brother's ill-gotten gains.

An advertisement in 1804, offered for sale a twenty-fourth share in the wad mine. Messrs Skinner, Dyke Co were to hold the auction which was to take place in Garraways Coffee House, Exchange Alley, Cornhill, London at 12 noon on the 12th of July 1804. The minimum revenue, so the advertisement said, that one could expect from this investment was £64 17s 6d

Stores of wad were still being held in London at the Essex Street warehouse, which was rented at that time for 10 guineas a year, which rental had been increasing steadily over the years. The current stock of wad was held in 560 casks containing various qualities, weighing 40,400 lb and valued at £54,450. The accounts in 1806 show a payment to the Bow Street officers of £23 6s 0d. This is a handsome amount to be paid and one must assume it was for the protection of the wad whilst being in the London warehouse.

The mine was, during this period, working basically flat out as the large pipes recently found were being wrought. The enormous production figures testify to the success: 37 casks of first grade weighing 4,940 lb plus 644 casks of inferior weighing 87,276 lb were mined from Ridgeways Sop and Dixons Pipe, below and north of the Old Mens Stage.

Another smuggler of the time was a ne'er do well named Smith, a shifty, dirty type who visited Borrowdale valley from time to time, selling illicit whiskey. He had also been seen selling wad in the ale houses of Whitehaven, and it was suspected that agent Mark Ridgeway was his contact at the mine although this was never proved. After wad mysteriously vanished in 1809 however, the mine was quickly closed and the reserves hidden in Benjamins Pipe, which was allowed to flood to the collar for added security.

In January 1810, wad was being shipped to London via Whitehaven in the brig Farne in the charge of Captain Blamire. On this voyage 494 casks were transported at a cost of £107 0s 8d and the cartage from the mine and wharf came to £22 7s 0d. The main dealers in wad at this time were Messrs Ludwig and Warner, Emen and Israel, Lewis Lazarus and Messrs Taylor and the wad was still taken to the vaults in 85 Essex Street, near the Strand.

In April 1810, Crossthwaites Sop was located rising up from what is now known as Waltons Stage, and to give the miners due credit, they worked diligently.... to produce just 6 lb of wad, but the area in and above this pipe was later to prove most lucrative. The infamous Anthony Wright was still around, and apparently still full of information about the wad mine. This time he was offering Joseph Whitridge the whereabouts of a wad trial hidden on Seatoller Common, where he boasted that in two weeks he could fill two casks of wad by himself. However, William Dixon heard of this, and called Wright's bluff by offering him £5 0s 0d to show him this wonderful source of wad, but after searching the common for hours, Wright was unable to locate the spot.

10 The Saga of Benjamin Gregory

William Dixon was a man dedicated to the company, and who found some self gratification in doing his job well. He was also a man who liked his own way. One of the agents, Benjamin Gregory was junior in status to him but had worked at the mine for a number of years. He was a miner of experience, having worked in the Northwich salt mines and other places. Because of his status at the mine, he was required to live at the mine house as part of the security, and for some reason had not always hit it off with William Dixon, who certainly had the ear of Mr Henry Bankes. Bearing in mind the underhand goings on with Mr Ladyman a few years prior, Mr Gregory may perhaps be seen to be not exactly whiter than white.

Benjamin was a deft hand at making things of wood, and had brought with him to the mine a small lathe on which he made various types of furniture, toys etc. So skilled and prolific at this work was he, that he started to use part of the mine house to store his wares and naturally, the other men complained. At this, Gregory, normally a quiet and sociable man insisted that a store could be made at the end of the house. This, apparently, William Dixon did agree to but only after an exchange of words. Gregory, who had got a girl with child at this time, was evidently feeling very low possibly through concern for the girl's welfare and future, but was content to while away the evenings with his woodworking. He fashioned a puppet set, and apparently this was so imaginative that word got around, and eventually parties of people were visiting the mine to see this, and no work was being done. This was the last straw as far as Mr Dixon was concerned, and remonstration with Gregory developed into a full scale row resulting in Benjamin Gregory leaving his employment on the 5th of April, 1810. In consequence of this, a report was sent by William to Mr Bankes in London, apprising him of the facts of the matter. This however, was not the end of the affair, as Mr Gregory, being quite an educated man, wrote to Mr Bankes with his side of the story. In his letter he stated that William Dixon was a two-faced drunkard, as were his sons and his wife, and that his only aim in life was to acquire total power at the mine and become the sole mine manager:

"My position on leaving your employment was applied for by two men, Lance Roose a slater, and Rev M Thompson, both in my opinion not suited to such hard manual work, but these could be moulded into Dixon's ways of hard drinking as does his wife, and his two sons are as wild and debauched as one could wish to meet. He also makes false accounts and charges small items to the company for himself, he takes coal for use at home which also belongs to the company, he is not an honest man. Whilst at the mine, I have repaired the leather on the bellows for the smithy, built a wheelbarrow and constructed part of an extension to the house, even making window frames. All these jobs I did without pay. The wood for these jobs was obtained from Keswick on the mine account. Mr Dixon was to say I had bought cheaper wood from the wood yard, and had no right to say it was for the mine as I had no letter of authority. Other instances of Mr Dixon's cruelty to me whilst employed at the mine are as follows: I paid for fresh food and meat, this was often so rotten that I had to give it to the dogs; as a skilled miner, I wanted to help William Dixon in the success of the mine and I once suggested a place for a wad trial but he just laughed, telling me this was special mining and I knew nothing. Later a trial was made and this was successful. I suggested to him that we should use a riddle to sort the smaller wad, as this way we could retain many of the smaller pieces, but he was not impressed. Wad would be left outside on the dump for days before it was sorted and this, I suggested, would create a security problem, but again, his attitude was totally off hand. Perhaps worst of all was regarding the ability of the men he employed. Some are related to him, whilst others are infirm, all are devious and unsavoury characters and are all dishonest, and this includes Mr William Dixon himself. During 1806, he made an illicit agreement with John Airey, a pencil manufacturer in Keswick, his transactions were never in the accounts. The men employed by him to work the mine were a motley crew, one was Jonathon Crossthwaite who is an ex-sailor and was badly wounded in action; James Coates, a skilled local miner, took up work in a quarry when the wad mine was closed, and here he received frightful injuries to his leg. He deals illicitly in wad and is also married into the Bennett family. James Bennett is Dixon's son in law, who was working Greenside during another closed period and had his eyes blown out. William Dixon now steals coal for him. Matthew Bennett is the landlord of the Miners Arms public house in Rosthwaite and John Leck, a Patterdale miner was found selling wad for £10 0s 0d. All these men are under the spell of Dixon; they are his friends and relatives, they are without doubt a band of men who dislike outsiders intensely. I realise that I have left the company, but would like to return but not under Mr W Dixon. He forced me to leave and it has cost me £9 0s 0d to bring my chattels to Marple, Stockport where I am now living, and I feel I should be reimbursed with this amount."

Poor Benjamin seems to have been hard done by, but in truth William Dixon always appeared to have had the best interests of the company at heart, and certainly his son John was remarked upon as being a "very quiet and pleasant young fellow". After several letters of the same nature to Mr Bankes, Benjamin seems to have finally given up his crusade and allowed the matter to lie.

It was during 1811 that some bullets of wad were found high on Seatoller Common, and this decided the company that a serious trial should be made. This was aptly named Common Stage at OD 1420 feet and intersected a vein called Johns Vein. It appears to have been something of a failure apart from a small sop found in the sole of the level and called Waddy Pipe. The level was pursued but little was found and the venture was given up. Indeed, 1811 was a barren year and running costs for the mine were £389 14s 1d.

It seems that pencil making had existed in Keswick prior to the turn of the century, possibly as a cottage industry run by individuals who could afford to purchase wad legally from the merchant houses, or illegally from the numerous sources. Little documentation can be found to support this however, until around 1811. By this time there were certainly three pencil mills in operation, those of John Airey, Jacob Banks and John Ladyman, all of whom had started out as woollen manufacturers and were gradually changing over to the very lucrative business of producing pencils.

The mine was still being developed and an important crosscut level was commenced just below the top of the Grand Pipe being driven forward in a northerly direction. The level was initially called Daniels Drift (later Roberts Drift and finally Fareys Stage) and was driven internally from the Grand Pipe. The miners would ascend or descend onto a platform of wooden planks which was slung across the yawning chasm of the Grand Pipe, and from here they blasted their way forward in barren ground, their prize now but a few fathoms distant. They would cut Thompsons, Stuarts, Winkles and Grisedales Pipes all in the space of a few yards of each other. Meanwhile, 55 feet below, the Old Mens Stage was being driven further north by miners Wilson and Leck and the extension to the old drive was called Kents Drift which would eventually cut into the head of the massive Dixons Pipe.

Unlike conventional mining there is little or no indication of where the sops or pipes were. The tendency of the miners was to drive through the barren ground in faults or veins in the hope that they would cut into the wad. This added much to the frustration of the miners, who blasted and picked the rock out, sometimes driving yards of level and missing a sop by feet. What they were certain of was that the Grand Pipe had been for sure the area of the best wad, and the work of the ancients had now given them relatively easy access into the belly of the mine.

On the re-opening of the mine in 1812, the agents were John Winkle, Samuel Barbour and Thomas Walton. A major find at this time was on Waltons Stage when Winkles Pipe and Barbours Sop were discovered and named for their finders. These produced 87 casks of best wad which weighed in at 94 cwt 6 lb (10,534 lb) and brought 35/- per lb, and a further 495 casks of inferior wad were mined weighing 68,849 lb. The expenses for this period were £788 18s 11d. With the re-opening came yet more devious goings on. The wad cart, creaking slowly on its way to Kendal, was met accidentally at Staveley by agent Thomas Walton who, on approaching the cart, noticed that the guard was the agent Winkle. When challenged as to where the real guard

"Riding shotgun" J Tyler

was, Winkle threatened Thomas Walton to forget the meeting ever took place, otherwise he could expect some terrible misfortune would befall him one dark night! Thomas was so shaken and distraught by this very real threat that he wrote a letter to his friend John Gilbert in Northwich to tell him about it. It was shortly after this incident that the agents Winkle and Barbour, devious and deceitful men both, left the mine. They had each asked for a substantial raise which was not forthcoming, and they were given short shrift and subsequently paid off by William Dixon, each receiving outstanding monies of £20 12s 9d, whereupon they set off for Staffordshire. Both of these men were suspected of illicit wad dealings and the theft of wad, which was another reason for their speedy dispatch.

Much of the recently mined wad was transferred to London by ship, again on the brig Farne, which took 467 casks of coarse wad to Mr Cane of London

The mine was now at full working pitch and rich prizes followed. In 1813 Winkles Pipe was developed and produced 8 casks of very high grade wad weighing 965 lb and 89 casks of inferior weighing 10,680 lb. During the next few years or so, the area of prime production was to be Dixons Pipe and the uprise workings from Waltons Stage. These were Winkles Pipe and Crossthwaites Pipe which had been bisected now by Bankes Stage 40 feet above Waltons. The work in this area of driving over the years had been done by the miners Daniel Dixon and his partners. The 13th of November, 1813 was a lucky day in Seathwaite Wad Mine, for this day marked the discovery of Robinsons Sop on Coates Drift. Not a major find but one of exceptional quality and 5 casks of super excellent wad were extracted plus 15 casks of coarse, all of which was carried in bags from the sop directly to the dressing room. All this consignment was dispatched to London and sold to one consignee.

Because of the strict security in the mine, and the shortage of main adit levels to day, the transportation of the wad internally was a laborious, time-consuming and dangerous job, involving the descent of hundreds of feet of ladders with a heavy bag carried on the back. Thomas Walton had an idea to simplify the journey from the middle section of the mine by the construction of wooden trunkings, the equivalent of ore passes in metal mining. For example the 200 feet of descent from Barbours could be done more speedily if the wad from Barbours Sop could be collected from Jacks Uprise on Waltons Stage, from where it would be wheelbarrowed to Dixons pipe to be sent down the trunking onto Dixons Stage. From here it would be barrowed to the Grand Pipe and put down the next trunking where it would fall the 100 feet down to Whitridges Stage. At this point a labourer would be required to assist the material on its way using either a hoe, rake or shovel, when it would then crash down the final 50 feet to Gilberts Stage. From here, as normal it would be transported the length of Gilberts Level in wagons and on arriving at the mine house, it would then be carried in whiskets up into the changing room to be roughly sorted. The largest and best would be sent up to the dressing room and the coarse and vein material trammed out to day through the mine doors, and unloaded onto the picking tables. The method of carrying wad in bags had gone on for years and this new method was vehemently contested by William Dixon, both for the time needed for construction of the passes and the cost, which would be in the region of £60 0s 0d for the boards of wood 15 feet long and 10 inches wide, stemples and nails etc. It seems that Thomas was able to sway Mr Dixon to his idea possibly backed up by the men, and no doubt the fact that the wad was confined for much of its journey had been a deciding factor. The wooden 'wad pass' was duly installed, however it was shortly after this that Thomas left the mine.

During this year two trials were made on the common just above Gill Head, and shafts were sunk to a depth of 20 feet but due to the sumps filling with water, the trials were abandoned.

The wad being as we know, such a richly prized commodity, the guardhouses were now manned twenty four hours a day by men armed with blunderbusses. Some of the wad was transported to London by wagons drawn by six-horse teams, and protected by at least half a dozen armed men. These men stayed overnight in the warehouses, never leaving their precious cargo. It appears that when the loads had arrived as far as Kendal, a new set of guards and drivers took over to deliver the wad to London. Much of this still appears to have been delivered to Essex Street in London, where cellars were still being rented from a Mr Belsham at a new, increased rent of £31 10s 0d a year. The carriers of course, were under a considerable bond to ensure it arrived safely. Because all the wad was now being distributed from London by merchants, even wad intended for local use, it made it more difficult for the would be pilferer to dispose of his ill-gotten gains.

The mine re-opened again in 1814 and five casks of inferior wad were taken from off Dixons Pipe just above Gregorys Stage, weighing 600 lb and then a further 15 casks were drawn out, again of similar quality weighing 1,871 lb. By now Roberts Drift (Fareys Stage) had arrived at Thompsons, Stuarts and Grisedales. Despite all this underground success, William Dixon, long in the tooth, had always been a believer in traditional mining methods such as trenching. His belief in this particular method had been firmly re-inforced when Robert Watson had discovered, on the peat road at Trail Gap, a solid piece of wad weighing nearly 4 lb. This sample had been extremely soft and of the purest quality, which was ideal for the finest grade of pencils. Convinced of the possibility of success, William directed a number of his men to commence trenching and on this occasion a little wad was revealed. The resulting finds became known as 'Flote Wad' but little else was found, although it is worthy of note that this method had already revealed fifteen different veins.

The mine re-opened in the spring of 1815, and a new sop, Williams was discovered off Bankes Stage just 4 yards north of Winkles Pipe. This produced 117 casks of neat wad weighing 14,170 lb and 323 casks of inferior weighing 38,760 lb.

During 1816 at Hollows Farm, which was also a pot-house and the home of Anthony Wright the ex-miner, Mrs Wright took in lodgers. One such was a Mr Bakewell, a mineralogist, and Wright offered to sell him numerous samples of wad although his association with the mine had by now ceased. It seemed that Mr Wright had a considerable store of wad of his own with which to supplement his income!

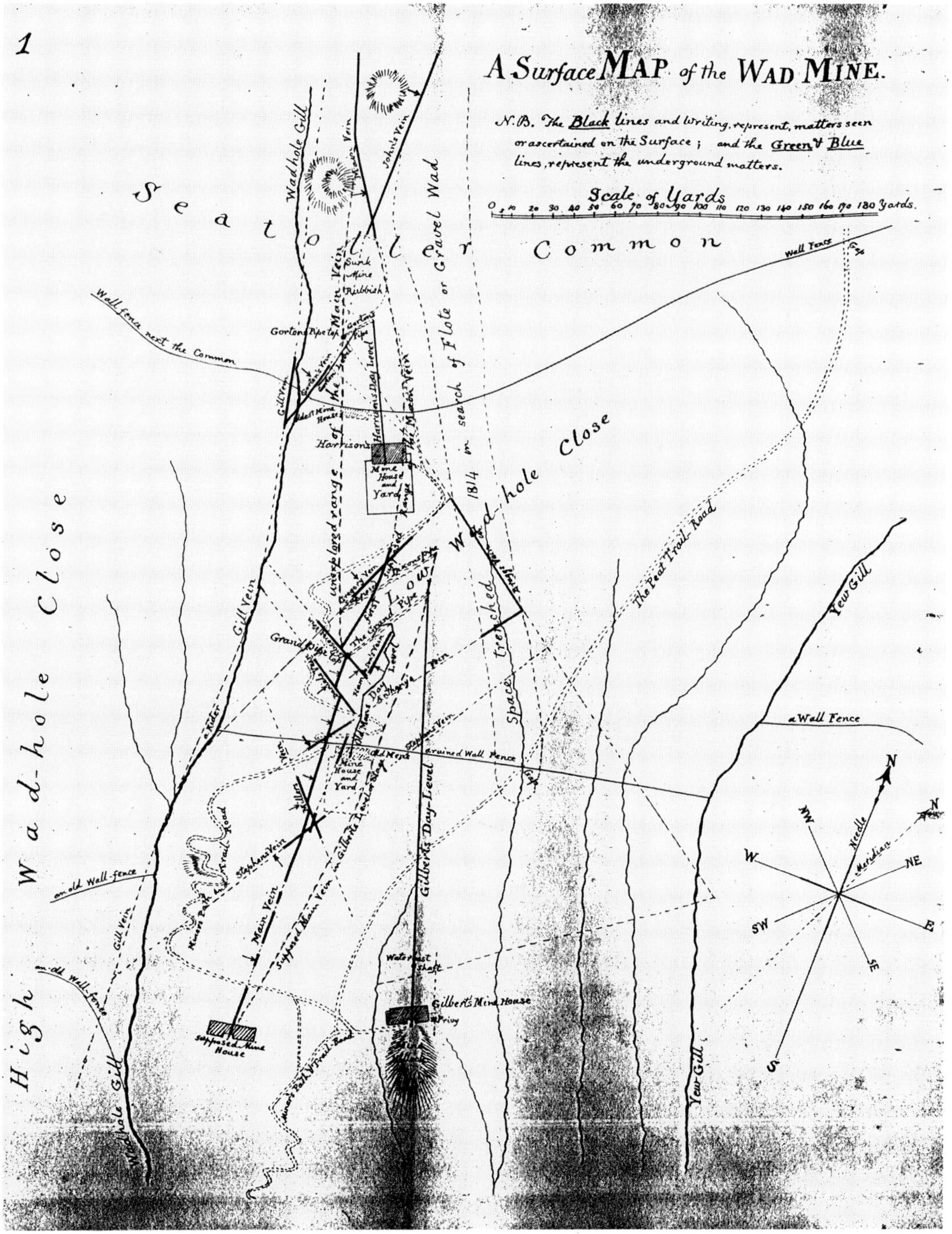

Surface plan of Wad Mine showing veins and main surface levels by John Farey circa 1818. Courtesy of D R O.

11 Enter Mr Farey

For years the mine had been run by William Dixon, and although efficient in most aspects of mine management, he had upset numerous miners over the period, and on more than one occasion had perhaps not been quite as straight as he might have. He was however, more than a match for his critics, having intimidated most of them into silence. Perhaps in these next few years, the likes of Benjamin Gregory and Thomas Walton would have enjoyed the taming process which was to take place.

John Farey was a different kettle of fish entirely from William Dixon. He was articulate, literate and a powerful shareholder, and more than a match for the Dixons. He was himself an experienced miner and surveyor, his father having been of the same profession, and John ran a successful business from Rowland Street, London. He came to the mine on the 26th of April, 1818 to commence a survey and to meet the mine agents and the miners in order that he could appraise all aspects of the mine. The direction in which the mining at Seathwaite would proceed would depend entirely on his findings. In order to get to know all the people involved with the mine, he actually lived at the mine house for a month, working between 12 and 14 hours a day, and for the other ten weeks he lived with the Dixon family in Beck House in Seathwaite. (The house had been purchased by Mr John Bankes from the Braithwaite family some years before).

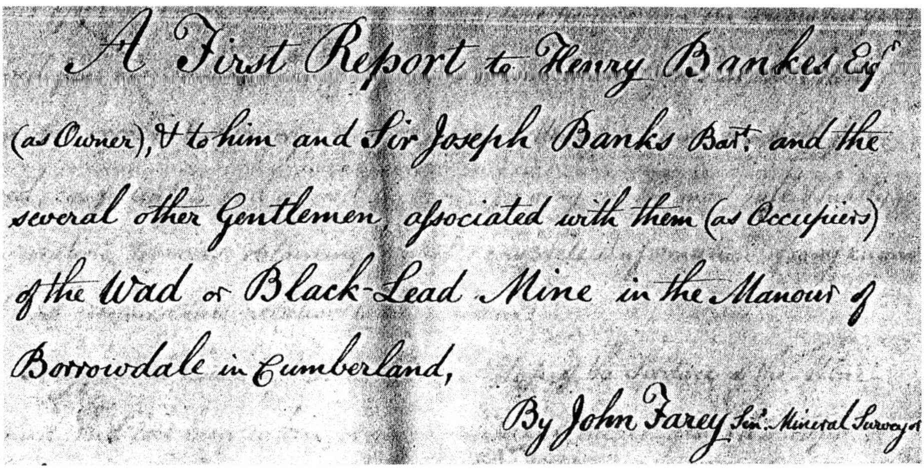
A First Report to Henry Bankes Esqr
(as Owner), & to him and Sir Joseph Banks Bart. and the
several other Gentlemen associated with them (as Occupiers)
of the Wad or Black-Lead Mine in the Manour of
Borrowdale in Cumberland,
By John Farey Senr. Mineral Surveyor

To ensure that, based on his survey, the mine would in future be run efficiently, Mr Farey wrote a 'Book of Directions' so that subsequent agents, superintendents or other managers would be in no doubt as to where their responsibilities and loyalties lay. During this period, John Farey wrote no less than twenty five letters to William Dixon in connection with details of the mine, to which he received twenty seven letters in reply.

The workforce at the mine was appraised and John Farey noticed very quickly that out of the thirteen people working at the mine, eight were related to William Dixon.

MINE WORKERS, 1818

NAME	AGE	OCCUPATION	WAGE	STATUS
WILLIAM DIXON	66	AGENT	5/3d*	MARRIED, LIVING SEATHWAITE
JOHN DIXON (SON)	31	ASST. AGENT	3/6d	MARRIED, LIVING ROSTHWAITE
WILLIAM DIXON JNR (SON)	28	MINER	3/6d	MARRIED, LIVING THORNYTHWAITE
DANIEL DIXON (SON)	20	MINER	3/6d	MARRIED, LIVING SEATHWAITE
JAMES BENNETT (SON IN LAW)	41	MINER (BLIND)	3/6d	MARRIED, LIVING SEATHWAITE
THOMAS BENNETT (GRANDSON)	13	LABOURER	1/6d	LIVING WITH PARENTS
MATTHEW COATES (BROTHER IN LAW)	24	MINER	3/6d	MARRIED, LIVING ROSTHWAITE
BENJAMIN DIXON (SON IN LAW)	32	CARPENTER	3/6d	MARRIED, LIVING GRANGE
JAMES ROBINSON	40	MINER	3/6d	LIVING CASTLELODGE
CHARLES STEWART	28	MINER	3/6d	LIVING SEATHWAITE
EDWARD BARRON	40	MINE	3/6d	LIVING SEATHWAITE
JOHN BARRON	62	MINER	3/6d	LIVING SEATHWAITE
JOSEPH GLOVER	67	MINER	3/6d	LIVING HIGH HOUSE SEATHWAITE

*Plus £30 0s 0d annual salary.
Wage of the miners is for an 8 hour day

It was noted by Mr Farey that any reductions in the workforce should commence at the bottom of the list and work up.

The mine officially re-opened during April 1818, and John Farey attempted to inspect all parts of the mine but could get no higher than Waltons Stage, as the ladders were in a poor and dangerous condition. Various areas were backfilled as a security measure, thus restricting his access to other possible working areas. Little is recorded of mine maintenance, but it is obvious that during these periods of inactivity the mine did, in certain areas, fall into disrepair. During these next months, a rough plan was drawn up of the surface area and the accessible parts of the mine, and John Farey's first report and recommendations made on the 17th of September 1818, noted that there were some inaccuracies in the existing plans. This was brought to William Dixon's attention, and Mr Farey also let it be known how frustrated he was by the fact that many of the workings were inaccessible due to the back filling. It was however, possible to confirm that seventeen new openings had been made over the last forty nine years.

Mr Farey enquired as to the method William Dixon used to survey the mine, and as this was not to his liking he instructed the Dixons in the proper method of surveying: in future the compass box was to be put on a high stool away from the metal rails, and a string stretched across the level parallel with the floor. The side of the compass box touching the string obtained the horizontal bearing, and a further string suspended from the roof of the level would obtain the forward bearing.

It was also noted that the levels were cluttered with rubbish and the floors uneven, having been packed with waste so that barrowing could be more easily effected. However, this practice prevented the surveyor seeing the vein unless it was in the skirt of the level or the roof.

John Farey soon found Mr Dixon and his son somewhat unsupportive regarding his ideas for running the mine, he being old fashioned in his ways, and they constantly contradicted him on the names of the veins etc., and his methods of surveying. To this end, he took them both underground and actually explained the methods of surveying until they could no longer refute them. Mr Farey insisted that in the future surveying, either William Dixon, his son John or one of his brothers accompanied him to ensure that it was done his way and accurately. To assist in the surveys, John Farey authorised the purchase of some basic equipment at a cost of £4 0s 0d including a compass which was presented to the Dixons.

It was now considered that, due to the depth of the Grand Pipe the old binding put in by John Gibson could be removed from Bills Stage. This work was carried out by William Dixon, the material carefully removed and two casks of graphite were obtained. The extraction of wad continued and the finest wad ever taken was removed from a small wad sop near the top of the Grand Pipe at a stage known as Whitmores. The central area of the mine was totally unventilated as the workings had now extended a considerable way north and here the air was stale and hot and the men were complaining. The complaints were treated with sympathy and sections of air-trunking were fed in from Dixons Stage down to Deans and Wakerleys.

By the end of September 1818, John Farey was able to present Sir Joseph and Mr Henry Bankes with further points for immediate consideration, for the more efficient running of the mine. With regard to security, which obviously was still of prime concern, he recommended that the main adit levels and crosscuts to sops where wad was still available, should be secured with solid iron doors. Future levels were to be driven to a standard size, so that the doors could be transferred, and worked out areas were to be completely backfilled to ensure maximum security.

Nearly all the theft took place either in winter or during periods when the mine was closed. Another problem was that honest miners and workmen were obliged to seek work elsewhere during these closed periods, many going to the quarries to more dangerous work. John Dixon had been seriously injured on his last lay off period and John Grisedale, one of the best miners, had been enticed away with a guaranteed seven year contract. To prevent this drifting away of the work force Mr Farey suggested that underground work could continue during winter, and any wad found could be stored in the most inaccessible parts of the mine and secured by bindings. This would ensure continuity of a loyal workforce, and control of a greater supply of graphite to the merchants.

The act of tipping waste from the workings before checking it, even if considered barren, was to cease as it was far too easy for wad-rich lumps to be hidden and the trammer to remember where he had tipped it and return later to remove it. In future, no graphite was to be washed or sorted outside the mine house as had been done in the past, for dressers were known to have hidden piles under the grass and collected it during the night. The mine hillocks were to be kept steep to make them difficult for pilferers to scale. The storing of loose graphite within the enclosing walls, garden and peat stores was to cease, as the thieves simply came at night, and hiding behind the walls were able to sort the graphite in peace by lantern light, which could not be seen for the walls.

It was noted that Harrisons guardhouse was now in a poor state of repair, having been punished badly by the weather, and the level should be secured with a steel door to prevent access to the upper mine. Backfilling had been proved effective in the bindings but not in the levels, and in the past, the villains would scrape away the top 18 inches of the fill and wriggle their way into the best secured stages. Unfortunately, it seemed that the driving of the Gilberts Level was not in the best place, and Mr Farey would have suggested a few yards to the south at a similar horizon and following the main vein to bisect the set. Here, he stated that he would have also built a large house to accommodate all the workforce. A fixed ladderway should also be made from Gilberts Stage up to Whitridges, and another section from here up to Dixons for ease of access, these to be manways only and not for transferring material, as this could injure the men and damage the ladders. The wad pass put in by Thomas Walton was treated with complete derision. Mr Farey considered it to be a slow, ineffective method which contaminated and mixed any pure graphite with all sorts of waste rubbish, and recommended that the wood be re-used or committed to the guardhouse fire where, for a short period, it would serve a better use!

Such were the immediate feelings of Mr John Farey, and the Dixons, who for the last hundred years had more or less been allowed to run their own show, had now come under scrutiny. Mr Farey's Book of Directions was to be given to Mr Dixon, to be a 'bible' for him to refer to, on any aspect of running the mine in the future.

By October 1819, a manway had been blasted the 150 feet up from Gilberts Stage through to Whitridges, Gregorys etc. and eventually connected with Dixons Stage. This was to be used for the transportation of wad and for access to the middle workings. As the mine was developed, some of the disused pipes were converted, where convenient, to simple manways however these were not fixed with expensive ladders, but stemples secured across the shaft at regular intervals for the men to climb. It was during this month also that Mr John Farey commenced a full and detailed survey of the mine, which was to take all of three months. The overall assessment of the veins and wad deposits however, would take years. Samples of superior wad, some weighing as much as 3½ lb each, were discovered whilst the work was being carried out, and other samples, some no more than glazed pieces of rock, were all carefully noted and catalogued. William Dixon was instructed to pack these samples carefully into a gunpowder barrel and dispatch the contents, numbering twenty five samples and weighing some 50 lb, to John Farey's house in London, where he would be able to study them more closely when he returned home. Whilst doing this work at the mine, he was assisted by John Dixon and an old miner. It appears that Mr Farey had high hopes for William Dixon's son John and evidently sought to help him on his way in the business of mining. He wrote personally to Mr Bankes, recommending that John's wage be increased by 1/- per day to 4/6d, to help him with his young family, provided that he carried out his job as agent properly and effected the rules according to the Book of Directions. Not all John Farey's observations were of praise though, and he did not hesitate to tell William Dixon of his shortcomings, and that these would be noted and there must be no repetition. One operation which Mr Farey did not take kindly to, was the practise of sorting wad samples outside the mine house. This was to cease, and all wad was to be sorted behind the locked doors of the house. In fact this was endorsed by its inclusion in the Book of Directions. Although it had been originally recommended that the mine houses should have iron doors, in view of the expense it was decided that oak should be used, and this work was completed by December 1819.

It must also be remembered that up to now the Grand Pipe totally secured the internal level known as Daniels Drift. This was soon to be re-named Fareys Stage for it was he who recommended that the level be opened up the 19 yards of barren rock southwards out to day. This would mean that all the development material, instead of being sent down the Grand Pipe, as had been the procedure up to now, could be trammed straight out to day. It was Mr Farey's intention to drive the level forward to open up the middle of the mine. The result of the recent survey had indicated various veins which convinced Mr Farey that wad was available, so the fell area above Fareys was trenched and by all accounts their suspicions were confirmed.

Fareys Stage was railed out with angle iron rails at a gauge of 24 inches and the tubs running on this system would not have had flanged wheels. The level was cut 6 feet high and 5 feet wide, and by December 1820 had drawing hoppers in the roof of the level taking wad from the uprises of Stuarts, Thompsons and Grisedales Pipes, this last having so far this year produced 18 casks of best and 268 of coarse. These had been worked continuously by William Dixon and partners, and all of the wad had been transported on the miners' backs in leather bags to the guard house at Gilberts Level. Fareys Stage was, without doubt, going to be one of the most productive adits of the mine system as it was the main drawing adit from the heart of the mine, where many large sops of great value had been discovered both in the level sole and roof. It begs the question why did it not have a guardhouse? It is possible that Harrisons, strategically placed above, would provide some protection and although Gilberts Level was many feet below, the field of vision from both these houses would give a tremendous view of the terrain. Also, and perhaps most importantly, was the fact that Fareys Level was not yet fully developed, having only now become accessible as an adit from day.

By now, Thompsons, Stuarts and Grisedales Pipes had been taken out in the roof (a system known as up-piping) and in the level sole Winkles was now being extended (known as down-piping). Eventually, Thompsons Pipe would corkscrew its way out to day in the bank of Wadhole Gill. Stuarts Pipe, after up-piping for 20 feet would strike across and join Grisedales Pipe, this connection being known as Rhoydes Stage (Rhodes Stage). It was from this stage that most of the development work was done in a northerly direction, taking out the upper middle part of the mine at this point and using the Grisedale Pipe as an uprise and a way into the upper workings, known as the Labyrinth. Once the connection had been made above at Gills Stage, it would mean that one could transfer wad from this high point down to Gilberts Level without coming out to day, a total vertical height of 400 feet!

The Grand Pipe had been fully opened, and was now a horrifying, black abyss dropping 290 feet into the murky depths of the mine's lower areas. The simple drawbridge spanning the top was strengthened and barren material was pushed across it and dumped outside on the mine hillock.

It was to be found in the Book of Directions, that all future letting of work (ie bargains) were to be worked by cubic measure. Driving was to be done by gangs of four miners, two at the forfield noggering, blasting and melling down and the others wheeling and waggoning the rubbish, and all working shifts were of 8 hours duration. Nogger holes were to be 1 to 1¼ inches round and 10 to 12 inches deep. Noggering four holes was a good shift, and one hole would wear out 2¾ noggers. (The cost of noggering a hole was a ½d an inch on a 1 inch round hole). In future, noggers too short and worn were not be sent to the Edge Tool Maker in Keswick, where they were welded together and re-tempered at a cost of 5/- per day. This work was now to be done at the mine. All levels had to be cut to a uniform size, and recorded as follows: 1.94 to 2.09 yards high and 1.40 to 1.20 yards wide. Mr Farey, in his official capacity of owner, was very pleased with his mining skills, having on the 1st of July discovered Daniels Sop, his first find. This was not, however, a bonanza and produced only 2 casks of best and 7 casks of coarse wad.

Exploration continued and old workings were again investigated for any wad which may have been left by the ancients. To this end, further work was being done in Coates Pipe just below Dixons Stage when a back filled sump was discovered. The poor miners, unfortunately, found that this had been used as an underground privy. To their dismay, they were ordered by Mr Farey to clear it out "on some Saturday afternoon or other", and ensure that all the filth and water were flushed down the Grand Pipe! The sump had then to be backfilled with CLEAN deads.

Another new directive was that from now on, in the interests of security, all wad when extracted from a sop, would be placed in leather knapsacks with backstraps and a stout cord for securing the top, and with the capacity for carrying a 56 lb load. The wad was to be loaded into the bags which would be supported on a bag frame (like an upturned stool), enabling the miner to place the wad directly into the open bag. There would be only six wad bags and three supports, all kept stored in the guardhouse in between times of use. For its removal, the bag would be loaded onto the miner's back by the agent or a responsible person and given a tally indicating its quality. The wad would then be carried through the mine to the dressing room where it would be sorted, placed in casks and transported daily to the security of two side drives off Gilberts Level, referred to as Anthonys and Stephens stores. These had been driven especially for the purpose, and were secured by stout, locked doors.

No miner was to be allowed out of the mine during the working shift, and the mine entrance and guardhouse doors were to remain locked for the duration of the shift. An inside privy had now been built to preclude the excuse of needing to go outside. All workers were to be thoroughly searched by the agent or superintendent before they were allowed to leave the mine house. The mine superintendent or agent must, without fail, inspect the mine every day to ensure that all doors were locked and secure, and should he be away or fall ill, his deputy was to make sure that a proper inspection was carried out.

It appears that the 'Blue Miller' became redundant as now all dressing and sorting was to take place within the mine house. Dressing areas, where the wad was bucked to reduce its size, and all washing areas and store rooms were to be swept and the wad placed in casks. The dressing of wad outside the confines of the guardhouses must cease, and the dressing floors below Harrisons, Fareys and the Old Mens Stages were to be abandoned. Under no circumstances should the silly practice continue of giving poor grade wad to shepherds and visitors, or selling it for a few shillings for ale money! Specimens could be given to mineralogists under the direction of the agent. The practice of people visiting the mine was to be discouraged, and bona fide mineralogists could visit provided they were given a written introduction by the local Keswick mineralogist, William Jonathon Otley (also a clock and watchmaker), and the application had to be approved by Henry Bankes. No details were to be given of the mine or its rocks, and it was also essential that the wad mine did not become a 'Laker's Lion' (tourist attraction) for the idly curious!

Due to the snow and frost, the wad could not be sorted during the winter of 1820 and much of it was just thrown down from Grisedales onto the floor of Fareys Stage. Likewise, a similar heap was dumped on Waltons Stage where it lay as common rubbish. This, however came to the notice of the owners and a severe reprimand was meted out to the stewards for allowing this careless action.

It was around this date that a further section of Fareys Stage was laid with rails from beyond Grisedales pipe onwards. William Dixon was again reprimanded by Mr Farey for the twisting and winding way the level had been cut, informing Dixon that this would soon wear out the rails and the new mine tubs. He also maintained that the level was not cut wide enough, and that in future William was to personally see to it that the levels were cut straight and in the meantime, he was also to get this section of level straightened out! The rails and wagon wheels were being supplied at this time by Seaton Iron Works in West Cumbria, the 130 yards of rails and oak sleepers costing 8/- a yard not including labour. Also a special iron bracket had been made to support the tubs when tipping down the pipes in the sole. Two connections had now been made in the sole of Fareys from Bankes Stage 25 feet below, one the large

Winkles the other a small uprise known as Bills which connected with Fareys just beyond Grisedales.

Naturally, miners and other indigenous tradesmen enjoyed, whenever possible, a few 'wets' in the local tavern or pot-house. Ale laid the dust and replaced body fluids lost through hard, physical toil besides providing some relaxation for the men. Certainly when the annual ritual drinking session and the inauguration of the 'King of Borrowdale' took place, the miners needed no second calling. Traditionally, this was held at the Miners Arms in Rosthwaite and in January 1820, the old miner John Youdale, now 86 years old and blind, still had the energy to take his eager entourage of mock subjects to the inn where he held his court. John had worked the mine way back in 1769 and had lived in the valley all his life and was just one of many characters living in Borrowdale in those far off days. Sarah Youdale or Old Sal as she was known, also lived all her life in Rosthwaite. It seems likely that she was John's daughter and was herself given the title 'Queen of Borrowdale'. In her youth there had been "no wheeled thing in Borrowdale" and everything was carried on "t'nag back". All clothing and clogs were home-made and to burn on the fire were sticks and peat but no coal. Everyone gathered at chapel for local news and after Joss Harry, who came regularly from Watendlath had died, his dog continued to come on its own! There were stories of wolves and boars in Langstrath, and women with bairns on their backs would go hunting. Great celebrations were had at Christmas and weddings with fiddlers and dancing and "rows of breet pewter plates on t' dresser" and there was snow on the fell tops until summer. Sarah died in Rosthwaite in 1869 aged 101.

As the valley prospered and more people came to live in Borrowdale, the company was aware that many of the workforce and their families lived close by, and the Rev A Heslop was pleased to receive a donation from the company of £25 0s 0d in March 1824 for his church and the local school.

Trial Seatoller Fell. Caldbeck Mining Museum Collection.

Remains of Harrisons Stage house. Caldbeck Mining Museum Collection.

Entrance to Gills Stage. Caldbeck Mining Museum Collection.

Miners from Seathwaite Wad Mine. Caldbeck Mining Museum Collection

Top: Seathwaite Wad Mine, looking into the Grand Pipe from Fareys Stage. The adit to day driven by John Farey can be clearly seen. Roy Fellows Collection.
Bottom: Miners' bait area on Verdons Stage. Caldbeck Mining Museum Collection.

Seathwaite Wad Mine, Fareys Stage laid with angled rail circa 1820. Roy Fellows Collection

Seathwaite Wad Mine, on Waltons Stage looking down Dixons Pipe.
Roy Fellows Collection.

Top: Entrance to Gilberts Level. Caldbeck Mining Museum Collection.
Bottom: Remains of Gilberts Level house in 1991 Caldbeck Mining Museum Collection

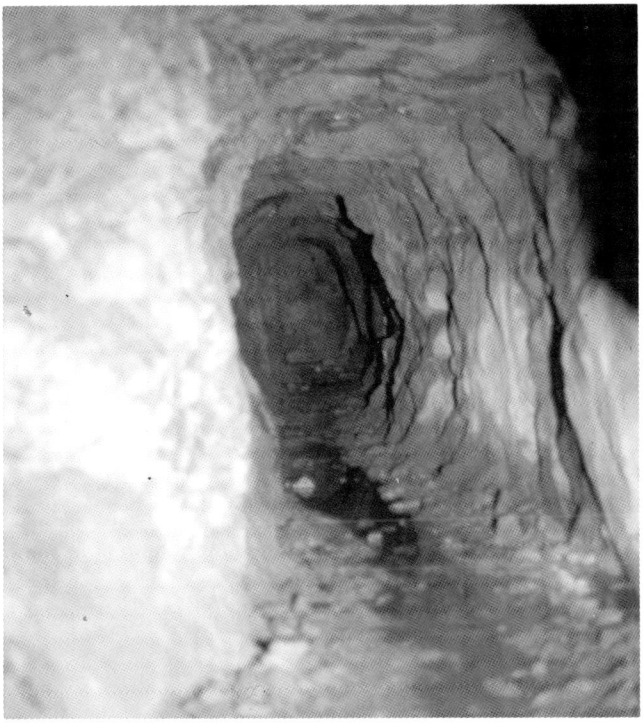

Top: Anthonys Store. Caldbeck Mining Museum Collection.
Bottom: Gilberts Level near Anthonys Store. Caldbeck Mining Museum Collection.

12 Back to Seatoller Fell

By 1829 the price of wad had risen to 35/- per lb and this was to rise even higher. By now, the pencil industry in Keswick was a thriving affair and there were fourteen manufacturers operating in the small town.

PENCIL MANUFACTURERS UP TO 1829

CHARLES WRIGHT	**JOHN SCRATCHARD**	**WM ROBINSON**
JOHN GREEN	**CHRIS HARRINGTON**	**WM ATKINSON**
JOHN HARRISON	**WM FORSTER**	**JOHN FOULKE**
JOHN LADYMAN	**JACOB BANKS**	**JOHN GATES**
JOHN AIREY	**JOSEPH GRAHAM**	

The most important of these were Jacob Banks at Greta Mills (Fitz Woollen Mill), Gates and Coupland at Greta Hamlet Mill and John Ladyman at Beckside Mill.

A local warehouse was being now being rented by the mining company for the storage of wad from a Mr Randleson of Keswick and he had recently been paid £5 12s 4d for its use.

Such was the demand for wad that efforts were redoubled to find more, and little expense seems to have been spared during the next few years with no less than four new levels being driven, and others being extended. The company turned its efforts once again to Seatoller Common, and started to open up three levels high on the moor in a desperate attempt to find wad at one of the original sites. One called Higher Stage at OD 1470 feet was started early in 1829 on an area of Seatoller Fell which is literally peppered with small trials, pits and surface trenching. It is impossible to tell which are company workings or those of the thieves or freeholders who had worked the common by day as well as night especially during the period when the mine was closed, also at this horizon they were completely out of view of the valley. This new level was driven forward by miners William Birkett, Thomas Bennett, Daniel Dixon and William Dixon and they all worked forty eight days, for which they were paid 3/6d per day. Unfortunately, this proved a worthless trial and no wad was found.

The company was obviously convinced that wad was to be found below the old pits, and therefore it was decided to drive a much bigger level slightly to the south and just above the Common Stage, which had been driven with little success in 1811. This second level was commenced about March 1830, and was to become known as Moors Stage at OD 1460 feet. The earliest driving was done by Daniel Dixon and partners, one of whom was William Birkett. They were paid 35/- per yard for one bargain, and were charged 6½d per lb of tallow making a total deduction of 7/7d from the bargain. Other miners were also driving the level for bargains of 25/- and 30/- thus showing how much the ground varied. The workday commenced with a slog up the hill from Seathwaite of virtually a mile, with a height gain of nearly 1,500 feet, and the miners of course, had to transport their heavy drill steels, powder etc up to this sodden, windswept place. After about 60 yards of driving they succeeded in striking a small sop, which was taken out. The level, on completion, was then connected down to Common Stage and the driving was continued, but in totally barren ground, for a distance of 18 yards.

Disappointed with this effort, but still convinced that the Moor had secrets to reveal, another small level was pushed into Seatoller Fell just above Moors Stage but slightly to the north at OD 1480 feet, and is unnamed. The size of the dump indicates a drive of about 70 yards, and on some of these trials a small amount of iron pyrite and some malachite staining is to be found, but in all cases, wad eluded them in any quantity worth further exploration.

By 1832, the Greta Bridge Mill, previously used for fulling had now been turned over to pencil manufacture by Hogarth and Hayes. This mill was the lowest on the river and consisted of two mills back to back which had been on the site since 1790 when used for bobbin making. Gates and Coupland who had originally made fancy waistcoats, were still producing pencils at Greta Hamlet Mill. Jacob Banks at Greta Mills had re-named his company the Greta Pencil Works and Black Lead Mills. The mill was very large occupying a prominent site on the river, and its dominating feature was a large tower whose bell summoned the workers every morning to their pencil making. This company was in fact to continue for virtually a hundred years. The mill then being labour intensive employed many people, and the foreman was a Mr Thomas Tate. This company were also joint lessees of the Borrowdale Black Lead Mining Co. which acquired the lease of the wad mine. It was this company who decided to cut the middle ground between Harrisons Stage and Fareys Stage, for with the price of wad still rising, reserve stocks were urgently in need of replenishment. Gills Stage was at OD 1210 feet and although a trial had been made here some years ago, it was decided, in 1832 to drive a major level in order to drain and work up into any of the old workings. Meanwhile, 145 feet below in Fareys Stage the miners were still rising up in the lucrative Grisedales Pipe which eventually would connect with Gills Stage.

By 1833, although wad mining had peaked, prices for top grade wad were now up to a staggering 45/- per lb, and consequently, any new finds, bogus or otherwise were brought to the attention of the rich or famous. In one instance, the poet William Wordsworth was approached by a gentleman called Henry Lancaster, a shoemaker at Troutbeck, offering him a partnership in a wad mine he had recently discovered. On enquiring about samples of wad from the mine, Lancaster told William that all the samples of the wad he had, had been lent to other prospective investors, whom he hoped to bring into the partnership. The largest specimen he had kept for himself, but was unable to locate it just at that moment and was of the opinion that one of his children might have lost it or put it on the fire! Mr Lancaster was adamant that the sop was but a spade's depth from the surface and that he could assuredly obtain more. William, naturally not wanting to miss out on a good thing, consulted with a neighbour, Mr Benson Harrison who was himself a miner and on his advice wrote to Lord Egremont asking for his opinion. As no further records appear concerning this matter, it must be assumed that Mr Lancaster was indeed the charlatan that he appeared to be, and that hopefully, Lakeland's most famous literary son was not taken to the cleaners!

The driving in Gills Stage was hard, and the rock here fast blunted the noggers as the miners struggled to drive forward. Charles Stuart and William Dixon Jnr were being paid 50/- per yard, and were now nearly at the ancient Gortons and Woodmans Pipes. By January 1836, the total connection had been made from Fareys to Gills Stage, which had originally been followed up through Grisedales Pipe, however this had petered out. A shaft was sunk 30 feet down from Gills and connected through to the top of the Grisedales Pipe via a sub-level. This was driven a distance of 30 yards and included four prospecting drives. It was driven by miner Thomas Bennett for 45/- per yard, although the level was actually called Charltons Stage. This connection now meant that the whole of the mine from Harrisons Stage down to Gilberts Level could be gained without going out to day, and Gills Stage had now been opened a distance of 130 yards and was into good wad. The most productive area was just below the sole of Gills and here, in the Labyrinth, dozens of small sops were discovered. This exploration had now reaped the rewards and 133 casks of wad weighing 15,556 lb and a massive 1,360 casks of coarse wad weighing 173,600 lb were produced.

Whilst a lot of work had been done in the upper mine, the lower section had not been exactly standing still. By September 1837, the workforce had grown to thirteen miners and three boys some of whom were being employed in the expansion of the mine. Driving costs were now 47/6d per yard and no less than 371 wagon loads of rubbish were drawn from Gilberts Level. This was from the development work beyond the Grand Pipe where Hastings Pipe was discovered, and was now being put down in the sole. All the waste material had to be jack-rolled up the shaft to the level, then the heavily-laden tubs pushed the 240 yards along the full length of Gilberts Level, for which work trammer W Flemming was paid 3d a tubload.

The total production figures vary in certain account books and so absolute accuracy is not possible, but between the years of 1801 and 1837 around 270 tons (604,743 lb) of graphite were mined at an average price of 25/- per lb. which gives a total return for the period of £755,928.

By this time in Keswick, the pencil industry had extended further and Abraham Wren had opened his mill on Penrith Road.

Then, on the 30th of March 1837, Mr William Dixon Snr died. This was indeed a sad day for he had worked at the mine man and boy, had seen it all and there was little he had not done. However he had left fine sons who were already working the wad, so the true spirit of mining would carry on.

13 John Dixon Takes the Reins

The death of William Dixon was a great loss, and it was with a heavy heart that his son John Dixon, took over the running of the mine in a temporary capacity. His father would be a difficult man to follow, but John had worked side by side with him for many years and had learnt everything possible about the management of the mine. The rule in those days was no work no pay, so it was not many days before John was up at the mine overseeing the operation as his family had done for scores of years before him, but he was to wait for many months before he would see the first wad being brought out of the mine under his supervision.

Thankfully, the riotous attacks on the mine had now ceased, although there would be continuing pilferage. The mine owners were still aware of the necessity of emphasising the boundaries of their property, so now, the whole of the lower wad mine was to be encircled with a very substantial dry stone wall. A length of wall 232 yards long was therefore constructed by George Gillbanks, who was paid the sum of 1/4d per yard for this skilled and monumental task. The wall is about 6 to 7 feet high and runs up the fell on one side of the sett, along the top of the sett, separating the High Wadhole Moor from the Low and then runs back down the fell on the other side. It is a magnificent example of the art of dry stone walling testified to by the fact of it still standing in an area which invites severe weather patterns.

During this period, the company also had a house constructed at Seathwaite at a total cost of £96 4s 8d. John Birkett supplied eighteen loads of slates at 3/6d per load, George Gillbanks did all the rendering and the roof work for £25 2s 2d, whilst John Christopherson and John Atkinson glazed the windows and painted the premises for £4 1s 4d. It is possible that this house was constructed for John Dixon, just as had been done for his father all those years before. By November of that year, John was officially promoted to mine superintendent at a wage of 31/6d per week, and had a total of eight miners working for him.

To try to meet the demands of the manufacturers, the mining company was ever anxious to scour the areas where the old men had worked in the hope that during their prosperous tenure they had thrown away or backfilled useable wad. They were particularly keen when costly exploration work was failing to find new reserves as was the case now. During January 1838, the miners were sent by the new mine captain into the deep recesses of Harrisons Stage in the hope of finding some odd pockets missed, but it was not to be. The ancients had missed practically nothing and little was recovered. However, it was from this level that three casks of wad were eventually recovered, and these were the first to be extracted under John Dixon's management.

Exploration work still continued through 1839 in the high area of the mine. In Gills Stage, short crosscuts were being made and some of them had resulted in small amounts of wad being found. Gills Stage was still being driven forward, and was now well in and following a fault containing glutinous, clayey haematite sludge, which oozed out and mixed with the water in the level. This coloured the men's clothing and skin with a rosy-pink stain which was even worse than the silvery-grey graphite. Another part of the workforce was still working above in Woodmans Pipe in Harrisons Stage, but again little was to be found. However, daily work at the mine still had to continue and to do this tools had to be bought. John Postlethwaite supplied pick shafts for £1 17s 4d whilst Joshua Jackson supplied spades and John Thompson jumpers (noggers) for £3 12s 3d. For 3/- per day, William Dixon Jnr assisted at the smithy which had just been supplied with a new pair of bellows by Messrs J Allison at a cost of £4 10s 0d. Tallow candles were of course vital for underground lighting and these were purchased in dozens from Ann Guy, who had been their regular supplier for many years. Despite the dying out of the organised raids on the mine, five firearms were still retained, and William Wallace came to the mine from time to time to repair and maintain them. His most recent charge for this service was 17/6d. The wad, as and when it was available, was still being despatched from the mine in casks and these were being supplied new by Joseph Wright, although on some occasions disused beer kegs and butter barrels were purchased. Gunpowder was, of course a normal requirement at the mine, and was delivered regularly by Messrs Huddlestons of Elterwater, their last account being for £16 10s 6d.

Although little actual mining appeared to have been done during the previous few months, a small load of wad was dispatched to Kendal and John Dixon decided to send his son William with it on its journey; his overnight expenses came to £1 10s 0d. Another miner at this time, Thomas Bennett was relieved of his duties for a couple of days during November 1839 to cut peat and sled it from the common down to the peat store adjacent to the mine house, and for this chore he was paid 1/3d per load.

The following year saw the attentions of the miners being transferred from the high area of the mine to Fareys Stage, which was being railed out to the forehead. Despite all the activity, still there was little wad being found and so the Hastings Pipe in the sole of Gilberts Level was de-watered, this taking a total of forty seven days of sheer graft. The water was clear by June 1840, and an exploratory drive costing 55/- per yard was being made by Joseph Coates and partners, but this was proving fruitless. The mine was going through one of its worst barren periods, and no matter which area the miners took on, they seemed to strike a blank. This resulted in John Dixon being instructed to carry out the deeply distressing task of sacking some of the workforce and reducing it to ten men. These men were not only his workforce, they were his friends

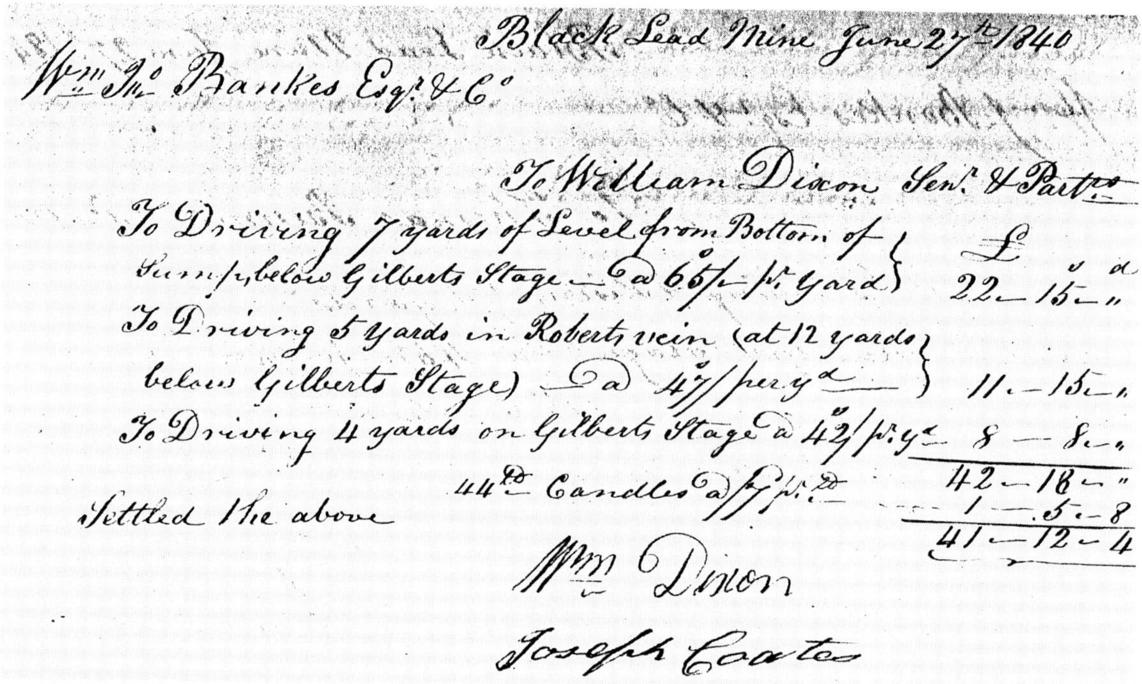

Black Lead Mine June 27th 1840

Wm Jno Bankes Esqr & Co

To William Dixon Senr & Partns

	£	s	d
To Driving 7 yards of Level from Bottom of Sump, below Gilberts Stage — @ 65/- pr yard	22	15	"
To Driving 5 yards in Roberts vein (at 12 yards below Gilberts Stage) — @ 47/ per yd	11	15	"
To Driving 4 yards on Gilberts Stage @ 42/ pr yd	8	8	"
	42	18	"
44 lbs Candles @ 7d pr lb	1	5	8
Settled the above	41	12	4

Wm Dixon

Joseph Coates

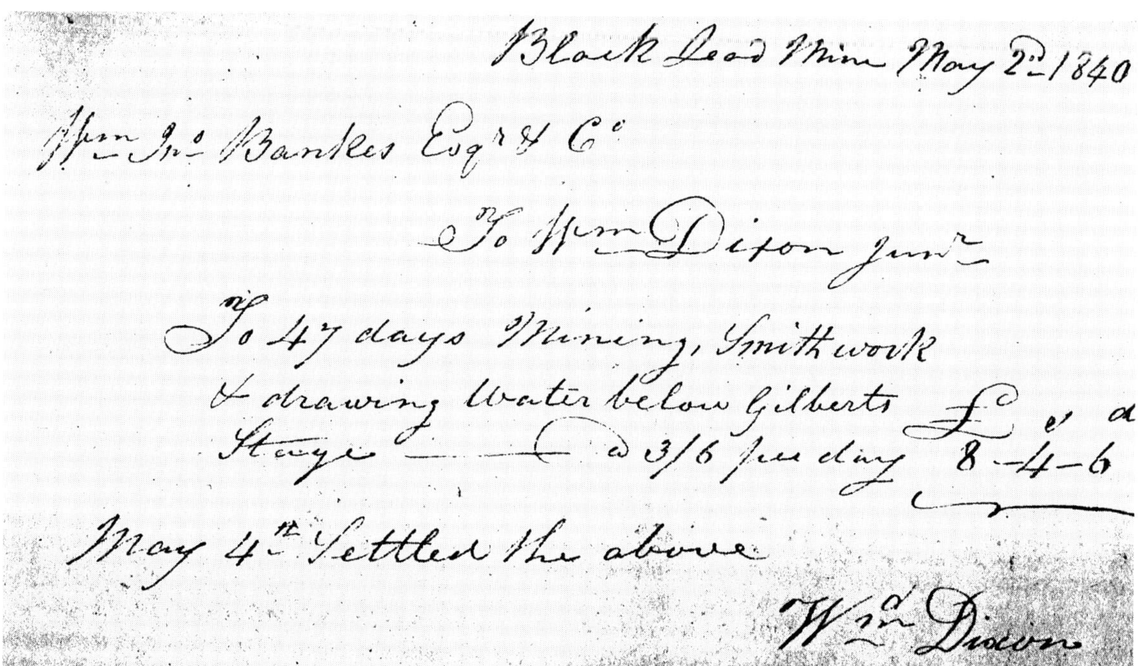

Black Lead Mine May 2d 1840

Wm Jno Bankes Esqr & Co

To Wm Dixon Junr

	£	s	d
To 47 days Mining, Smithwork & drawing Water below Gilberts Stage — @ 3/6 per day	8	4	6

May 4th Settled the above

Wm Dixon

Top: Bargain for Joseph Coates 1840. Courtesy of D R O
Bottom: Bargain for William Dixon 1840. Courtesy of D R O.

Contra Cr

		£	s	d
1840	Brought forwards	533	9	10
June 27	Paid Wm Dixon Senr & partrs for driving 12 yards of Level at 65/- 47/- & 42/ pr yd	41	12	4
	" Thos Bennett & Partrs 7½ yards @ 45/-	16	9	4
	" Wm Dixon Junr 29 days work @ 3/6	5	1	6
	" Danl Dixon 22 " "	3	17	"
	" Jno Dixon Senr 8 weeks @ 31/6	12	12	.
	" Adam Bird Jumpers &c	4	4	7
	" Jno Dixon Incidental expenses	2	5	7½
Aug 22	" Jos Coates & Partrs as per bill	34	3	2
	" Danl Dixon & partrs 14 yds Level @ 45/-	30	12	6
	" Wm Dixon Junr 16 days Smithwork @ 3/6	2	16	.
	" Jno Dixon Senr 8 weeks @ 31/6	12	12	.
	" Ann Guy Candles	5	12	.
Sept 5	" Jno Greenhow Kibble		6	.
Oct 17	" Jos Coates & Partrs Driving &c &c	33	10	5
	" Thos Bennett & Partrs Sinking &c	30	8	1
	" Wm Dixon Junr 19 days @ 3/6	3	6	6
	" Jno Dixon Senr 8 weeks @ 31/6	12	12	.
	" James Lowther 14 lb Nails		4	6
	" Lady Wm Gordon Stemples	1	9	.
		787	4	4½

Wad Mine expenses circa 1840. Courtesy of C R O.

and the selection must have needed a great deal of soul searching to carry out. To cut costs further, the breaking of new ground was halted due to the excessive cost of gunpowder. The instructions from the board were clear: produce wad without major costs, rob any area of visible wad using picks, pull down back filled areas, scour the tips ..... things were certainly tight. Despite the cutbacks, the essentials of the mine carried on, Adam Bird the smith being paid £4 4s 7d for sharpening jumpers and W Fisher supplying stemples for 18/9d.

In Keswick however, the pencil manufacturing business seemed to have been in quite the reverse situation, with now something like fifteen mills operating. Most of these had been converted from their original use as woollen, bobbin or flax mills etc, and some of the work was fed out to local women working at home. This created a cottage industry very welcome in those days when women were often tied at home by very large families, and every penny was needed to fill those hungry, young mouths.

The mine still continued to work on, but at a very restricted level, as new wad locations still had not been found. During 1841, Joseph Coates and his partner were driving forward in Fareys Stage at 45/- per yard, and had driven through barren ground for 15 yards. Here the rock was hard and the drive was following the same ruddy mess that was to be found in the far end of Gills Stage 145 feet above. The upper middle of the mine above Fareys, was being pushed forward in Rhodes Stage by Daniel Dixon and Thomas Bennett and some wad was being found but not of notable amounts, and Grisedales Pipe was literally being stripped of any deposits that were left.

During 1842 further development at the mine continued in Rhodes Stage although as this drive continued on its northerly course the driving became totally barren. This was exactly what was happening at the far end of Gills above and Fareys below, although in Fareys a new small sop known as Hardys Pipe produced a little wad. Whilst the mine continued to work during 1843, it was still a very lean time and led John Dixon, in 1844, to send one of his oldest and most reliable miners Joseph Coates with his partners, to the Old Mens Level to commence a main by-pass drive in a southerly direction off the Grand Pipe. This was an area untried, and after a few yards the drive turned west to head towards the rich area of Winkles Pipe, discovered years before. The rate for the drive was 40/- per yard and the work was hard. It was a blind drive and conditions became worse as the tunnel was blasted forward. Here, the smoke and acrid fumes hung for hours before clearing, yet less than 30 yards behind at the Grand Pipe, the air was as fresh as day. Eventually, Joseph and his mates broke into the area at the back of Winkles Pipe, but here they found heartbreakingly little for all the back-breaking toil they had endured. This area around Winkles had been well excavated on its original discovery many years before and all the workings were backfilled and the old wad sops choked with debris. The only use for this drive now could be as added ventilation. A short drive was put through to connect with Shepherds Stage which was bisected by Winkles. This more or less fruitless task achieved it was thought, for some reason, that the driving of another 30 yards in a south-westerly direction was worth the effort, and amazingly they were rewarded with a small pocket of wad in the sole of the level.

A further prospecting drive by William Dixon was being made into Seatoller Fell at a price of 42/- per yard and later in the year, the work was undertaken by Thomas Bennett at 47/- per yard and continued until 1844. This appears to have been a rather extravagant undertaking as the overall mining operation was so much lower down the fell. By now, one would have thought, all the available wad would have been traced within the maze of tunnels which riddled this area. The level is not mentioned by name, and no doubt the miners cursed the manager as they trudged daily up the 1,200 feet of steep climbing carrying their tools and powder, especially when their mates were working hundreds of feet below.

Down the valley meanwhile, Keswick Town was still enjoying its peace and prosperity, and its fame and fortune as a tourist centre were becoming apparent. Another distinguished visitor at this time was none other than the the King of Saxony, who also visited the pencil mills.

14 Robsons - The Final Push

The last few years had been very unkind to the wad mine with production at an all time low, and by 1845 it had become obvious that the mine was virtually worked out. Further barren drives in Gills Stage had failed to produce anything of note, and it seemed as though the magic wad had disappeared. In Fareys Stage, a new level had been started in a north-westerly direction just past Grisedales Pipe and running nearly parallel to Fareys. This, it was hoped, would achieve success under Rhodes Stage, which had been a very productive area. In fact, so confident of success was the company, that this level was railed out and was later named Robinsons Level. These bold drivings cost money and valuable time, and still they were not striking any new sops. If the company was to survive, it seemed that a further exploration level would have to be driven to enter and open a complete new area of ground. Although not enjoying its previous mining success the company, because reserves of wad were still considerable, was able to continue trading. The partners though, were edgy about investing any more money, particularly in further expensive development work, and the managers explained that unless they were prepared to invest and speculate, as had proved successful in the past, they would have no future at all. The managers won their case, and plans were drawn up for the company to commit itself to a new drainage adit which would be driven 270 feet below Gilberts Level. This would be called Robsons Level after director William Robson from Wilton, Salisbury, who had come onto the board two years previously.

To pursue this venture, the miners needed more equipment and Greta Forge supplied various tools. Messrs Greenhow supplied a new kibble for 6/- whilst Ralph Douglas supplied £5 4s 0d worth of spirits, although it must be stated that spirits had been a regular item on the supplies account! Perhaps this time, they were to celebrate the start of this new venture. Ultimately, this level was to undercut all the above workings, and on completion would cover a distance of some 600 yards before it came under the Hastings and Benjamins Pipes, both in the sole of Gilberts Level. The hardness of the rock in these sumps reflects in the price of the bargains the miners had been able to negotiate, and were so far the highest paid. Thomas Bennett was being paid as much as 75/- per yard in Hastings, where he was putting in a crosscut 40 feet down. The driving of Robsons started at OD 540 feet, and to secure the level entrance a guardhouse was constructed of stone with a slate roof. This was smaller than the others, no doubt because of its close proximity to the hamlet of Seathwaite, so fear of armed attack was less likely.

The initial driving was through boulder clay and had to be supported by timber, and as the driving went forward and the air became foul, at 50 yards in a rise was put up to surface. The nearby Wadhole Gill provided sufficient water to effect a waterblast, which made life a little more bearable for the miners. As the drive pushed forward however, air trunking was required and the first batch cost a 1/- per yard and was supplied by J Bowman. Various miners undertook bargains here, John Robinson driving a 25 yard stretch for 52/- per yard, but the Coates partnership and the Dixons would all have their time here as well. The progress in the level was slow and certain areas had to be heavily timbered as the boulder clay was very unstable. As the level went further under Dickinson Bank, the air and general conditions became intolerable. The atmosphere was stifling and so a fan was installed to put air up to the face, and to ensure that water was in plentiful supply to drive this, a leat was dug from Sour Milk Gill a few hundred yards away and put down the shaft. This was an awful drive, the water streaming through onto the miners as they blasted and picked their way forward. The men were not at all happy working here, and would have much preferred to be in the more stable ground above.

The company, although by no means penniless, had miners working everywhere for wad, in order to offset the spiralling costs of driving Robsons. During September 1847, numerous places were being tried: William Dixon was driving forward on Whitridges Stage and Joseph Coates was driving in the far end of the Old Mens Stage for 60/- per yard. John Robinson and J Bowman were sinking in Hastings Pipe near the forehead of Gilberts Level which was beyond Benjamins Sop by a distance of 28 yards. It was now November 1847 and Hastings Pipe was really the only new ground the company had going for them, but even this was going to turn sour. The sump was always filling up with water and half the time was spent lifting the water out, and they were working with it continually sloshing around their clogged feet. The ventilation here was almost non-existent and even the Grand Pipe with its enormous updraught just a few yards away, failed to clear the air. Here they were a total of 250 yards inbye and 100 feet down. With the tallow smoke stinging their eyes and virtually soaked to the skin, the men were having a tough enough time when, almost without warning, as they were removing blast debris with bars a large block moved. Suddenly, gallons of water started to pour into the sump, and the two men headed rapidly for the ladders as the deluge increased. All that hard work was gone in an instant, and soon they were looking at a large, deep, black pool. Dismally, they wondered how on earth they were going to break the news to Captain Dixon, that the sump was now well and truly filled and would certainly have to be abandoned for the time being.

This disaster could not have come at a worse time, as this working was at the vanguard of the mining development programme. Below, Robsons Level had now been driven a total of 400 yards in and a drive, Jacks Crosscut was being driven in a north-easterly direction to undercut Hastings and Benjamins. Here, the rock was some of the hardest encountered, the type which had been already seen in the workings directly above, however, this was safer ground and required no timbering. The crosscut encountered two veins which were tried, and became known as H vein and K vein and a small amount of wad was discovered, but nothing of major significance.

The winter came and went, and the year of 1848 started with renewed vigour, the attention of the company once again turning towards Robsons Level. Here the driving continued forwards in the main drive, in Jacks Crosscut and other side drives. Messrs Tuck and Ley were supplying rails in 6 foot lengths, candles were costing 6/6d per dozen (these had to be purchased by the miners) and gunpowder was also in great demand, 111 lb being supplied at 6½d per lb. Messrs Bowman supplied a further 100 yards of air-trunking at 1/- per yard. Another urgent priority was the de-watering of the flooded Hastings Sump, and in Gilberts Level a windlass was constructed and the business of draining the sump began. John Robinson and his men worked at this for no less than 79 days, for which John was paid 3/6d per day, making him £13 16s 6d. All was not plain sailing however, and a 23 yard section of Robsons became unstable and required immediate attention. This was dealt with by J Robinson and his partners, the oak timber for the repairs supplied by William Litt. It must be remembered that Robsons Level was a blind adit with only one way out, and the level was now something like 440 yards in from day.

Robsons Level was still a hive of activity and during November 1849, John Robinson and his partners were driving in at 70/- per yard towards the Grand Pipe. Due to the hardness of the ground this was one of the highest paid bargains recorded. Messrs McGlasson supplied wood, sleepers and a new wagon for £3 16s 0d, which had been long awaited by Mr Dixon and had been the cause of much correspondence. Joseph Coates was again driving forward in Jacks Crosscut at 70/- per yard. Gunpowder for blasting was costing 6½d per pound and tallow candles were £2 5s 6d for 84.

Wad was still being transported to Keswick and 12 cwt was sent from the mine at 8d per cwt. The carrying cost from Keswick to Kendal was 2/- per cwt and a small consignment of 173 lb was despatched to Messrs Gough in Essex Street, London. During 1849 two gentlemen visited the mine, a Mr Taylor and a Captain Eddy, both local mining men. What their interest in the mine was at this time is not clear. They may have been there in an advisory capacity, intending to invest in the project or perhaps they were friends of the owners. Whatever the reason for the visit, all their expenses and lodgings were paid for by the company.

The winter of 1849 must have been a fearfully hard one, for Samuel Ladyman, erstwhile pencil maker, had collecting boxes out around Keswick to provide soup kitchens for the poor. Two of them were stationed on Lake Road and when he went to empty them, he estimated that 2,000 people were skating on the frozen surface of Derwentwater!

INVENTORY OF MINE EQUIPMENT 1850

		£	S	D
418 YARDS OF RAIL	8D PER YARD	13	18	8
470 YARDS OF RAIL	12D PER YARD	27	8	4
420 YARDS OF AIR PIPE	6D PER YARD	10	10	0
ONE WAGON		1	5	0
TWO WHEELBARROWS		1	0	0
ONE PAIR OF BELLOWS		2	10	0
ANVIL		1	10	0
DRILL STEELS 57 LB WEIGHT	4D PER LB		19	0
2 PRICKERS			2	0
2 SCRAPERS			2	0
4 BORING HAMMERS			6	0
4 SHOVELS			5	0
2 COAL RAKES			2	8
2 MALLETS			4	0
2 SMITHS HAMMERS AND TONGS			4	0
3 WINDLASS			4	6
3 ROPES			9	0
5 FIREARMS		2	5	0
2 CHAIRS			2	0
3 TABLES			9	0
4 CUPBOARDS			8	0
WOODEN LADDER		1	15	0
TOTAL VALUE OF GOODS		65	19	2

15 The Pencil Makers

As we know, graphite was probably being used as a writing medium as far back as the 15th Century when the monks of Furness Abbey supposedly used it in the Coucher Books. The first writing stylus had been described in 1565 by Esner and graphite was being used in the Michaelangelo School of Art in Florence from 1580.

However, it seems safe to say that the pencil industry proper began in the small town of Keswick just down the valley from the purest source of graphite in the world......the Seathwaite Wad Mine. It is possible that the start of the pencil industry as a commercial venture was as early as 1792, but the information available is a little tenuous.

We can firmly establish that John Ladyman, John Airey and Jacob Banks were operating mills by 1811 and that the industry continued to grow steadily and provide much needed work in Keswick. By 1829, manufacturers were:

John Airey	Jacob Banks	Gates and Coupland
Joseph Graham	Joseph Ladyman	John Foulk
Charles H Wright	John Scratchard	William Robinson
Christopher Harrington	John Green	William Forster
William Atkinson		

The mills operating were Beckside, Greta Mills (Fitz Woollen), Greta Hamlet, Greta Bridge and by 1837, Abraham Wren was established with partners Michael Falcon and Henry Dodgson at Penrith Road (now the site of the petrol station). An independent, Robert Thwaite was at Brigham and the company of the Fosters were also making pencils. In 1842, Robert Gibson purchased the Greta Hall estate which encompassed the Banks' mill but the name Banks and Co was retained. Greta Mill was possibly the largest pencil factory at this period, and the town of Keswick was now becoming known throughout Europe as the home of pencils.

In 1851, the Temple of Art and Industry was established at Crystal Palace, London and here, it was the Keswick firm of Banks & Co who gained distinction with their pencils and production was now rapidly approaching the six million mark. The wood used in their manufacture was not local, but cedar wood from the Americas, and was actually re-claimed from disused railway sleepers. Rare local examples of these trees can be seen on Vicar Island on Derwentwater, and in the grounds of Barrow Cascade House beside the lake.

At this time, the three main manufacturers of pencils were Greta Bridge Mill belonging to Hogarth and Hayes, Southey Hill (Greta Hamlet) belonging to Robert Coupland, and Greta Mill (Fitz Woollen) which was Banks, Foster & Co. Other manufacturers were:

John Airey	App and Harrison	William Guy
Samuel Ladyman	Henry Powley	Jefferson, Thompson
Abraham Wren	Christopher Harrington	Crosthwaites, Lancaster & Co

However, competition was fierce and certain unscrupulous companies would claim that their pencils were made from the Borrowdale wad, the printing on the side of a pencil stating that they were 'Warranted Pure Cumberland Lead', when often they were made from inferior, foreign material.

In earlier days, the pencils had been hand-made, but by now machinery was being used to great effect, and seemingly it was the long-established firm of Banks and Co who led the way in this innovation. In 1854, the Greta Hamlet Mill, Southey Hill was taken over by three men, Joseph Gatey, John Dodgson and John Hudson, for which they paid £70 0s 0d per annum rent, and they stayed here for three years. The mill was then taken over by Messrs Abraham Wren and Michael Falcon, who still had ownership of the mill at Brigham, higher up on the river Greta and on the site of the old lead smelter of 1809.

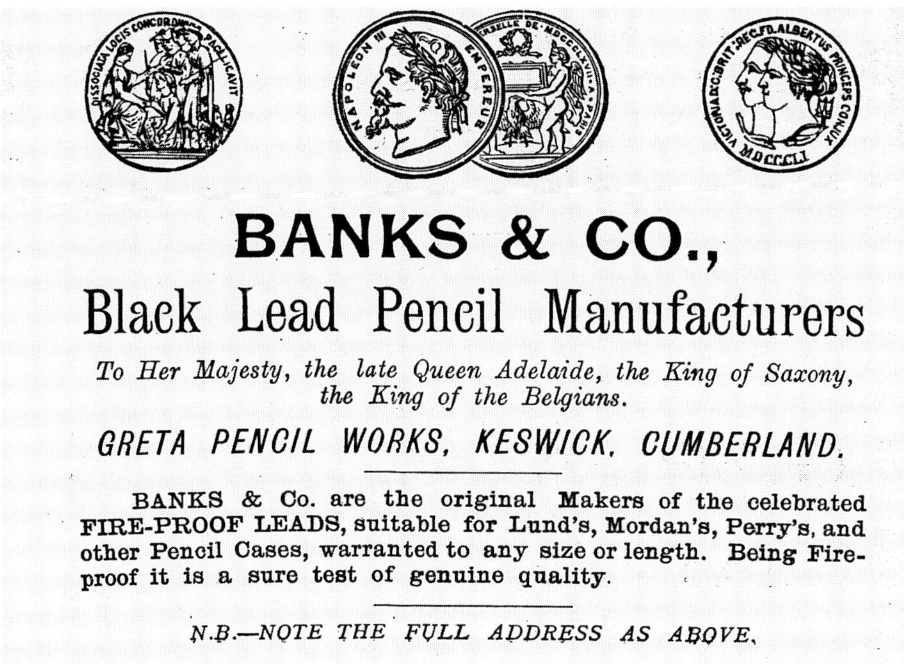

Advert for Black Lead pencils circa 1890. Caldbeck Mining Museum Collection.

In January 1857, the Greta Bridge Mill was in the hands of Messrs Banks, Foster for pencil manufacture, and during this year production was marred by a fatal accident when a worker fell into the waterwheel. In this year also, Greta Mills was visited by Edward, Prince of Wales, later King Edward V11.

Over the last few years, the wad mine had fallen into decline, and in 1859 only three casks were produced, and another small amount was sold locally to a fuller. The cash was running out and even some of the most stalwart investors, including Mr Bankes had obviously started to lose faith, or perhaps they just wanted to quit whilst they were still ahead. Robsons Level was becoming a millstone, and although a mining showpiece, it was a massive drain on resources. It seemed that enough was enough and although the miners had put their hearts into the venture, risking their lives every day, the investors had decided that no more money was available. This meant that the existing operation would be wound up, the current lease having just three years to run.

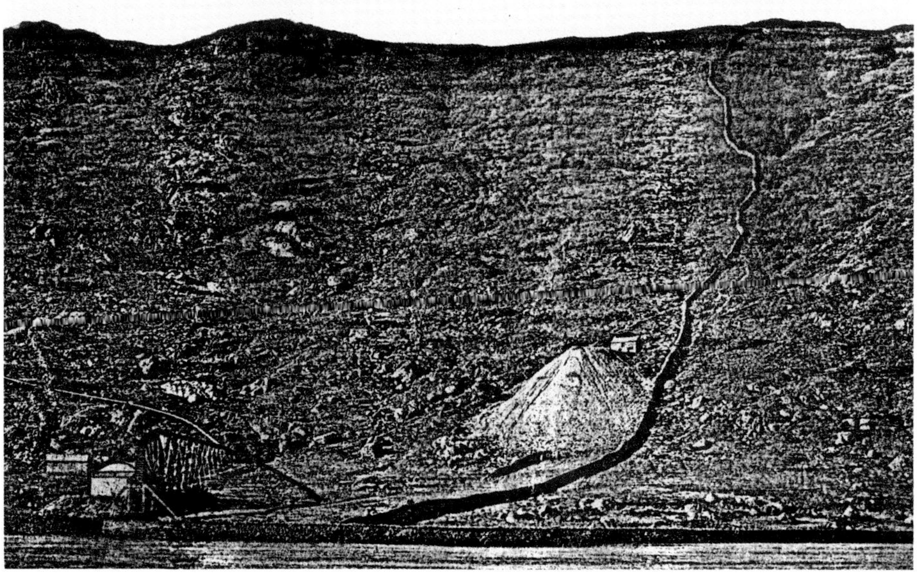

Top: Seathwaite hamlet; houses originally built by J Braithwaite.
Stan Edmondson Collection
Bottom: Early photograph of Robsons Level and mill site circa 1888.
Caldbeck Mining Museum Collection.

Top: Robsons Stage at water-blast shaft. Ian Hebson Collection.
Bottom: The ruins of Robsons Stage house. Caldbeck Mining Museum Collection

Top: Robsons Stage, general view of the level. Note air trunking supports.
Ian Hebson Collection.
Bottom: Robsons Stage, area of pack-wall just before unstable ground.
Ian Hebson Collection.

Top: Southey Pencil Mill, Keswick. The Jackson Library.
Bottom: Greta Bridge Pencil Mill, Keswick. The Jackson Library.

Top: Ann Banks Greta Bridge Pencil Mill, Keswick circa 1890.
Cumberland Pencil Co Collection.
Bottom: Retail shop in Ann Banks Greta Bridge Pencil Mill circa 1890.
Cumberland Pencil Co Collection.

Pencil makers at work, Greta Bridge Mill, Keswick, circa 1890.
Cumberland Pencil Co Collection

Top: Grinding stone used for crushing the wad, the Greta Pencil Mill, Keswick. Caldbeck Mining Museum Collection.
Bottom: River Greta, Keswick. Site of Greta and Forge Pencil Mills. Caldbeck Mining Museum Collection.

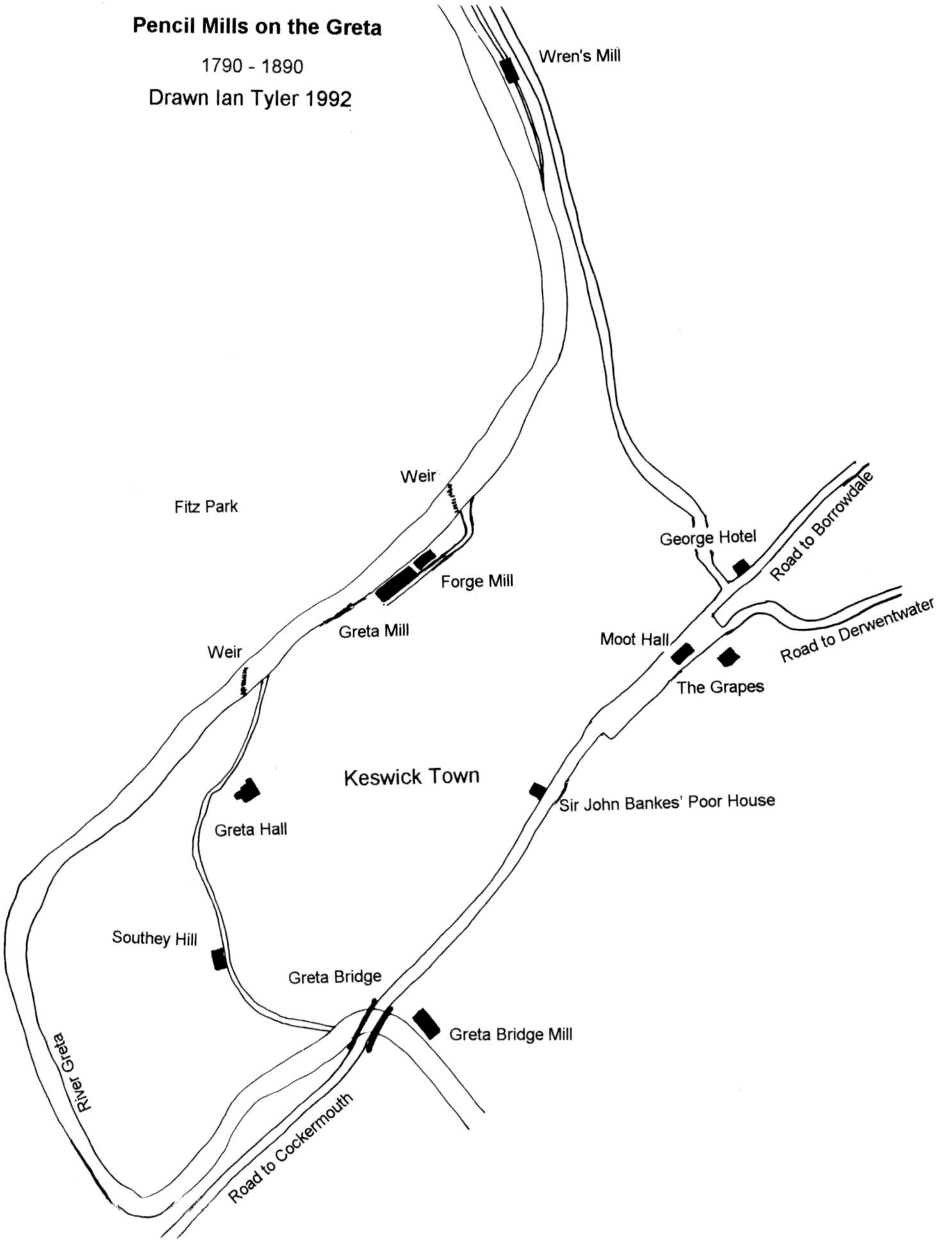
Pencil Mills on the Greta
1790 - 1890
Drawn Ian Tyler 1992
Wren's Mill
Weir
Fitz Park
Forge Mill
Greta Mill
Weir
George Hotel
Road to Borrowdale
Moot Hall
The Grapes
Road to Derwentwater
Keswick Town
Sir John Bankes' Poor House
Greta Hall
Southey Hill
Greta Bridge
Greta Bridge Mill
River Greta
Road to Cockermouth

16 The Cumberland Black Lead Mine Co Ltd

Despite the lack of interest in Borrowdale wad, a new company was eventually formed in 1859 by a group of men who were convinced the mine had potential. The company name was to be The Cumberland Black Lead Mine Co Ltd and the directors were R Eales of Exeter, D T Johnston of London, W Watkins of London and C Worthington of Brighton. The agent and mine manager was to be John Dixon. Money for the venture was raised through floating 4,000 shares at £5 0s 0d each, which would produce £20,000 equity if all the options were taken up. The new investment certainly instilled enthusiasm and confidence.

The mine had lain dormant over the last few years, and as a result of irregular maintenance, certain areas had become unstable, sumps had flooded and the weather had taken its toll on the buildings. Now that the new company was here however, and the workforce almost all re-employed, work could once more continue.

This year saw Robsons Level cleared out to the face and already driven 440 yards. The level was in the Rake Vein and at about 400 yards in, Jacks Crosscut was being continued north. Here the rock, known as grey wacke, was unbelievably hard and the sparks were flying off the jumpers as the men hammered their way forward. The miners hated this place, for it was wet and the air was poor. The air-trunking supposedly bringing fresh air from the water blast some 350 yards behind, was woefully inadequate because of the distance to the face. To make matters worse, due to the severe shortage of cash during the last period of working, the level had not been railed right up to the face. This of course meant that the muck from the face driving had to be barrowed part of the way back and then transferred to the waiting tub, despite Mr Dixon's request for more rail.

Jacks Crosscut was being driven in the hope of cutting further pipes, particularly Hastings Pipe which had already been sunk in the sole of Gilberts Stage, and which it was hoped would compare with the Grand Pipe for richness of wad, although so far the signs of graphite were minimal. Mr Dixon was very enthusiastic about the new development, though this early optimism and speculation could well have been for the benefit of the new shareholders. Naturally, if a find as great as the Grand Pipe could be discovered it would certainly secure the future of the mine.

The connection of the virgin ground between the two levels of Gilberts and Robsons was the ultimate aim. This would of course, de-water and ventilate Hastings and Benjamins Pipes and all of the new ground made available. The miners were pursuing their grim and arduous task at the forehead of Robsons one day, when they were suddenly deluged with water. Gallons washed out of the face through the newly blasted rock, and the men, bedraggled, soaked through, tired and above all dejected, made their weary way back to Robsons entrance. As they stripped off their sodden clothes at the house trying to warm themselves by the fire, a commotion was heard outside and one of the men from Gilberts Level arrived, shouting that they had broken through and the sump was de-watering. Congratulations were obviously short lived as the truth started to dawn...the men working in the lower level had cut a feeder and released the water from the sump in Gilberts! This would certainly not enhance the conditions in Robsons and if this was a natural spring, the extra water would continue to hinder the men. The bonus would be that the flowing of the water might help to stimulate some air movement. However, the men in Gilberts Level could now start to re-work the Hastings sump and any associated pipes. The distance was still 168 feet between the two workings, and when this connection was made there certainly would be cause for rejoicing. Wad production at the mine was still poor with few new finds apart from the ones in Hastings. During 1859 the selling of the wad was still the priority of the company and 448 lb was sold to D J Johnson of Cannon Street, London. It appears that during this period deals were being made with local manufacturers in Keswick and a delivery was made to Messrs Elles of Keswick at 30/- per lb. Another recipient of the quality pencil wad was Messrs Robert Wilson of Keswick.

Still the pencil industry continued to thrive, and various mills in Keswick were changing hands. In the year of 1859, Samuel Ladyman's mill and the large Greta Mill amalgamated creating a united power of three waterwheels, one wooden and two cast iron, the largest being 16 feet in diameter with a 10 foot breast. This last would have developed something like 120 hp, and its main use would have been to drive the grinding wheels to crush the graphite. With this amalgamation came a new name, that of the Banks Pencil Mill Co.

During 1861 Mr R Wilson took over Greta Bridge Mills and during his tenure the company was very successful gaining Gold Medals for pencils produced. The Keswick Greta Pencil Mill, under the watchful eye of manager Mr Henry Birbeck was doing well. It was now under the control of Miss Gibson, but still wisely trading under the Banks name, and so successful was this lady, that the company collected Gold awards during 1872.

Eventually, a new mining company was formed, the Borrowdale Plumbago Mines and Manufacturing Company, and a new lease was signed on the 12th of May 1875. The main shareholders were Ralph Banks, J Barratt, J Shepherd Sawrey and Alan Backhouse Salmon. This company also leased Beck House in Seathwaite and various grasslands. The new source of funding soon got the mine re-opened and by now John Dixon's son William was the new manager. His daily correspondence with Mr Salmon F G S, the director from Ulverston, shows the efficiency and dedication of the man.

There were requests for zinc air-trunking and timber for Robsons Level, and Marshalls were supplying larch wood for sleepers which were cut to 2 feet 8 inches by 5 inches by 2½ inches. This was fine for the 20 inch gauge intended, but the cutting of these was costly. Also a new horse was purchased and was now being used to transport all the heavy goods for the mine, and this also meant a whole new load of tack.

By July 1875, above Fareys Stage the areas of Grisedales Pipe, Rhodes Stage and Charltons Stage had been tried for wad but had produced little and it seemed this ground was now completely worked out. A little random driving was carried out by two miners in a desperate attempt to win a new find, but again, this produced virtually nothing. In order to increase overall production, a strong wooden hopper was installed at the bottom of the Grand Pipe in Gilberts level. Again the miners were sent to scavenge all the workings and the backfill of the old workings in Dixons, Winkles, Ridgeways, Wilsons and Crossthwaites and any wad found was to be dispatched directly down the Grand Pipe regardless of quality!

Fortunes change in mining either through lack of money, loss of the vein, loss of the market or a change of management and now William Dixon was basically alone. Gone were his old associates and the new regime were hard businessmen who put the old man under considerable pressure. Things were bad, production was appalling and William Dixon was without doubt in fear of losing his job. This was the situation which obtained in 1875, when William, in a quivering hand wrote a letter begging for his position as mine manager to be retained and assuring the Board of his loyalty and his ability to find the elusive wad. To make matters worse a major collapse of 16 yards had occurred in Robsons Level at 236 yards in from the portal. This was the second time this area had given problems and the last time the miners had repaired this section, it had taken six months with four and sometimes six men working. A further section of 98 yards of the level was railed out and this was laid in 6 foot sections. William Dixon still battled for the mine's requirements and wrote copious letters to obtain another underground wagon, preferably one of the new iron ones. The request for 400 more rail sections was also made. Further work had been done in Verdons Stage, 12 feet below Fareys Stage, and in the old working area of Winkles and Williams Pipes the miners had found a small area showing signs of wad. In the Labyrinth below Gills Stage around Gortons Pipe, another area was being tried with a little success, and a small sop had been located just east of the Grand Pipe near Braggs Drift.

Below, at Robsons, the joiners who were cutting the sleepers out of 12 inch logs were cursing the wet weather. The continuous rain had left the logs sodden and this was making the work doubly hard. The man in the bottom of the saw pit cursed the weather more than his mate above for not only was he standing in the muddy water, but with every draw of the two-handed blade he was covered with a shower of wet sawdust.

By the end of 1875, it seemed as though William Dixon had weathered the period of uncertainty as it is obvious that money for further investment had been found and although little graphite had been discovered, a large amount of development work had continued. The ritual of the 'King of Borrowdale' was still maintained and the new king, William Fisher had recently been crowned at the Royal Oak at Rosthwaite (formerly the Miners Arms). The name may have been changed as a result of the new influx of tourists, the previous name possibly being felt to be too indicative of the industrial background of the valley.

It appears that the distribution of graphite was, in the main, still the same. Most of the mined wad was transported to the London warehouse from where it was distributed. This is borne out by the most irate response of a representative of Messrs Hogarth and Hayes of Greta Mill, Keswick who travelled to the mine to purchase graphite. William Dixon informed him of the company policy of all graphite being sold and distributed from London. At this the representative became most offensive, but a phlegmatic William suggested he write to Mr Salmon, Hen Howe, Ulverston. He was the only person who had the authority to sanction arrangements for the purchase of wad at a local level, and until Hogarth and Hayes had made the necessary arrangements with him, William Dixon was not going to budge!

The weather in Seathwaite had turned from its usual torrential rain of the last few weeks to that of a more seasonal nature, and the snow fell thick and fast transforming the mine and its accompanying waste into a Christmas card scene under a thick layer of sparkling, clean, white snow.

With the coming of the New Year, William Dixon was a much happier man. All the rails were now laid to the forehead of Robsons, and he had just taken delivery of two new mine wagons. Not only had all the general work been progressing, but the mine had produced nearly seven casks of wad. During March, it was reported that the snow was disappearing from the fell and this would enable work to continue more easily. In May 1876, fifteen men were being gainfully employed at the mine, and William Dixon's wages were now £2 0s 0d per week whilst the miners were being paid around 4/- per day. Joseph Dover and William Jenkinson were working on Rhodes Stage just above Fareys Stage near Grisedales Pipe. Joseph Dover was also employed as the groom, for which work he was paid an extra 6/- per month.

On the 17th of June, the director Mr Barratt made an unexpected visit to the mine, and was most impressed with the work done in Robsons. He too was convinced that the connection up to Gilberts would be the best way to develop the mine. William mentioned to him that the showings of wad in Hastings Pipe below Gilberts could turn out to be a fine prize and in the last six months had

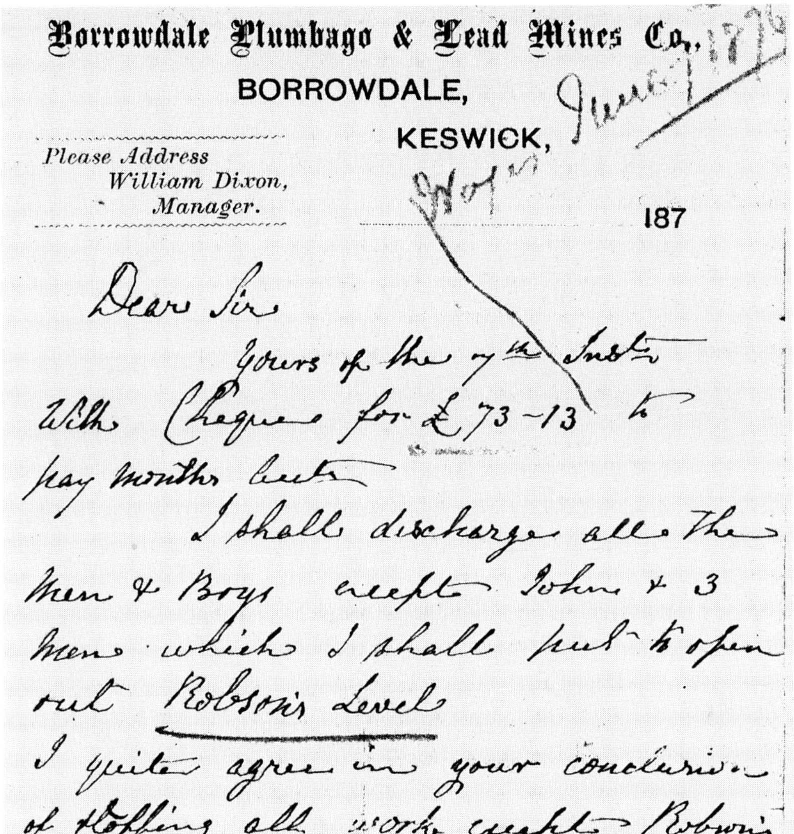

Borrowdale Plumbago & Lead Mines Co.,

BORROWDALE,

KESWICK, 187

Please Address
William Dixon,
Manager.

June 1876

Dear Sir

Yours of the 7th Inst

With Cheque for £73-13 to
pay months lent

I shall discharge all the
Men & Boys except John & 3
men which I shall put to open
out Robson's Level

I quite agree in your conclusion
of stopping all work except Robson's
I only wish this day was over as
the men do not know before
I come from Bank

I shall keep 3 best men
& the amount to pay the other
men's back time is £7-19

Yours Obediently

William Dixon

Letter from Wm Dixon regarding the dismissing of the men 1876. Courtesy of C R O.

produced 3 tons of wad. Mr Barrett left in what appeared to be a satisfied mood, however this speculation was soon to change for the worse and the mercurial business of mining took another bitter twist.

By the end of June, the company seemed to run into more difficulties, for in a letter from Mr Salmon, William Dixon was instructed to lay off most of the men and enclosed with the letter was a cheque for the wages of £73 13s 0d. William set off to the bank in Keswick with a heavy heart, and whilst on the journey he brooded over the nine men and boys he had to sack. On his return to the mine, William summoned the men one by one to his office where he gave each man his back pay of £7 19s 0d, and within the hour his workforce consisted of only his son and three men. This had been an awful day as these men were not only reliable and trustworthy, they were his neighbours and friends. Dejectedly, he sat at his desk to write and confirm that the men had been dismissed and that there were enough casks of powder for the present. William's wage for all this misery was a monthly £8 0s 0d plus £1 7s 6d to visit the Glenderaterra mine every four weeks.

Apparently the company had decided to concentrate all their efforts on Robsons Level, as virtually all the workable wad from other areas had now been removed. In anticipation of the success of Robsons Level, a new mill was planned to be constructed near the old ford and bridge. At present, the bridge was in total disrepair and two large millstones complete with iron fixings were lying on the river bank as it was impossible to get them any further.

By March 1877 however, it was obvious that things were going very badly wrong indeed, and even the company's headed note-paper was all gone and had not been replaced. Then, on the 23rd of March William Dixon was asked by Mr Barratt to accept a reduction of his wages to £1 0s 0d per week. Poor William could do little but accept as his only other income was £2 16s 0d a year from a grass letting. The mine was now at a standstill, and this situation was to continue for the next two years. By January 1879, the creditors were knocking at the door. The blacksmith's bill was long overdue as was the joiner's account for repairs to a cart broken two years previously, while carting heavy timber to the mine. William had had to borrow a cart ever since. In order to keep expenses down, he managed to sell 80 feet of timber to Abbotts, a local merchant and cleared the joiners invoice by giving him 39 feet of timber in lieu, this being surplus to requirements. Things were looking grim and little or no interest had been shown in the mine. This was starting to fall into dereliction and the buildings, now left open to wild and tempestuous weather on that high, bleak fell were gradually being ravaged and destroyed.

In Keswick, the Greta Bridge Mills were taken over by Hogarth and Hayes during 1880 and by 1884 only three mills were operating in Keswick: Banks and Co, A Wren and Co and Hogarth and Hayes. These three employed about 100 men and women between them and at that time the average wages were

25/- for men and 12/- for women. Nothing was wasted from the factories, spare wood being sold to Thomas G Newby, 34 Main Street and John Tangye of 115 Main Street, Keswick who made toys and souvenirs. Even the cedar wood sawdust was re-cycled and sold to a soap company, presumably for scenting.

In 1886, Hogarth and Hayes took over the Abraham Wren company and following this, a new company was established, that of Mrs Ann Banks and Co at Greta Bridge. This new firm had apparently no connection at all with the other Banks company, and having immediately installed the most up to date machinery, then boldly advertised that only 'Genuine Borrowdale Black Lead' was used in their product. Their supplies of wad had been purchased from Professor Brockedon of London who was evidently now the sole distributor.

17 *One Last Go*

The Borrowdale Plumbago Mines and Manufacturing Co Ltd, continued under a new Board of Directors comprising Sir Charles Clifford, Lt Col Feilden, John Harrison and A R Robertson. The agreement was signed on the 12th of January 1887 and the purchase price was to be £7,750 plus the purchase of 37,250 fully paid up shares and a dead rent of £100 rising to £300 a year. The royalty was one tenth for all wad and one twelfth for other minerals and the lease had 34 years to run.

This company had a whole new concept in mind. Pencils were an absolute necessity and could easily be manufactured and sold for between two guineas and £2 8s 0d a gross, but wad had now become a useful commodity in other fields, and the company were intent on diversifying. It proposed to manufacture blacking for grates etc, crucibles, paint, plumbago lubricant and other products.

To accommodate the venture, a mill and blacksmiths shop were erected at OD 440 feet by the river near the ford and bridge, just below and to the south of Robsons level. Here a large shed was constructed with a concrete base which would house the crusher, and power for this was provided by a large overshot waterwheel. To ensure a steady head of water for the wheel, wooden troughs on trestles were erected to launder the water from Sour Milk Gill and as a back up, a leat was cut and water brought from Wadhole Gill. It is thought that the wad once sorted and ground was to be stored in a rented barn at Seathwaite just as it had been all those years ago.

Once again however, the mining operation was in trouble when in September 1887, a letter was received from Dibb and Co, Solicitors of Leeds conveying the information that the new mill and waterwheel were actually on land not owned by the mining company. The land was in fact, the property Jopsons High Bank owned by Mr John Marshall of Derwent Isle and tenanted by a Mr Richardson. The mine manager was now one Henry Vercoe, late of Brandlehow Mine, an entrepreneur in his own right and a very capable miner of many years experience in the Lake District, and it was he who took up the struggle on behalf of the company. The wrangling was still going on in June 1888 when he received a letter from Mr Marshall expressing his concern regarding the "dangerous state of the waterwheel etc", and requesting that this and other erections on the site be removed altogether. Seemingly unperturbed by these problems, the company carried on with its venture, and the main objective of pushing forward Robsons Level was partially achieved. The level was cleared and secured for 500 yards and railed out with bridge rail, but the vital rise up into the heart of the mine and through into Hastings Sump was never completed. It is shown on some plans that a large sump was cut in the sole of Robsons Level, however in all the documentation researched there is no mention of this work actually being carried out. What is also puzzling is why a development drive of the scale and importance of Robsons should be diversified into a sinking in the sole, thus creating an extra de-watering problem. Also, assuming no further work had been done, they would still have only been 168 feet from making the connection with Gilberts, which was of course the reason for the drive. This would also have allowed them to explore and develop this new area of ground. The sinking in the sole may have been done in the final years but I would state again this is not reported in any of the company documents.

Graphite was now in very short supply and although there were still reserves in the warehouses, a final effort was made on the main crosscuts of Gilberts, Fareys and Gills. The miners were once again sent to work in the places they had worked and re-worked, lifting rocks and backfill which had now been gone through time and again. Back they went to the old haunts of Gortons, Verdons, Rhodes, Dixons, Grisedales, Winkles and Charltons. Some wad was found but this could only be described as rubbish, and it was beginning to look as though this was the end of the road. Whilst the miners toiled dejectedly away under the management of Henry Vercoe, the legal pursuits were still continuing, but it seems that the company finally decided enough was enough. Wad was still proving elusive and so at 11 am on the 16th of June 1891, Company Chairman J S Sawrey called an extraordinary meeting in room 470, 20 Bucklersbury, London and the Company Secretary wound up the business.

That was the end of wad mining in the Lake District, but the story does not end there, for the pencil industry continued to survive in Keswick. By this time, Banks and Co had been owned and very successfully run for some years by Miss Gibson. In 1906, she decided to sell the company to her factory manager Henry Birbeck, and during this period there was a complete change in the manufacture of pencils. It seems that stocks of the Borrowdale wad must by this time have been exhausted, as graphite was being imported from countries as far away as Korea, Ceylon and Mexico and instead of being pure, it was now mixed with a special clay.

The pencil trade in 1910 still had three independent mills in Keswick, Hogarth and Hayes of Southey Hill, the Cumberland Pencil Co owned by C Greenwood which was in Ann Banks' former mill by Greta Bridge, and Banks & Co with Birbecks as the proprietors at Forge Mill. This last company continued to trade under Simon Birbeck until 1928 when the firm closed down. The last surviving company is the very successful Cumberland Pencil Company still on its old site at Greta Bridge. From its humble beginnings nearly two centuries ago, the pencil making business still thrives in Keswick and employs some 100 people. From the discovery of that first gleaming, grey wad by those illiterate shepherds back in the dark mists of time, evolved an industry of mining and manufacturing unique to the area and the envy of the world

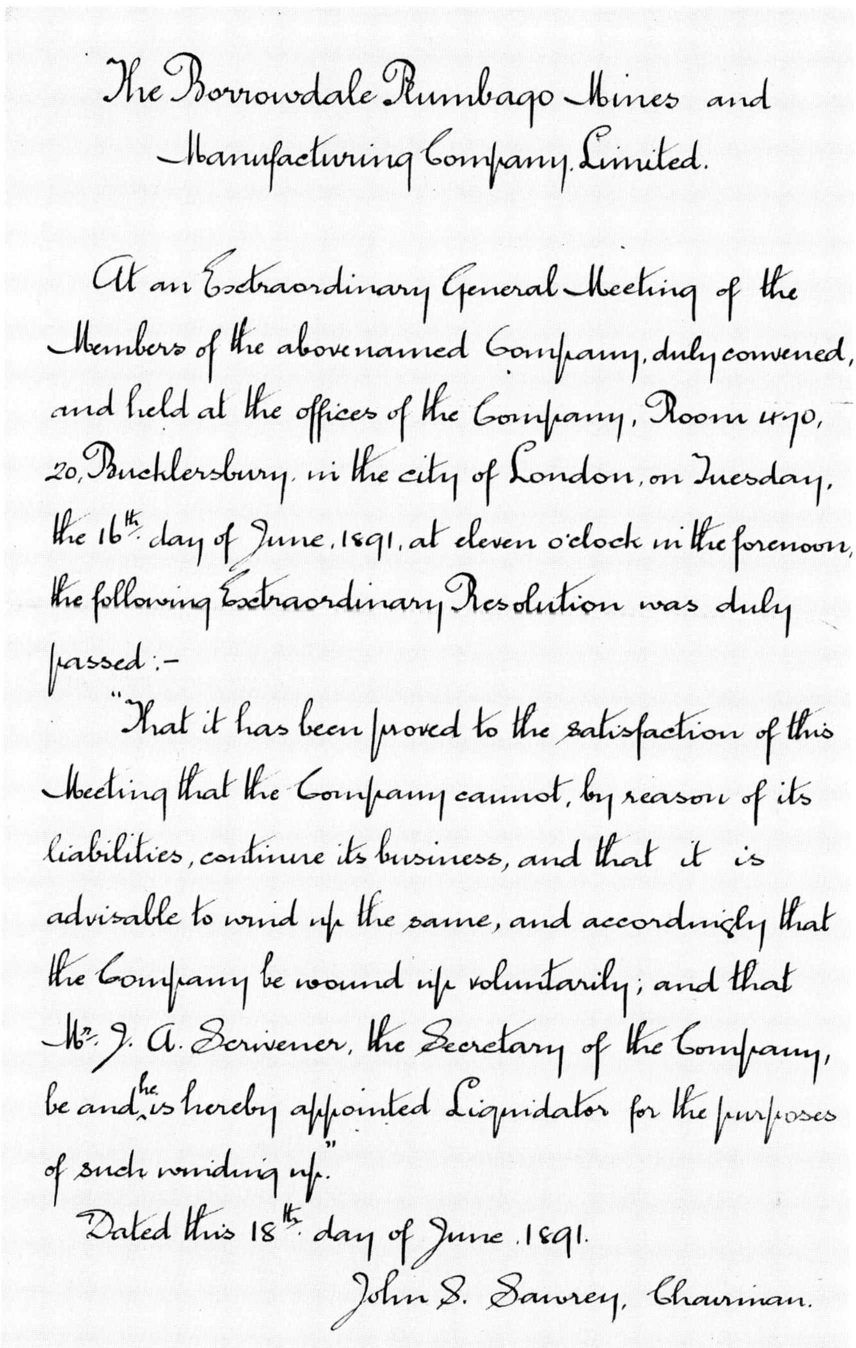

The Borrowdale Plumbago Mines and Manufacturing Company Limited.

At an Extraordinary General Meeting of the Members of the abovenamed Company, duly convened, and held at the offices of the Company, Room 470, 20, Bucklersbury, in the city of London, on Tuesday, the 16th day of June, 1891, at eleven o'clock in the forenoon, the following Extraordinary Resolution was duly passed:-

"That it has been proved to the satisfaction of this Meeting that the Company cannot, by reason of its liabilities, continue its business, and that it is advisable to wind up the same, and accordingly that the Company be wound up voluntarily; and that Mr. J. A. Scrivener, the Secretary of the Company, be and he is hereby appointed Liquidator for the purposes of such winding up."

Dated this 18th day of June 1891.

John S. Sawrey, Chairman.

Out To Day

.........wet, bedraggled and tired, we emerged from the adit entrance into the ruined remains of Gilberts House. We had commenced at Gills Stage and descended through the mine, down the famous Grisedales Pipe onto Fareys Stage, down the Grand Pipe to the Old Mens Stage, from here round the bye-pass level via Waltons Stage to Dixons Pipe and down, down, down through Ridgeways, Temperleys, Gregorys, Whitridges, Hursts, Fredricks and finally Gilberts. We had passed through hundreds of years of history and seen at first hand the tremendous complications of this unique mine, and what obvious frustrations the miners suffered by the dozens of insignificant short drives into barren areas. The thought of descending those many hundreds of back-breaking feet with the heavy wad bags tugging at the shoulders, makes one really appreciate how fit and tough those miners must have been.

Behind are the huge mounds of purply-shaded spoil, radiating across the fell and revealing the positions of the various adits and dressing floors. The pony track can be seen, zigzagging its relentless way up to the high workings, and just behind the house is the boundary stone erected in 1752 although sadly, someone has managed to damage this in the last few years.

Looking down from Gilberts mine hillock, Robsons Stage, the last major working can be clearly seen though it is now partially hidden in the trees. Below and across the river Derwent are the terraced houses at Seathwaite, once occupied by the Jopsons and now home to the Edmondson family (who are descended from the very old Birketts) with behind, Beck House, built for the occupation of mine manager William Dixon. Nestling in the trees beyond is High House where old wad miner Joseph Glover lived.

The valley is unchanged, the enduring mountains embracing the small hamlet still, as they have done for all those years. Few visitors know of the existence here of wad and the untold wealth that it created for generation after generation, in possibly the most beautiful, wild and romantic place in the Lake District........ we hope that you are now wiser.

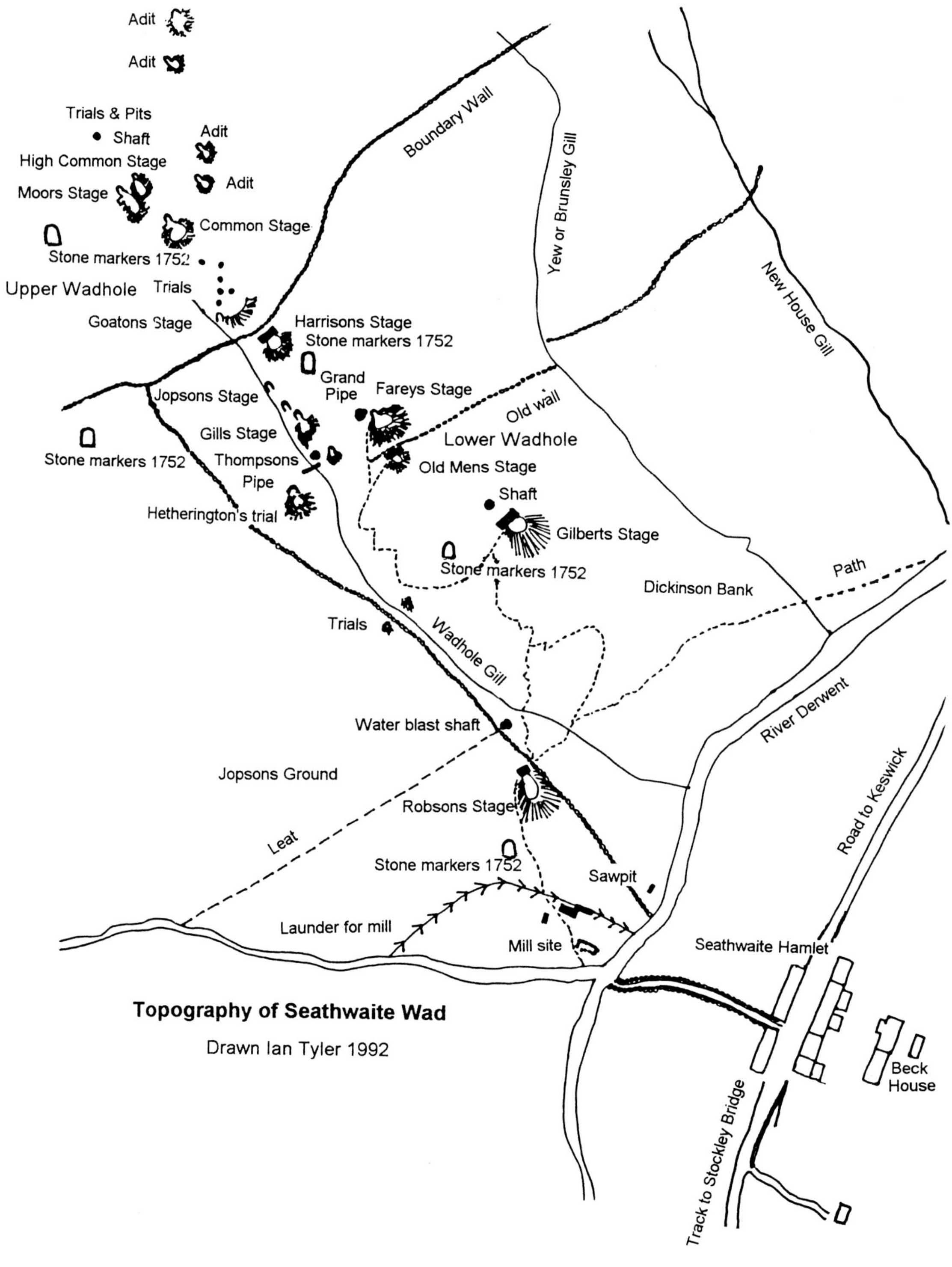

Topography of Seathwaite Wad

Drawn Ian Tyler 1992

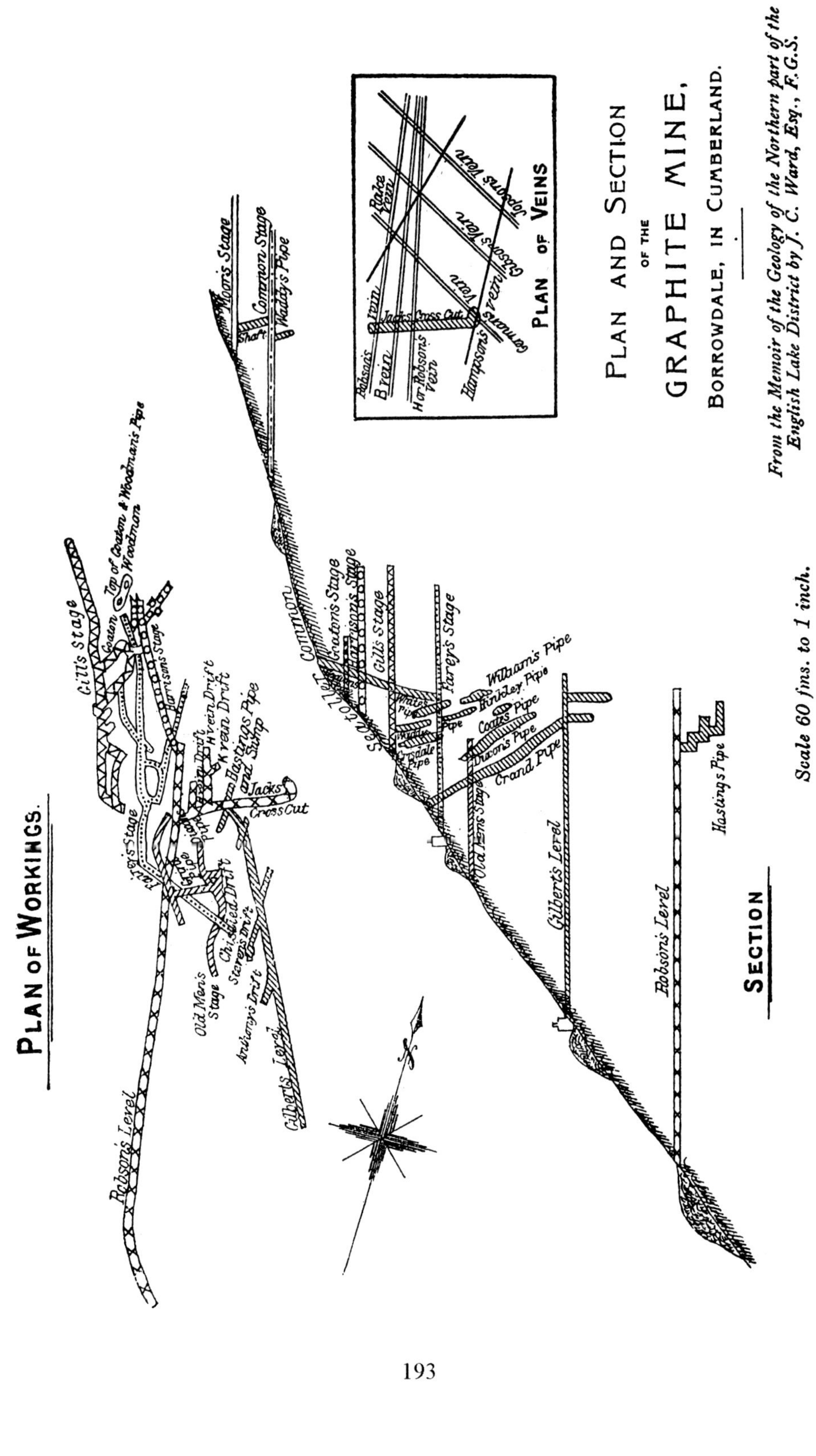

Plan of Workings.
Section
Plan of Veins
Plan and Section of the Graphite Mine, Borrowdale, in Cumberland.
From the Memoir of the Geology of the Northern part of the English Lake District by J. C. Ward, Esq., F.G.S.
Scale 60 fms. to 1 inch.
Robson's Level
Gilbert's Level
Hastings Pipe
Common Level
Gill's Stage
Farey's Stage
Old Men's Stage
Moar's Stage
Common Stage
Waddy's Pipe
Shaft
William's Pipe
Grand Pipe
Jack's Cross Cut
Hampson's Vein
Gibson's Vein
Rake Vein

Seathwaite Mine

Robsons Stage

Surveyed I Hebson, drawn I Tyler. 1995

Scale: 1/32nd = 1 yard

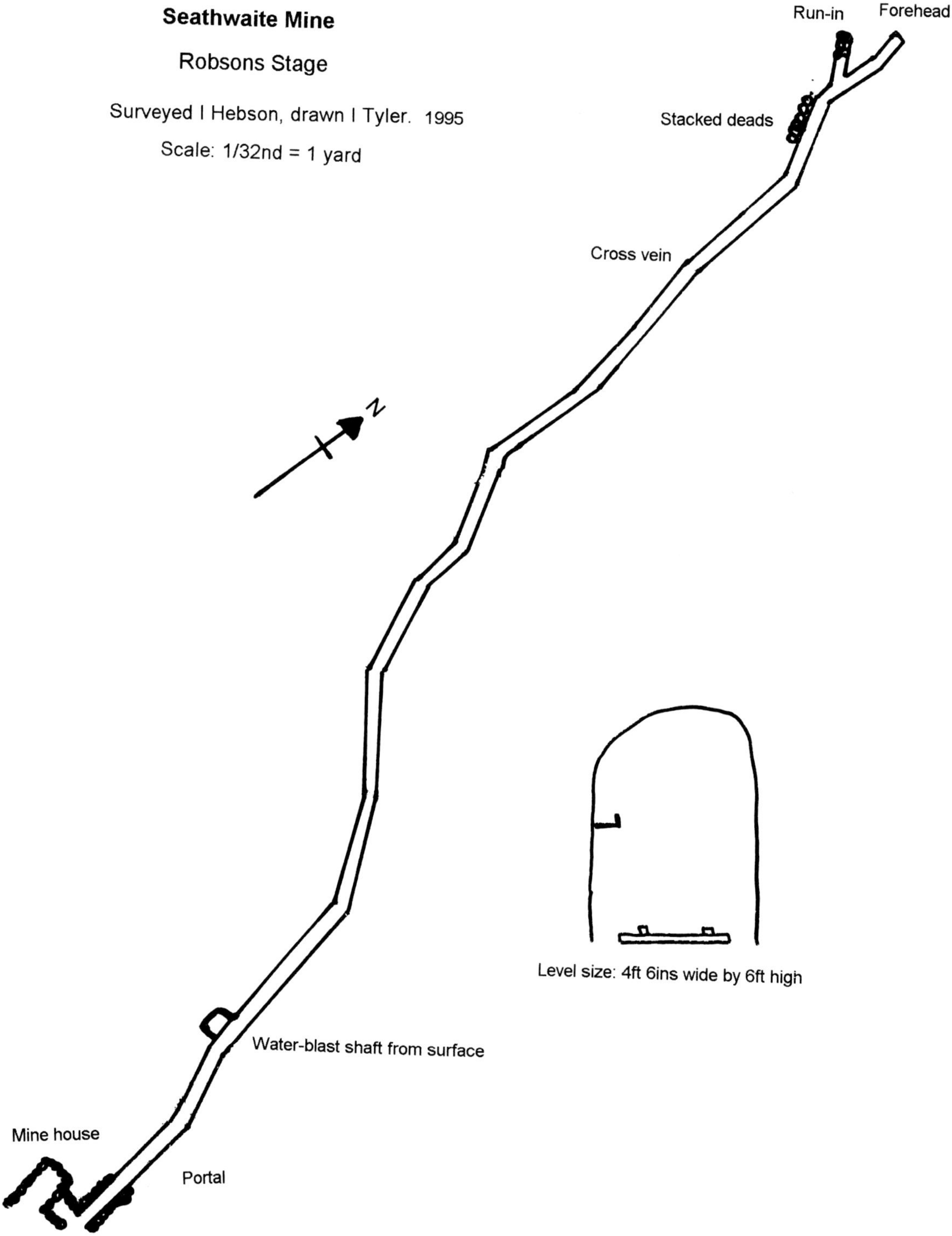

Level size: 4ft 6ins wide by 6ft high

Section Seathwaite Wad Mine between the Old Mens Stage and Gilberts Stage

Drawn by Ian Tyler 1994
Height span between Gilberts - Old Mens 200 ft

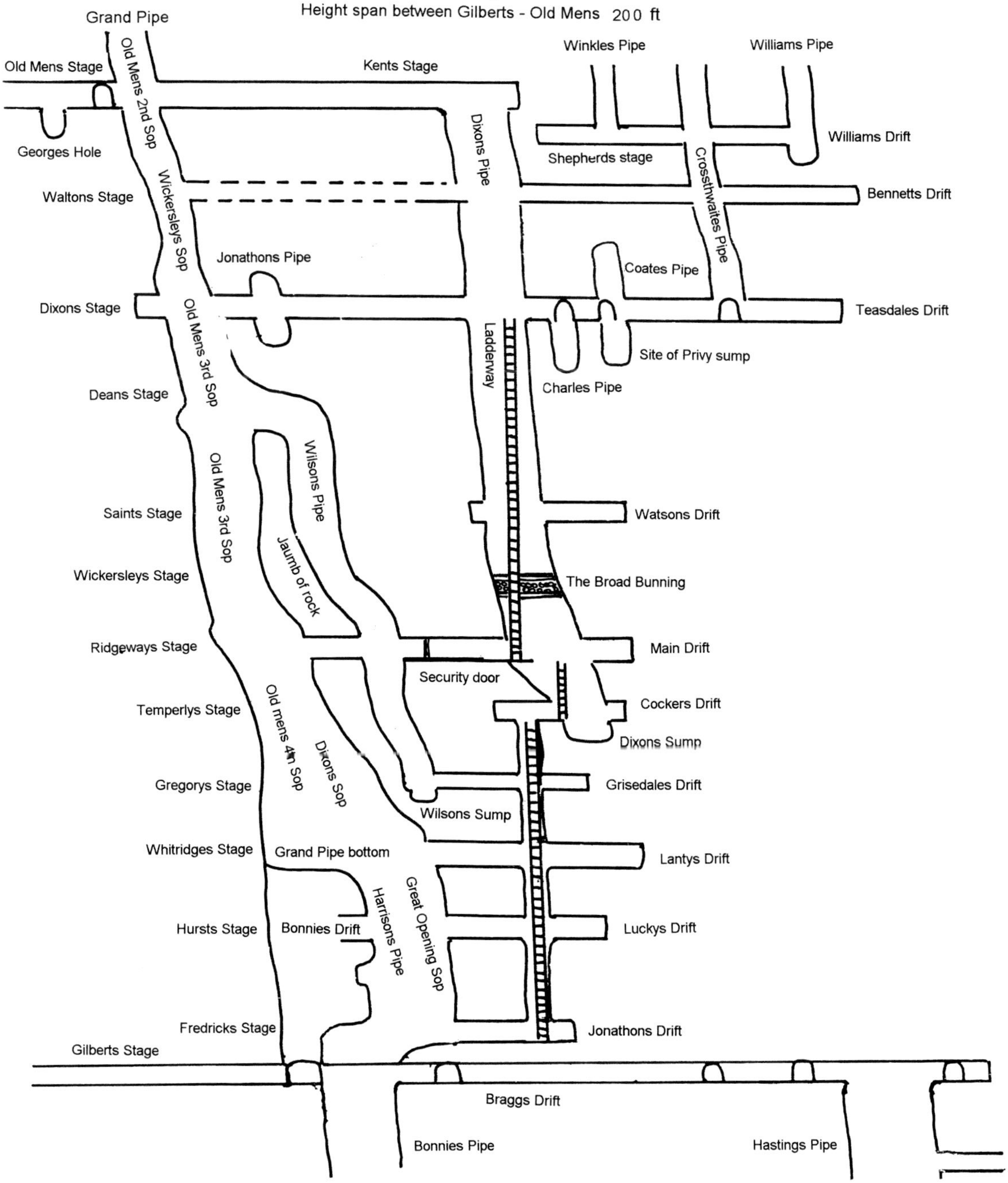

Seathwaite Wad Mine   Harrisons Stage house

Surveyed Ian Tyler, Pete Blezard 1994

Scale 1/16th inch = 1 foot

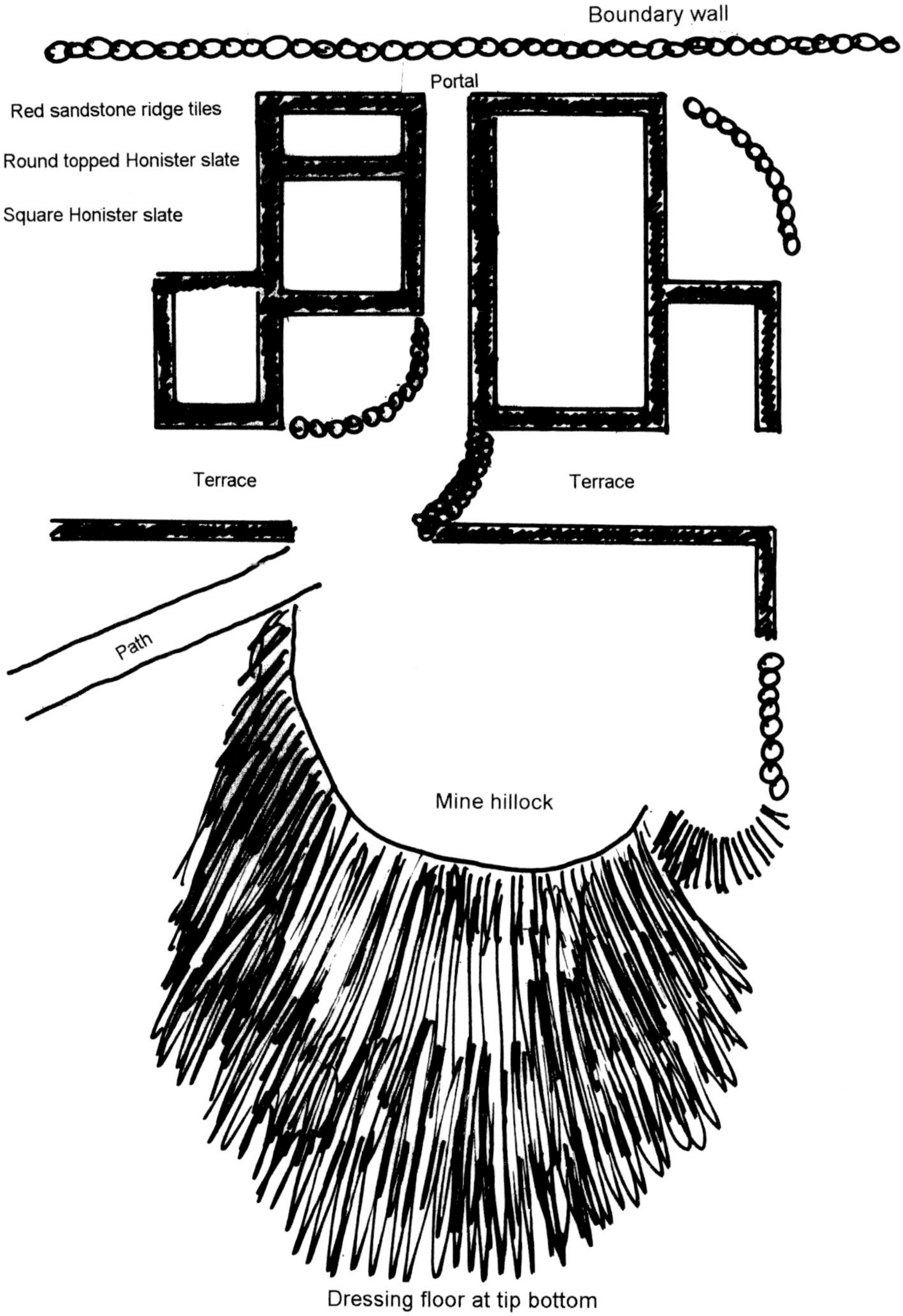

Seathwaite Wad Mine   Robsons Level house

Surveyed Ian Tyler, Pete Blezard 1994.

Scale 1/16th inch = 1 foot

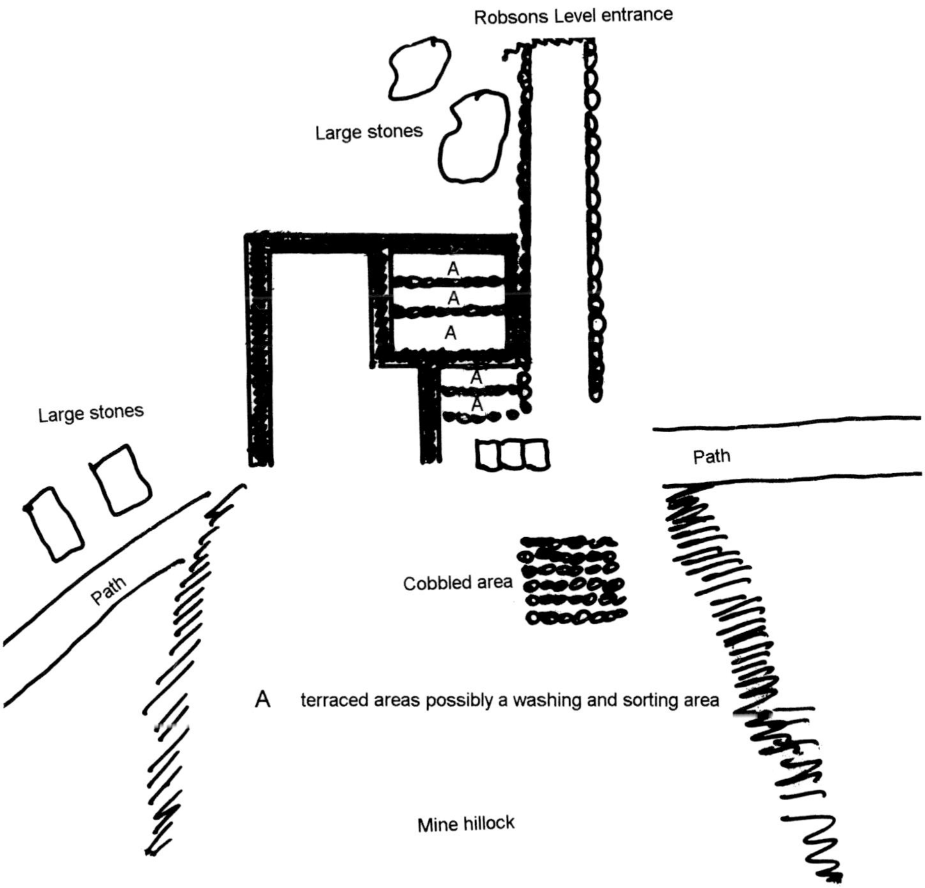

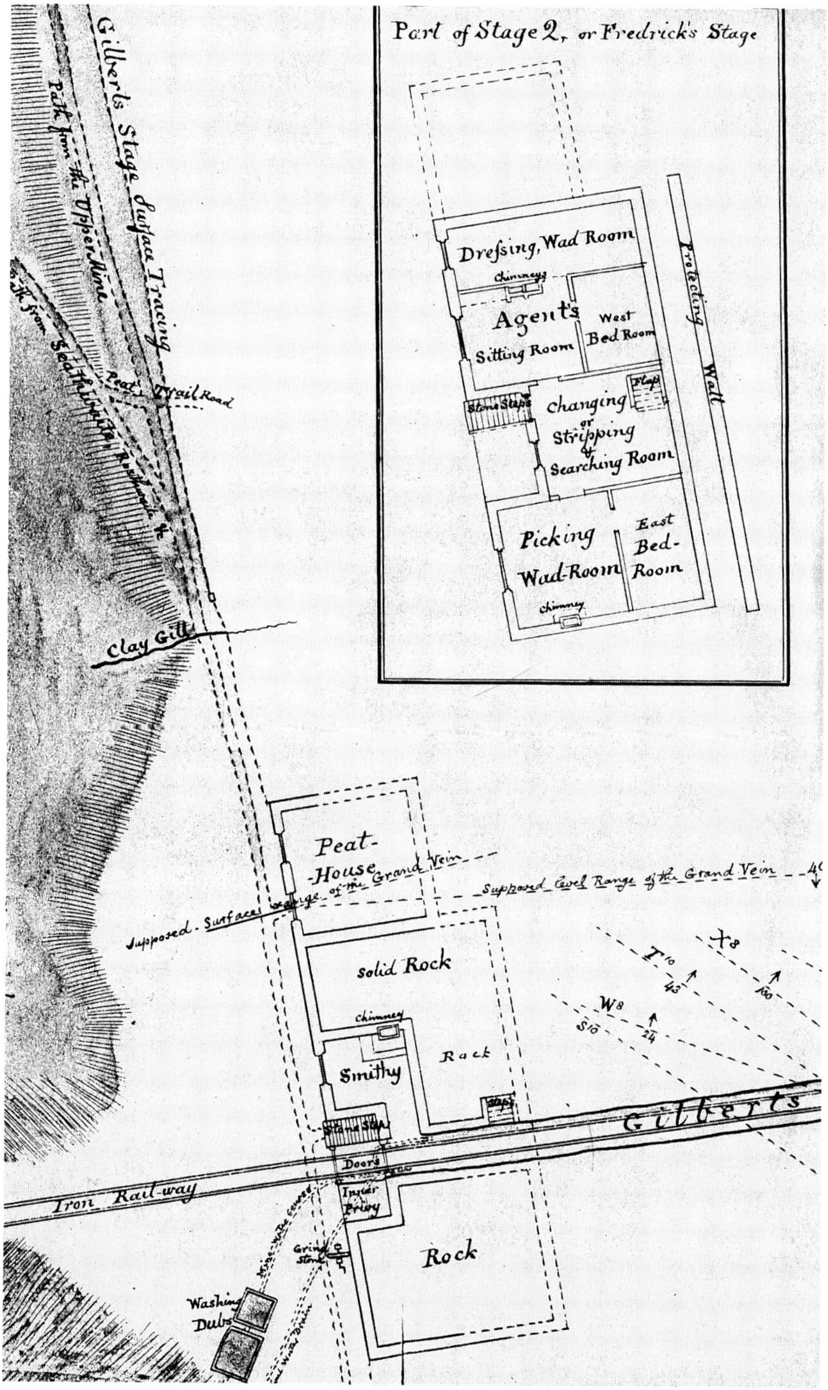

Gilberts Level house. Plans of upper and lower floors drawn by John Farey circa 1818. Caldbeck Mining Museum Collection.

Gilberts Level house circa 1850. Caldbeck Mining Museum Collection.

Topography of the Wad Mine

Top Workings Above the Wall - High Wadhole Close

Ordnance Datum	
1510ft	Trial
1500ft	*Adit with hut
1465ft	Adit with hut
1455ft	Pit
1480ft	Adit
1480ft	Area of surface trials
1470ft	Very old shaft working
1465ft	Adit
1465ft	Adit
1465ft	Adit
1465ft	Very old bell pit shaft
1470ft	High Stage
1460ft	Moors Stage...connects to Common Stage by unnamed shaft
1455ft	Shaft working
1455ft	Adit
1450ft	Adit
1445ft	Adit
1445ft	*Adit
1440ft	Adit
1420ft	Common Stage...Waddys Pipe
1410ft	Surface trials
1360ft	High Shaft
1360ft	Old Shaft
1355ft	Adit with hut
1355ft	New Shaft
1350ft	Surface trial and hush
1350ft	Wilgoose Shaft
1330ft	Hetheringtons Shaft
1320ft	Goatons Shaft (area all collapsed)
1320ft	Surface trials (area of surface collapse)
1300ft	Goatons Stage...bisected by Goatons Pipe-Wilgoose Pipe-Hetheringtons Shaft-Bowes Shaft.

The workings above this point are numerous and too close together for a detailed and accurate survey, consequently all are not listed.

* Open flooded levels.

Workings Below the Wall - Low Wadhole Close

Ordnance Datum	
1260ft	Harrisons Stage...bisected by Goatons Pipe
1230ft	Trial beside the gill
1220ft	Jopsons Level
1210ft	Gills Stage...bisected by Waddys Pipe-Goatons Pipe-Woodmans Pipe
1210ft	Gills Stage first trial
1200ft	Old hand dressing floor for Gills and Harrisons
1190ft	Top of Thompsons Pipe in Gill side
1160ft	New Level trial in Gill side
1140ft	Hetheringtons trial
1100ft	Grand Pipe at surface
1065ft	Fareys Stage...bisected by the Grand Pipe-Thompsons Pipe-Stuarts Pipe-Winkles Pipe-Grisedales Pipe
1030ft	New Level trial in the Gill side
1030ft	Old hand dressing floor
1010ft	Old Mens Stage...bisected by Georges Hole-the Grand Pipe-Dixons Pipe-Crossthwaites Pipe
850ft	Trial pits
830ft	Gilberts Stage. air shaft
810ft	Gilberts Stage...Anthonys Drift, Stephens Drift, intersected by the Grand Pipe-Benjamins Pipe-Hastings Pipe
570ft	Robsons Stage. Air shaft
540ft	Robsons Stage. Hastings Pipe in the sole? Jacks Crosscut
440ft	Seathwaite dressing mill
421ft	Seathwaite hamlet

The main stages listed here are the levels coming out to day, also indicated are the main pipes which these drives intersected.

Wad Mine Stages Looking South-North

STAGE	FT	DAY/INT	MAIN PIPE	CIRCA
HARRISONS	1260	DAY LEVEL	GORTONS	1791
GILLS	1210	DAY LEVEL	GORTONS	1830
			WOODMANS	1830
CHARLTONS	1150	INTERNAL	GRISEDALES	1814
RHODES	1120	INTERNAL	STUARTS	1820
			GRISEDALES	1814
BILLS	1100	DAY SHAFT	GRAND PIPE HEAD	1560?
BILLS		INTERNAL	THOMPSONS	1820
BILLS		INTERNAL	STUARTS	1820
			GRISEDALES	1814
FAREYS *	1065	DAY LEVEL	GRAND-OLD MENS	
			FIRST	1600?
			THOMPSONS	1820
			STUARTS	1820
			WINKLES	1812
			GRISEDALES	1814
WHITMORES	1060	INTERNAL	GRAND-OLD MENS	
			SECOND	1610?
WHITMORES		INTERNAL	WINKLES	1812
VERDONS	1055	INTERNAL	GRAND-OLD MENS	
			SECOND	1610?
VERDONS		INTERNAL	WINKLES	1812
			WILLIAMS	1814
BANKES	1040	INTERNAL	GRAND-OLD MENS	
			SECOND	1610?
BANKES		INTERNAL	WINKLES	1812
			WILLIAMS	1815
			TEASDALES	1816
PERROTS	1030	INTERNAL	GRAND-OLD MENS	
			SECOND	1610?
PERROTS		INTERNAL	WINKLES	1812

STAGE	FT	DAY/INT	MAIN PIPE	CIRCA
PERROTS		INTERNAL	WILLIAMS	1814
PERROTS		INTERNAL	CROSSTHWAITES	1810
NORMANS	1020	INTERNAL	GRAND-OLD MENS SECOND	1610?
NORMANS		INTERNAL	DIXONS	1803
NORMANS		INTERNAL	WINKLES WILLIAMS	1812 1814
NORMANS		INTERNAL	CROSSTHWAITES	1810
OLD MENS**	1010	DAY LEVEL	GEORGES GRAND-OLD MENS THIRD DIXONS	1778 1630 1803
OLD MENS		INTERNAL	WINKLES	1812
OLD MENS		INTERNAL	WILLIAMS	1814
OLD MENS		INTERNAL	CROSSTHWAITES	1810
SHEPHERDS	1000	INTERNAL	GRAND-OLD MENS THIRD GRAND-WICKERSLEYS	1750 (RW) 1769
SHEPHERDS		INTERNAL	DIXONS	1803
SHEPHERDS		INTERNAL	WINKLES	1812
SHEPHERDS		INTERNAL	CROSSTHWAITES	1810
SHEPHERDS		INTERNAL	WILLIAMS	1814
WALTONS	990	INTERNAL	GRAND-OLD MENS THIRD GRAND-WICKERSLEYS DIXONS WINKLES BARBOURS CROSSTHWAITES	1750 (RW) 1769 1803 1812 1812 1810
DIXONS	960	INTERNAL	GRAND-OLD MENS THIRD	1750 (RW)

STAGE	FT	DAY/INT	MAIN PIPE	CIRCA
			JONATHONS	1810
			DIXONS	1800-03
			CROSSTHWAITES	1810
			WICKERLEYS	1769
			COATES	1814
DEANS	940	INTERNAL	GRAND-OLD MENS THIRD	1750 (RW)
			WILSONS	1802
DEANS		INTERNAL	DIXONS	1803
SAINTS	920	INTERNAL	GRAND-OLD MENS THIRD	1750 (RW)
			WILSONS	1802
SAINTS		INTERNAL	DIXONS	1803
WICKERSLEYS	910	INTERNAL	GRAND-OLD MENS THIRD	1750 (RW)
			WILSONS	1802
WICKERSLEYS		INTERNAL	DIXONS	1803
RIDGEWAYS	900	INTERNAL	GRAND-OLD MENS THIRD	1750 (RW)
			WILSONS	1802
			DIXONS	1803
TEMPERLEYS	890	INTERNAL	GRAND-OLD MENS FOURTH	1769 (RW)
			GRAND-DIXONS	1803
TEMPERLEYS		INTERNAL	WILSONS	1802
TEMPERLEYS		INTERNAL	DIXONS	1803
GREGORYS	880	INTERNAL	GRAND-OLD MENS FOURTH	1769 (RW)
			GRAND-DIXONS	1803
GREGORYS		INTERNAL	WILSONS	1802

STAGE	**FT**	**DAY/INT**	**MAIN PIPE**	**CIRCA**
WHITRIDGES	**860**	**INTERNAL**	**GRAND-GREAT OPENING**	**1778 (RW)**
			HARRISONS	**1778**
HURSTS	**845**	**INTERNAL**	**GRAND-GREAT OPENING**	**1778 (RW)**
			HARRISONS	**1778**
FREDRICKS	**825**	**INTERNAL**	**GRAND-GREAT OPENING**	**1778 (RW)**
			HARRISONS	**1778**
GILBERTS	**810**	**DAY LEVEL**	**BENJAMINS HASTINGS**	**1800**
ROBSONS	**540**	**DAY LEVEL**	**HASTINGS**	?

(RW) = REWORKED

The stages were horizontal drifts connecting the various pipes, consequently there could be two stages called "bankes stage" in a completely different part of the mine and not connected but at the same horizon.

Circa the date shown is the earliest date recorded, however in many cases the workings were re-named during the 1818-1821 survey. Consequently it would be fair to assume they were worked at an earlier date and this has been indicated thus "?"

* Also known as Daniels or Roberts Drift

** Also known as Kents or Main Drift

Miners at the Wad Mine

1541	Ambrose Dormer	Owner
1606	Edward Boraston	Owner/Miner
1606	Thomas Fanshaw	Owner/Miner
1607	Daniel Hechstetter	Owner
1607	Emanuel Hechstetter	Owner
1607	Joseph Hechstetter	Owner
1619	Thomas Kalcher	Miner
1619	Anthony Teyller	Dresser
1619	Martin Zuckmantell	Dresser
1622	Sir John Bankes	Owner
1622	William Lamplugh	Owner
1622	Charles Hudson	Owner
1622	Ralph Hawtrey	Owner
1622	John Williamson	Owner
1622	John Masefield	Owner
1622	Francis Hechstetter	Owner
1630	John Birkett	Owner
1630	Gawen Helm	Owner
1632	Robert Jopson	Owner
1632	William Braithwaite	Owner
1644	Sir Ralph Bankes	Owner
1656	John Jopson	Owner
1661	Roger Griggs	Agent
1667	John Hudson	Owner
1678	John Bankes	Owner
1678	Joseph Beck	Agent
1697	John Shepherd	Owner
1718	Gorton	Miner
1718	Gorton	Miner
1735	William Shepherd	Owner
1736	Hugh Workman	Miner
1736	William Hetherington	Miner
1739	W Davis	
1739	John Martin	Miner
1739	Charles Bowman	Miner
1739	John White	Miner
1745	James Bowes	Agent
1745	Gowan Youdale	Agent
1748	Robert Hetherington	Miner
1748	Nicholas Little	Miner
1751	J Mackentire	
1752	John Sharpe	Agent
1752	Mr Littledale	Agent
1752	John Braithwaite	Owner

1752	Mr Simpson	Agent
1752	James Spedding	Agent
1752	Spedding Jnr	
1752	Mr Dawson	
1752	Mr Scott	
1752	Samuel Levie	
1755	D Hamilton	
1758	William Bankes	Owner
1758	Robert Banks Hodgkinson	Owner
1758	John Rhoydes	Owner
1758	George Perrott	Owner
1758	Thomas Lloyd	Owner
1758	Daniel Fox	Owner
1758	Gascoigne Fredrick	Owner
1758	Robert Bill	Owner
1758	Charles Bill	Owner
1758	Rev John Bill	Owner
1758	William Bill	Owner
1758	Thomas Gilbert	Agent
1758	John Gilbert	Miner
1765	John Wilgoose	Agent
1765	John Hodgson	Assistant Agent
1765	Caleb Fisher	Assistant Agent
1768	John Wilson	Guard
1769	Henry Bragg	Guard
1769	George Frear	Guard
1769	Robert Beck	Guard
1769	Joseph Key	Guard
1769	John Grave	Miner
1769	Edward Birkett	Miner
1769	William Tyson	Miner
1769	John Tyson	Guard
1769	Jonathon Jopson	Guard
1769	William Jopson	Guard
1769	Robert Thursby	Guard
1769	John Bushby	Guard
1769	Benjamin Taylor	Guard
1769	Thomas Holmes	Guard
1769	Thomas Lloyd	Agent
1769	John Wren	Agent
1769	Thomas Green Snr	Guard
1769	Thomas Green Jnr	Guard
1769	John Bush	Guard
1769	George Ramsey	Guard
1769	Benjamin Taylor	Guard
1769	William Wakerley	Agent

1769	John Birkett	Dresser
1769	Francis Bill	Agent
1769	John Greenup	Miner
1769	Samuel Matthew	Miner
1769	Thomas Flint	Miner
1769	Joseph Brown	Miner
1769	John Gibson	Miner
1769	Edward Watson	Labourer
1769	Isaac Rumley	Miner
1769	Joseph Bownas	Miner
1769	Henry Wren	Miner
1769	John Sheldon	Labourer
1769	John Youdale	Miner
1769	Thomas Johnson	Labourer
1769	Joseph Workman	Miner
1769	Robert Smith	Miner
1769	Henry Rigg	Labourer
1769	Thomas Dixon	Steward
1769	John Dixon	Miner
1769	William Dixon Jnr	Dresser
1769	Simon Graham	Labourer
1769	Crispian Pharoah	Labourer
1769	Isaac Tyson	Smithy
1769	William Allen	Steward
1769	Charles Norman	Steward
1769	John Wren	Steward
1769	Robert Jopson	Freeholder
1769	Mr Langholm	Freeholder
1769	Joseph Fisher	Freeholder
1769	John Braithwaite	Freeholder
1769	Thomas Gatsgarth	Freeholder
1769	Joshua Scott	Freeholder
1769	John Hodgson	Freeholder
1769	Edward Watson	Labourer
1769	Matthias Vicars	Miner
1769	C Hudson	
1771	W Walker	
1777	Mr Miller	Miner
1777	W Woodwise	
1777	John Sharp	Agent
1778	John Wilson Harrison	Agent
1778	F Kent	Miner
1778	Thomas Kent	Miner/Surveyor
1778	Thomas Temperley	Miner/Surveyor
1778	Jonathon Jopson	Steward
1778	William Allen	Miner

1778	James Morris	Miller
1778	Joseph Bank	Miner
1778	Jonathon Hind	Miner
1778	Edward Watson	Miner
1778	John Fletcher	Miner
1778	George Tyson	Miner
1783	W Burrel	Labourer
1783	James Hurst	
1788	William Milnes	Agent
1788	J Wilson	Agent
1788	Jason Hurst	Agent
1788	Thomas Burry	Agent
1788	Benjamin Gregory	Agent
1789	John Harrison	Miner
1790	Jonathon Thompson	Quarryman
1791	Richard Dean	Miner
1791	Bill Dean	Miner
1791	J Furness	Miner
1791	William Charlton	Agent
1794	F Foulkes	Surveyor
1796	Joseph Saint	Agent
1796	Willy Woodman	Miner
1799	Joseph Bragg	Miner
1799	James Ferman	
1799	Anthony Wright	Miner
1799	M J Edmondson	
1800	T Workman	Miner
1800	Stephen Wright	Miner
1800	James Bennett	Miner
1800	John Leck	Miner
1800	John Wilson	Miner
1800	Ephraim Gregg	Miner
1800	John Dixon	Miner
1801	William Dixon Jnr	Dresser
1801	Betty Hunter	
1801	Robert Wilson	Miner
1801	Joseph Mawes	Miner
1801	John Dixon Jnr	Miner
1801	Lanty Dawson	Miner
1801	John Flash	
1801	John Leek	Miner
1801	Mary Dixon	
1801	John Mawes	
1801	M Watson	Miner
1801	J Nixon	
1801	J Hilton	

1801	John Plaskett	Miner
1801	John Simpson	
1801	Robert Watson	
1801	Robert Richardson	Miner
1802	Joshua Harris	Quarryman
1802	John Rawes	Miner
1802	J McKinney	
1802	Mr Fell	
1802	Thomas Taylor	
1802	J Edmondson	
1802	John Grisedale	Miner
1803	J Crossthwaite	Miner
1803	J Baines	
1803	Mark Ridgeway	Miner
1803	James Bennett	Miner
1810	Joseph Whitridge	Miner
1810	James Coates	Miner
1812	John Winkle	Agent
1812	Samuel Barber	Agent
1812	Mr Williams	
1818	Joseph Glover	Miner
1818	John Barron	Miner
1818	Edward Barron	Miner
1818	James Robinson	Miner
1821	Mr Mitford	Miner
1821	Mr Burry	Miner
1825	John Dixon	Miner
1825	William Thompson	Miner
1825	William Dixon Jnr	Miner
1825	James Robinson	Miner
1825	James Bennett	Miner
1825	Charles Stuart	Miner
1825	Matthew Coates	Miner
1826	William Birkett	Miner
1826	John Jackson	Labourer
1826	Joseph Jackson	Labourer
1837	Thomas Bennett	Miner
1837	John Dixon Snr	Superintendent
1837	John Dixon Jnr	Miner
1837	Daniel Dixon	Miner
1837	T Burrell	Miner
1837	Joseph Coates	Miner
1837	William Dixon Jnr	Smithy/Miner
1837	John Thompson	Smithy
1837	J Crossthwaite	Miner
1837	William Flemming	Trammer

1837	T Buckell	
1838	Thomas Birkett	Miner
1838	Isaac Bennett	Miner
1838	Mr Taylor	
1838	Adam Bird	Smithy
1847	John Robinson	Miner
1847	J Bowman	
1849	J Cross	
1849	John McGlasson	Miner
1859	William Dixon	Dresser
1859	Daniel Dixon	Miner
1859	John Coates	Miner
1859	Henry Dawson	Miner
1859	Wilson Dixon	
1859	J Coates Jnr	Miner
1859	John Plaskett	Miner
1859	William Brunskill	Miner
1859	Nathan Coates	Miner
1859	William Thompson	Trammer
1876	John Dixon	Agent
1876	William Jenkinson	Miner
1876	Thomas Edgar	Miner
1876	William Coates	Miner
1876	Wilson Tyson	Miner
1876	John Tyson	Miner
1876	Joseph Dover	Horseman/Miner
1876	Fletcher Wren	
1876	John Thwaite	
1876	Thomas Birkett	Dresser
1876	William Dixon	Dresser
1876	John Dixon	Dresser

All the names listed have been taken from official company records, but these are incomplete therefore it is not possible to ensure the whole of the workforce is listed. The earliest date has been recorded and of course many of the men were employed over many years. A problem also has been the fact that it was traditional for the father to name his first born with his Christian name.

Many of the agents were also competent miners and worked underground, also some of the miners were employed as guards and stayed overnight at the mine for extra pay.

Production Figures - Seathwaite

THE ACTUAL production figures are somewhat confusing, this has been due to the large amount of pilfering which continued through out the working period of the mine. Internally there were certainly some accounting errors, and during a period just prior to 1800 the accounts are missing which has helped to cloud the issue.

Another problem is that the wad was sold by quality in casks generally at so much per lb, however in the case of the lower grades these were sold at a special price per cask which bears no relation in value to the better grades. The original casks were small being old ale casks of the nine gallon size called a firkin and holding about 78 lb of wad. Around 1800, the casks became larger and weighed between 120 lb and 135 lb.

The wad produced at the mine was normally pre-sold and consigned to bonded warehouses virtually from the start of the mining operations. Large stockpiles were amassed underground to cover the closed periods when the wad was, in some cases, sold in a bonded time.

The production figures have been compiled from numerous sources and we have tried not to duplicate them. The weight produced and presumably sold is shown in pounds weight. It should also be noted that the price of wad fluctuated with the market of the day.

Over the years the various descriptions of wad produced changed thus making the comparisons of quality over the years impossible. Listed below are some of the names given to describe the various qualities or grades.

With regard to the locations for the wad being taken, the main pipe name has been used and not the individual sop, as some of the pipes were mined over many years and contained numerous sops.

YEAR	**CASKS**	**TYPE**	**LB**	**PRICE /LB**	**£ VALUE**	**LOCATION**
Cask weight 78 lb						
1597	200		15680		91	
1597	35		2800			
1607	1055		82880		1110	Grand Pipe
1607	1148		89600		1280	Grand Pipe
1619	143	Great	11200		135	Grand Pipe
1619	143	Small	11200		85	Grand Pipe
1619	143	Small	11200		85	Grand Pipe
1620	1148	Great	89600		1470	Grand Pipe
1620	574	Small	44800		85	Grand Pipe
1620	244		19040		36	Grand Pipe
1631	1148	Great	89600		1470	Grand Pipe

YEAR	CASKS	TYPE	LB	PRICE /LB	£ VALUE	LOCATION
1631	574	Small	44800			Grand Pipe
1631	14		1120		6	Grand Pipe
1642	574		44800			
1646	1435		112000			
1646	861		67200			
1655	1435	Superior	112000			
1655	488	Inferior	38080			
1663	172	Large	13440			
1663	258	Second	20160			
1663	516	Third	40320			
1663	947	Fourth	73920			
1663	114	Rough	8960			
1671	172	Large	13440			
1671	172	Second	13440			
1671	459	Third	35840			
1671	172	Fourth	13440			
1671	1435	Fifth	112000			
1678	1924		150080			Gortons
1715	1148		89600			
1735	27		2130			
1745	13		1014			Bowes
1760	201		15680			Gortons
1765	138		10810	10/6d	5675	Wilgoose
1765	24	Best	1872			Woodmans
1765	6	Coarse	468			Woodmans
1769	183	Best	14274			Wakerleys
1769	86	Inferior	6708			Wakerleys
1769	97	Inferior	7566			Wakerleys
1773	98	Inferior	7598			
1774	85	Best	6631			
1778	417		32526	30/-	43758	Great Opening
1792	5	Best	390			Deans
1792	7	Coarse	546			Deans
Cask weight 125 lb						
1800	109	Best	13883	30/-	20824	Grand Pipe
1802	395	Best	49465	30/-	74198	Wilsons/Dixons
Cask weight 135 lb						
1803	580		78726		11370	Ridgeways

YEAR	CASKS	TYPE	LB	PRICE /LB	£ VALUE	LOCATION
Cask weight 125 lb						
1808	105	Coarse	13125			Dixons
Cask weight 135 lb						
1809	37	Best	4940	25/-	6175	Barbours
1810	644	Inferior	87276			Ridgeways
1812	495	Inferior	66825			Winkles
Cask weight 120 lb						
1812	87	Best	10534	35/-		Winkles
1813	8	Best	965			Winkles
1813	89	Inferior	10680			Winkles
1813	2	Best	156			Watsons
1813	9	Coarse	1080			Watsons
1814	5	Best	600			Robinsons
1814	15	Best	1871			Coates
1815	117	Best	14170			Williams
1815	323	Inferior	38760			Williams
1815	2	Best	240			Stuarts
1815	65	Coarse	7800			Stuarts
Cask Weight 135lb						
1819	3	Best	405			Fareys
1819	7	Coarse	945			Fareys
1820	2	Best	270			Daniels
1820	7	Coarse	945			Daniels
1820	18	Best	2430			Grisedales
1820	268	Coarse	36180			Grisedales
1823	6	Coarse	810			Grand Pipe
1836	133	Best	17955			Gortons
1836	1360	Inferior	173600			Charltons?
1837	3		333			Harrisons
1838	3		435			Woodmans
1839	13		1734			Rhodes
1839	5		722			Fareys
1839	3		420			Waste Tips
1842	3		388			Rhodes
1846	2		248			
1847	5		720			Whitridges

YEAR	CASKS	TYPE	LB	PRICE /LB	£ VALUE	LOCATION
1847	3		399			
1847	6		809			
1848	2		206			
1848	10		1403			
1850	165	Rockrubbish	22400		100	
1850	1		41		41	
1859	3		448			Hastings
1859	1		59			
1861	14		1875			
1875	50		6720			
1876	6		750			

1891 Mine Closed.

The Keswick Pencil Makers

1800	John Ladyman
1800	John Airey
1800	Jacob Banks
1829	John Airey
1829	Jacob Banks
1829	John Ladyman
1829	John Scratchard
1829	William Robinson
1829	John Green
1829	John Foulke
1829	John Gates
1829	Christopher Wright
1829	Christopher Harrington
1829	William Atkinson
1829	John Harrison
1829	William Forster
1829	Joseph Graham
1832	Jacob Banks
1832	Abraham Wren
1832	Robert Coupland
1832	Hogarth & Hayes
1837	Abraham Wren
1837	Michael Falcon
1837	Henry Dodgson
1837	Robert Thwaite
1842	Robert Gibson
1851	John Airey
1851	App & Harrison
1851	William Guy
1851	Samuel Ladyman
1851	Henry Powley
1851	Jefferson, Thomson
1851	Abraham Wren
1851	Crossthwaites, Lancaster & Co
1854	Joseph Gatey
1854	John Dodgson
1854	John Hudson
1859	Samuel Ladyman
1861	R Wilson
1861	Miss Gibson
1887	Ann Banks
1906	Henry Birbeck
1910	C Greenwood
1928	Simon Birbeck

Glossary of Mining Terms

ADIT - A horizontal tunnel driven into the hillside for access to the vein or sop or to drain the mine.

AGENT - A title given to the day to day manager of the mine.

BACK-FILLING - Waste rock which is dumped into disused areas of the mine.

BAIT - Miner's lunch or break.

BARGAIN - An agreement reached by a group of men to do a particular job for an agreed amount of money over a set time.

BINDING - A false timber floor created across a shaft with rubble placed on top to prevent access.

BING - Unit of measurement - approx 896lb.

BLACK CAWKE - Another name for graphite.

BLACK LEAD - Another name for graphite.

BOTHY - Small hut on the fell where the miners would live.

BUCKING - A method of dressing wad with a flat hammer.

BUNNING - Waste material placed on top of the adit roof supports to prevent the surface debris covering the entrance.

CAPTAIN - A title given to the person in charge of the mine and the underground workings.

CLOG - Miner's footwear.

COFFIN LEVEL - A tunnel, coffin shaped in section dating from the Elizabethan period.

COMMON - An area of ground given to the local residents as their birthright for grazing their stock.

COPPER - A mineral.

CROSSCUT - A tunnel driven usually at right angles to strike the vein in the shortest distance.

COUNTRY ROCK - The rock of the area bearing the mineral vein or wad.

DAY - Underground term meaning outside ie out to day.

DEADS - Waste rock stacked neatly to support an area of the mine.

DIALLING - The art of taking bearings underground for surveying.

DRESSING - Part of the process of reducing the ore extracted from the mine to the size required.

DRIFT - A tunnel driven to gain access to the vein or sop.

FATHOM - A measured distance of six feet.

FIRKIN - A barrel or cask with the capacity for holding nine gallons of fluid.

GRAPHITE - The correct name for wad.

HORSE - A large jutting out wedge of rock.

HUSHING - An early method of exposing a surface vein by releasing a volume of water to remove the surface cover.

INSPECTOR - A title given to a manager of the mine.

JACK ROLL - A manpowered windlass for hauling or lowering kibbles in shafts or sumps.

JAUMB - As 'HORSE'

JUMPER - A hand-held drill steel.

KIBBLE - A large wooden or metal bucket used for lifting ore or water from shafts and sumps.

LEAD - A metal gained from the ore of galena. Graphite was referred to as Black Lead.

LEASE - A legal document agreeing the terms and conditions of the tenants.

LEAT - A channel cut into the fellside to carry water to waterwheels or dressing floors.

LEVEL - A tunnel driven to gain access to the mineralised area of the mine.

MELLING - Hammering down, crushing.

MINE HILLOCK - The waste heap out side the mine.

MOIETY - An area of ground which has been leased.

MUCKING OUT - Clearing out of rubbish after blasting or a fall.

NOGGER - A hand held drill steel.

NOG HOLE - The hole made by the nogger.

OLD MEN - Early miners, sometimes referred to as ancients.

PARTNERSHIP - A group of men headed by a spokesmen to arrange bargains.

PIPE - The name given to a wad sop normally of irregular shape and size.

PIPE DOWN - To extract the wad from the sop by working downwards.

PIPE UP - To extract wad from the sop by working upwards.

PLUMBAGO - Another name for graphite.

PRICKER - A copper or iron needle inserted through the packing in the shot-hole to insert the fuse.

RISE - A vertical shaft in the roof of the level, sometimes connecting to a higher level.

ROYALTY - An area of land determined by the lease, or a percentage payment demanded by the owner for the weight of mineral sold.

SETT - The area of land determined by the lease for the company to operate in.

SHAFT - A vertical or inclined tunnel either from the surface or within the mine used for access both up and down and for the transporting of materials or water for mine aeration (water blast shaft).

SKIRT - Edge of the vein visible in the level walls.

SLEDDING - A method of transferring materials down steep ground by hand, or being drawn across the fell by horse.

SOLE - The floor of the level.

SOP - The area or mass containing wad.

SPOIL - Rubbish which is taken out of the mine and dumped.

STAGE - A workplace or level in the mine of importance.

STEMMING - Waste material used to pack powder in the drill hole.

STEMPLE - A wooden support used in the roof or the sole of the level.

SUMP - A blind shaft in the sole of the level, sometimes cut to collect the mine water, thus preventing it draining to unwanted areas.

SUPERINTENDENT - The same title as agent, a person in charge at the mine, sometimes there would be several.

SWILL - A wicker basket for carrying wad in the mine and to and from the dressing floors.

TALLOW - Old style candles usually made from animal fats.

TAMPING - After the shot-hole has been charged with powder, it is pressed firmly into the hole by means of a tamping bar, usually made of brass.

TRAMMER - A man who pushes the mine tubs out of the mine.

TRENCHING - A method of exposing the vein on surface by using surface water generally not on the same scale as hushing.

TRIAL - A small surface excavation, or a short underground level to find the vein.

VEIN - Mineral body in a horizontal, vertical, or angled position striking through the country rock.

WAD - Another name for graphite.

WATER BLAST - A shaft usually from surface, down which water is allowed to fall creating an air flow and also removing dust from the mine.

WEDGE - A small iron tool used for splitting rock.

WHEELER - The miner who pushes the wheelbarrow.

WHISKET - A wicker basket for carrying the wad.

Bibliography

Adams J, *Mines of the Lake District Fells*, Dalesman, 1988.
Atkinson G & Barber J, *Lakeland Passes*, Atkinsons, 1928.
Bott G, *Keswick, The Story of a Lake District Town*, Cumbria County Library, Cumbria Supplies & Chaplin's of Keswick, 1994.
Bouch C M L & Jones G P, *The Lake Counties 1500-1830*, Manchester University Press, 1961.
Burt R, *The British Lead Mining Industry,* Dyllansow Truro, 1984.
Camm F J, *Dictionary of Metals and Alloys,* George Newnes Ltd, 1941.
C.A.T.H.M.S. *Beneath the Lakeland Fells*, Red Earth, 1992.
C.W.A.A.S *Transactions Vol LXXV1, An Early Tudor Coin Mould.*
Collingwood W G, *Elizabethan Keswick*, Titus Wilson, 1912.
Donald M B, *Elizabethan Copper*, Michael Moon, 1989.
Fisher J, *Old Borrowdale*, 1875.
Hammersley G, *Daniel Hechstetter the Younger, Memorabilia and Letters 1600-1639*, Franz Steiner, 1988.
Hoover C H & Hoover H H, *De Re Metallica*, Dover, 1950.
Jollie F, *Jollie's Cumberland Guide & Directory*, F Jollie & Sons, 1811.
Ladyman S, *Thoughts & Recollections of Keswick and It's Inhabitants during 60 Years*, Keswick, 1885.
Lefebure M, *Cumberland Heritage*, Arrow Books, 1970.
Mannix & Whellan, *History, Gazetteer and Directory of Cumberland*, Michael Moon, 1974.
Millward R & Robinson A, *Borrowdale and West Cumberland*, Macmillan, 1972.
National Trust, *Kingston Lacey, Dorsett,* 1988.
Parson W & White W, *History, Directory & Gazetteer of Cumberland & Westmorland.* Michael Moon, 1976.
Postlethwaite J, *Mines and Mining in the Lake District*, Michael Moon, 1980.
Rowe D J, *Lead Manufacturing in Britain, A History,* Croom Helm, 1983.
Shaw W T, *Mining in the Lake Counties*, Dalesman, 1970.
Sutton S, *The Story of Borrowdale*, Borrowdale Women's Institute, 1960.
Tyler I, *Honister Slate, The History of a Lakeland Slate Mine*, Blue Rock, 1994.
Tyler I, *Force Crag, The History of a Lakeland Mine*, Red Earth, 1989.
Tyler I, *Greenside, A Tale of Lakeland Miners*, Red Earth, 1992.
Wilberforce W, *Journey to the Lake District from Cambridge*, Oriel Press, 1779.
DX/294, Carlisle Record Office
D/BKL, Cumberland (uncatalogued*). Dorchester Record Office.
D/LEC 80,81, Carlisle Record Office.

*Due to this archive recently being made public, the references originally given are in the process of being re-numbered and consequently it has not been possible to quote individual reference numbers.